TRAVEL
FOR
STOICs

EMPOWERING THE SOLO TRAVELER
WHO IS OBSESSIVE, INTROVERTED,
AND COMPULSIVE

EVA ROME

Blue Morpho Press New Mexico
3201 Zafarano Dr., Suite C #218
Santa Fe, New Mexico 87507-2672
www.bluemorphopress.net

Library of Congress Cataloging-in-Publication Data
Rome, Eva, 1952–
    Travel for STOICs / Eva Rome
    p. cm.
    Includes bibliographical references.
    ISBN-13: 978-0-9678995-1-0

1.Travel. 2. Self-help. 3. Humor. 4. Memoir. 5. Mental health. I. Title.

Printed in the United States of America

Cover design by Jean-Manuel Duvivier
Book design by Laurie McDonald
Photograph of Eva Rome by Mark Dayka

Certain names and locations have been changed to protect the privacy of the author and others.

FOR VIRTÙ

and the airline that forgot to deduct
200,000 miles from my frequent flier account
for an around-the-world fare

Don't explain your philosophy, embody it. Don't seek to have events happen as you wish, but wish them to happen as they do happen, and all will be well with you.

—*Epictetus*[1]

The whole world is my home country.

—*Seneca*[2]

Anything that is humanly possible and appropriate lies within your own reach.

—*Marcus Aurelius*[3]

Roam-a-nation, not rumination.

—*Eva Rome*

CONTENTS

PREFACE

According to Stoic philosophers Epictetus, Seneca, and Marcus Aurelius, the ideas central to ancient Stoic philosophy provide tools for managing anxiety, specifically by cultivating a kind of indifference to events, good or bad—not by suppressing emotions, but by examining and understanding how emotions are connected to our opinions and actions. There are things we can control and things we can't, but we can always regulate our reactions to what happens to us. And to conquer our anxieties, the Stoics believed we must get out into the world and do fieldwork. As Epictetus wrote, "We are eager and loquacious in the schools; but drag us into practice, and you will find us miserably shipwrecked."[4] Exposure to the strange and unfamiliar via travel is the perfect means for attaining mastery over our personality challenges. Amending your will to suit the world, not amending the world to suit you, will lead to the blissful condition of Stoic virtue, and as the Stoics believed, virtue is sufficient for happiness.

Part travel guide, part self-help book, and part memoir, *Travel for STOICs* is *the* book for the **S**olo **T**raveler who is **O**bsessive, **I**ntroverted, and **C**ompulsive, informed and empowered by ideas borrowed from ancient Stoicism. As an obsessive-compulsive (O-C), you know the power of habits, so being a STOIC will provide valuable training that you'll be able to apply to all areas of your life.

The need for empowerment implies that power has been taken away. Power is not a word often used to describe the obsessive, introverted, and compulsive person, a person who may have suffered from these conditions from a very young age and been made to feel powerless because of them. The clinical focus tends to be on intervening compulsions by mitigating obsessions. Because of this shift of focus away from empowerment, STOICs feel anything but mighty and robust, and this condition must be addressed as well. Teetering on the edge of agoraphobia, even the idea of leaving the house may be fraught with anxiety. Written specifically for those who dream of escaping, or at least being granted a temporary furlough, from the prison of the obsessive-compulsive and introverted, *Travel for STOICs* chronicles a sampling of STOIC experiences and illuminates the ways in which Stoic wisdom can strengthen, as Marcus Aurelius puts it, "the ruling power within us."[5] Consider me your scout, the person who's gone and gathered the information you need to confront your anxieties and defeat them. Imagine yourself as a Stoic traveler, then get out there and do it!

Suppose we were to send you as a scout to Rome. But no one ever sends a timorous scout, who, when he only hears a noise or sees a shadow, runs back frightened, and says, "The enemy is at hand…" Get you gone and prophesy for yourself; our only fault is that we have sent such a scout. Diogenes was sent as a scout before you, but he told us other things…"There is no enemy near," he says; "all is profound peace." How so, Diogenes? "Look upon me," he says. "Am I hurt? Am I wounded? Have I run away from anyone?" This is a scout worth having. But you come, and tell us one tale after another. Go back and look more carefully, and without fear.

—*Epictetus*[6]

Stoicism is the original cognitive behavioral therapy, and solo travel is anxiety disorder exposure therapy par excellence. What better way to confront and mediate your condition than to throw yourself, solo, into the world at large, a world full of strangers and perceived threats? If I can do it, so can you.

—Eva Rome

To see photographs of objects, places, and products
mentioned in *Travel for STOICs*, visit
www.travelforstoics.com

INTRODUCTION

For an obsessive-compulsive (O-C for short), the idea of traveling is usually nothing more than that, an idea. An O-C actually doing the traveling is a terrifying prospect; we are far too circumscribed and self-regulated to accomplish the planning, get on the planes, find our accommodations at our destinations, and actually enjoy the process. Fold in introversion, and you've got a crippling combination. Solo travel? Forget it.

Travel for STOICs is both a travel book and a survival manual, but of a different sort. It's not about which great restaurants to patronize or what sites are a must-see in a given place; it's about how to master solo travel challenges that happen in between those activities while successfully managing your O-C, introverted self. This book is especially for the STOIC—the **S**olo **T**raveler: **O**bsessive, **I**ntroverted, **C**ompulsive—and for those who care about our well-being and happiness.

Many of us have used the word "Stoic" to describe a difficult or challenging situation that requires a firm grip on our emotions and reactions. But Stoicism is much more than what we typically think it is. Yes, it's about wisdom, courage, justice, and temperance (the four cardinal Stoic virtues), but it's also pragmatic, self-deprecating, funny, and cheerful. STOICs identify with the Stoics from the classical world because in order to function as a traveler,

STOICs must possess qualities valued by our ancient colleagues. These qualities include, among others: patience, endurance, acceptance, resilience, kindness, honesty, and, most important, indifference to things beyond our control. If this sounds like you, or if you want to be more like this, you've chosen the right book.

Stoicism was founded by Zeno of Citium (Cyprus) around 300 BCE. Diogenes Laërtius, a biographer of the ancient Greek philosophers, wrote that Zeno's interest in philosophy began when he consulted an oracle to learn what he should do with his life. The oracle told him "to take on the complexion of the dead."[7] Zeno understood this to mean that he should study the ancient philosophers, which he set out to do, and soon he had a chance encounter with the most famous living Cynic, Crates of Thebes. Crates became an important influence, and Zeno's philosophy emerged from a blend of the Cynics, the ethical teachings of Socrates, and the philosophy of Plato. Around 301 BCE, Zeno began teaching in the Stoa Poikile ("the painted porch") in the Agora of Athens. His disciples were the first Stoics.

Throughout *Travel for STOICs*, you will find quotes borrowed from three of the ancient Stoic greats: Epictetus, Seneca, and Marcus Aurelius. You will discover contemporary concepts embedded in the ideas of the ancient Stoics and helpful advice to contend with challenges that arise during present-day travel. For all of our STOIC quandaries, nothing beats the wisdom of our Stoic triumvirate.

Stoic philosopher Epictetus was born in Hierapolis, Turkey, and died in Nicopolis, Greece. He lived from 55–135 CE. Epictetus was a slave owned by one of Emperor

Nero's secretaries and obtained his freedom after Nero's death. According to Epictetus's student Arrian, Epictetus was a powerful orator. Arrian recorded (on paper), transcribed, and compiled his discourses; no writings by Epictetus himself have ever been discovered. Epictetus distinguished between things in our power (*prohairetic*) and things not in our power (*aprohairetic*):

That alone is in our power, which is our own work; and in this class are our opinions, impulses, desires, and aversions. What, on the contrary, is not in our power, are our bodies, possessions, glory, and power. Any delusion on this point leads to the greatest errors, misfortunes, and troubles, and to the slavery of the soul.[8]

Epictetus's handbook of Stoic philosophy, the *Enchiridion,* encourages readers to have his teachings close at hand at all times, just in case life starts to spin out of control. And when, during the history of humankind, has it not?

Seneca was born in Córdoba, Spain, in 4 BCE and died in Rome in 65 CE. He was a Stoic philosopher, Roman statesman, and dramatist. Seneca was perhaps the World's Most Interesting (Stoic) Man. In his most famous work, *On the Shortness of Life*, he expressed his disdain for comb-overs, the first century CE's version of air guitar, pointless enthusiasm for useless knowledge, and people who maintain giant collections of books to make themselves look smart. Seneca hated pretensions. He believed that solitude and being part of a group of people should be mingled and varied: solitude being the cure for our dislike of a crowd and being with a crowd the cure for boredom.

All the greatest blessings are a source of anxiety.[9]

Marcus Aurelius was born in Rome in 121 CE and died in either Vindobona or Sirmium, two Roman provinces, in 180 CE. The last of the so-called Five Good Emperors of Rome, Marc-A was a Stoic practitioner heavily influenced by Epictetus. Even though he borrowed extensively from his Stoic predecessor, his work known as *Meditations* is considered a significant source of our modern understanding of Stoic philosophy.

Today I escaped anxiety. Or no, I discarded it, because it was within me, in my own perceptions—not outside.[10]

. . . . .

If you're reading this book, chances are your behavior lies somewhere on the obsessive-compulsive spectrum. In case you've never read the clinical definition of obsessive-compulsive disorder, here's what the DSM-5, the *Diagnostic and Statistical Manual of Mental Disorders, Fifth Edition*, has to say:

DSM-5 Diagnostic Criteria for Obsessive-Compulsive Disorder (300.3)
A. Presence of obsessions, compulsions, or both:
Obsessions are defined by (1) and (2):
    1. Recurrent and persistent thoughts, urges, or impulses that are experienced, at some time during the disturbance, as intrusive and unwanted, and that in most individuals cause marked anxiety or distress.

2. The individual attempts to ignore or suppress such thoughts, urges, or images, or to neutralize them with some other thought or action (i.e., by performing a compulsion).

Compulsions are defined by (1) and (2):

1. Repetitive behaviors (e.g., hand washing, ordering, checking) or mental acts (e.g., praying, counting, repeating words silently) that the individual feels driven to perform in response to an obsession or according to rules that must be applied rigidly.

2. The behaviors or mental acts are aimed at preventing or reducing anxiety or distress, or preventing some dreaded event or situation; however, these behaviors or mental acts are not connected in a realistic way with what they are designed to neutralize or prevent, or are clearly excessive…

B. The obsessions or compulsions are time-consuming (e.g., take more than 1 hour per day) or cause clinically significant distress or impairment in social, occupational, or other important areas of functioning.

C. The obsessive-compulsive symptoms are not attributable to the physiological effects of a substance (e.g., a drug of abuse, a medication) or another medical condition.

D. The disturbance is not better explained by the symptoms of another mental disorder (e.g., excessive worries, as in generalized anxiety disorder; preoccupation with appearance, as in body dysmorphic disorder; difficulty discarding or parting with possessions, as in hoarding disorder; hair pulling, as in trichotillomania [hair-pulling disorder]; skin picking, as in excoriation [skin-

picking] disorder; stereotypes, as in stereotypic movement disorder; ritualized eating behavior, as in eating
disorders; preoccupation with substances or gambling,
as in substance-related and addictive disorders; preoccupation with having an illness, as in illness anxiety
disorder; sexual urges or fantasies, as in paraphilic disorders; impulses, as in disruptive, impulse-control, and
conduct disorders; guilty ruminations, as in major de-
pressive disorder; thought insertion or delusional
preoccupations, as in schizophrenia spectrum and other
psychotic disorders; or repetitive patterns of behavior,
as in autism spectrum disorder).[11]

If you recognize yourself as described in section D, this
book may be too light weight for you. If you nodded your
head in the affirmative while reading sections A through C,
read on.

To summarize, an obsessive-compulsive person experiences unwanted thoughts, urges, and impulses and tries to
control them with certain neutralizing actions. So how can
a person who is obsessive-compulsive possibly be a Stoic,
in the way Stoicism's founder, Zeno of Citium, meant it?
Zeno proposed that virtue equals happiness and that our
judgments should be based on behavior, not what comes
out of our mouths. (We have a contemporary idiom for
this idea: action speaks louder than words.) He also maintained that we have no control over external events and can
only rely on ourselves and our responses to what happens
to us. Zeno's Stoicism reminds us of how unpredictable the
world is and how brief our lives are—and that the source of

our countless dissatisfactions lies in our impulsive reactions to what we encounter via the senses.

Let's stop right here. "Impulsive reactions to what we encounter via the senses." Dear reader, does this resonate? Isn't impulsivity part of being obsessive-compulsive; the initiating leap down the rabbit hole of compulsions? As obsessives well know, we express our compulsions in the form of putting things in order, checking (*Did I unplug the iron? Is the door locked?*), and repetitive behaviors. Something terrible will happen if you don't do these things. Or will it?

Zeno believed that the key to Stoic virtue lay in controlling our impulses with rationality, because when we throw logic out the window, we're in trouble. I propose that solo travel is a great way for the obsessive-compulsive introvert to confront and conquer those problems that limit our lives, and it's a lot more fun than going to the psychotherapist. Because you place yourself in unfamiliar situations, solo travel means adjusting your behavior at all times, and this can lead not only to Stoic virtue but also to relief from obsessions and compulsions. We must rely on only ourselves and our responses, sometimes moment to moment, and that doesn't leave much time to check that timetable twenty times or to stay in the bathroom scrubbing your hands while the Leonardo you've waited your entire life to see beckons. When you insert yourself into situations that run on a different clock than yours, you adjust.

Stoicism also teaches us how to be steadfast, strong, and in control—in other words, how to be a recovering obsessive-compulsive. But traveling puts us in a world populated with external events and ones with which we may not be familiar, and any barrage of alien input can send the obsessive-compulsive into a tailspin. Why is it important for a STOIC to travel, especially when it presents so many obstacles? If you want to know the answer, just examine how much your obsessions and compulsions inform your daily life.

Habit is a powerful influence.
                                              —Epictetus[12]

Here's how it works for me. I wake up at 6:50 a.m. every morning regardless of the season. The first thing I have to do is walk over to the window, raise the shade, and inspect my teeny but beautiful Zen-inspired backyard. Within twenty minutes of waking I must ingest three-quarters of a cup of coffee, a mixture of half espresso and half decaf espresso, and eat a bowl of oatmeal with blueberries. I must spend an hour reading the news, the current *New Yorker*, and/or my current science or music read (I seldom read novels). I must work out every other day at 10 a.m. at the local gym, where I do two miles on the elliptical in twenty-two minutes, five laps of the indoor track, the rowing machine for ten minutes, and squats, three reps of twelve each, placing a giant inflatable ball between my back and the east-facing wall. After showering, on some days it takes hours of trying on various shirts and jeans combinations to arrive at the one that feels right.

When I go to the grocery store I become supremely agitated if the cookies and crackers have been moved from their familiar location. When the Perrier was neither in the water nor the soda aisle but in a little enclave all by itself, ensconced in the soup aisle, I wanted to hunt down the store manager to bring the gravity of the error to his attention. But because I'm an O-C introvert, I don't make a scene. I just fume. I must eat certain fruits in specific seasons, like apples in the winter and pineapple in the summer; blueberries are a year-round requirement.

When I get into my car to drive to the office, looking at the mountains gives me a hefty squirt of dopamine regardless of the season. I must take the same route to my office, touching the gear shift knob every few minutes, or I become agitated. I must glance into the backyard of a house I pass that has a mysterious, octagonal gazebo overgrown with vines. When a driver immediately in front of me turns a corner and coasts instead of accelerating into the street, I heave a huge, indignant sigh.

I know these examples of O-C seem fairly mild, but when certain patterns of expectations are thwarted, like more serious O-C sufferers, I can spiral into a bad place. I am *rigid*, and for many of us, rigidity is a guard against anxiety. But to keep from being driven beyond normal rigidity to CRAZY, I *must* make myself vary the routine and vary it dramatically. Travel is the perfect remedy.

Something I learned how to do a long time ago as a documentary filmmaker was to be inconspicuous, even with a camera in my face. Learning this skill was advantageous because I mastered the observer effect, disturbing the quantum system in which I was participating as little as possible. Being a quiet bystander effecting minimal influence is a skill that also serves the solo traveler well because as an obsessive-introverted-compulsive, we avoid perturbations of any kind that may call attention to ourselves, we leave practically no footprint, and we are sensitive to people who may be one of us. We can enjoy our travel experiences while interacting with people and the world as little or as much as we want. On the other hand, and to continue with the science metaphor, if we O-C introverts were an atomic element, we'd be iron (Fe), which is the most efficiently bound and stubbornly stable atom in existence. But just because you are stable doesn't mean you must be chemically inert. This is another reason why travel works well for people like us. Tossing ourselves into a matrix of unfamiliarity and uncertainty can create the paradoxical effect of making us comfortable because it loosens our electrons and allows them to bond with other elements out there in the world that otherwise we would never bump up against.

Let it be thy earnest and incessant care… to perform whatsoever it is that thou art about, with true and unfeigned gravity, natural affection, freedom and justice: and as for all other cares, and imaginations, how thou mayest ease thy mind of them.
—*Marcus Aurelius*[13]

As I've mentioned, the Stoic philosophies of Zeno and Seneca and my personal favorite, Epictetus, represent early forms of cognitive behavioral therapy (CBT). The Stoics were all about challenging irrational beliefs and making us understand that the worst rarely happens in actuality—a difficult concept for the obsessive-compulsive, but one that's not impossible to grasp. CBT is all about changing perceptions; making you see that the way you perceive a situation has more to do with how you react than with what's actually going on. The Stoics engaged in a practice called negative visualization, or spending time imagining that we've lost the things that are of value to us, like our home, our car, our friends, our children, our money, our life. Or, if you want to take the drama down a notch, you could imagine losing a favorite pair of shoes or your grandmother's hand-crocheted afghan or the slip of paper on which you wrote the phone number of the person of your dreams. The person you met on a plane who sensed your introversion, engaged you in a discussion about your current read, and complimented you on your superior ability to converse. But you have to make the negative visualization meaningful enough so that when you're engaged in the process, you don't just feel wistful; you feel an actual sense of serious angst. Otherwise, it won't work. The purpose of negative visualization is to develop a modicum of indifference to the things that cause the angst, thus relieving anxiety and attenuating possible eruptions of obsessive-compulsive behavior.

CBT also acknowledges that we all engage in these negative thought processes and often confuse events themselves with the meanings we give them. If you believe you can't travel and that something terrible will happen if you do—so you stay home—you won't have the chance to prove your prediction. On the other hand, you'll have shining floors free of stray hairs, the clothes in your closet will be arranged according to color, and all glass surfaces will be smudge- and dust-free. Important stuff.

A final word about introversion, which in itself is neither good nor bad. It's a personality trait, period. Like many mental conditions that challenge our social skills, introversion has its own spectrum that informs our behavior in a variety of ways. Whenever I travel, introversion is what makes me stay in my room most nights and write. Seneca was an introvert; not only did he not seek the company of others, he even tried to decamp from himself.

I have withdrawn not only from men, but from affairs, especially from my own affairs; I am working for later generations, writing down some ideas that may be of assistance to them. There are certain wholesome counsels, which may be compared to prescriptions of useful drugs; these I am putting into writing; for I have found them helpful in ministering to my own sores, which, if not wholly cured, have at any rate ceased to spread.

—Seneca[14]

Like Seneca, my hope is that these words I'm putting into writing, plus the quotes I've incorporated from the Stoics, will help you manage your solo traveler: obsessive, introverted, and compulsive issues as it's helped me manage mine. I also hope that in the process of reading *Travel for STOICs* you will be validated, informed and entertained, and find some of your own truth within its pages.

CHAPTER I

DEAL WITH WHAT HAS BEEN GIVEN YOU

Seneca reminds us that all we have is "on loan" from fortune and can be reclaimed at any time.[15] Back in April of 2002, I learned this lesson in one of the most in-your-face ways possible. Because I lived through this experience, I don't need to do negative visualization because I need to be kind to my amygdala, the almond-shaped cluster of brain cells responsible for the fear response. My amygdala is like an adorable miniature Chihuahua abused by its owner and hiding under the bed, shaking. You try to coax it out with a hot dog, and it takes two years before it sticks its nose out to sniff it. I know what I have on loan and I know how fragile its ownership is; I know it in my bones.

Pre-April of 2002, I worked in my home as a writer and media producer, proud of my independence. No commutes, no corporate politics, a flexible schedule. On April 26, at about 3 p.m., I was in the front room of my house, my de facto office, working on a piece of writing. The wooden front door was open so I could see out through the glass door, my M.O. whenever I was working. A man appeared on the porch; the mailman, I thought, but what was he doing carrying a shotgun? Before I could react, the man and an accomplice forced the door and burst into the room, demanding money and "jewels." They tied my hands behind my back and forced me to lie on the floor, held a shotgun to my head, and questioned me regarding the whereabouts of my husband (I fabricated one) and my children (daughter Virtù was at college out of state). When I convinced them there was nothing of value in the house, that it was all in the bank, they wrapped my head in a towel and walked me out to my car. I heard kids walking home from school and people playing in the park across the street, but I guess that a woman with an orange towel around her head and her hands tied behind her back, being led to a car by two young men, one of them armed, was nothing unusual. Because no one reacted. Forced into the cramped back seat of my car, the three of us headed for the bank, normally a ten-minute excursion from my house, to make an ATM withdrawal. We drove around for what seemed like an eternity, me lying face down in the back seat thinking through possible escape scenarios. We arrived at the drive-through. (The bank later released a harrowing security camera photo of me, as described, which became evidence in the kidnappers' trial.) When the gunman botched the transaction and the ATM impounded my card, that's when serious panic set in. I suggested that we try to cash a check, so we drove around for another eternity while they considered their options. I talked them into unwrapping my head and unbinding my hands. ("How can I write a check behind my back and without being able to see? Besides, my hands are asleep.") I also talked them into putting me in the driver's seat, an idiot move on their part, and we headed back to the bank.

You have the abilities to deal with that which has been given you.
—*Epictetus*[16]

Thank goodness it was Friday. The lines at the drive-through were long and slow-moving. This offered my best shot at escape, and I was ready to risk it. I decided to play a distraction game with the gunman, now sitting in the passenger seat, and asked for items from my purse. "Do you think I could have my lipstick?" While he rummaged around in my purse I released the seatbelt undetected. When I sensed the gunman was sufficiently distracted, I made my break. He'd neglected to lock the doors, an oversight which saved me a precious couple of seconds. So I bolted, or tried to. He grabbed my waist while I squirmed and twisted and struggled and finally escaped, bursting from the car.

I learned that yelling "HELP!" frightens people, and when you're trying to engage someone's attention, it creates the opposite effect. No one reacted to my cries. Even my guardian angel must have been on an extended coffee break. I stumbled over to the next lane where a man sat in a green truck, his elbow resting on the ledge of the window. I grabbed his arm and shook it frantically, saying, "Those men kidnapped me and they're stealing my car!" He ignored me and stared straight ahead. By then I'd attracted a lot of attention, but everyone was still doing their best to ignore me. The kidnappers were escaping with my car and purse, but not before ramming the passenger-side door of the man's truck. That got his attention, but he continued to sit in his truck, frozen.

I ran to the teller's window, a big, plate glass, bullet– and soundproof barrier, to alert her to the crime in progress, but pounding on the window made me look like a crazy person. Finally an ancient bank security guard came strolling out of the building, hiking up his pants and checking to see if his gun was still in its holster, to investigate what the ruckus was all about.

After twenty-four hours had elapsed and the adrenaline rush of my escape had worn off, this is how I felt: exiled from my home and disengaged from my soul. Concepts like "individual will" and "future" and the idea of sovereignty over my life seemed strangely remote. Living in the place that had been my home and my work space for over two decades didn't seem like an option anymore. I spent nights with my ex-husband and his wife and with various friends and never slept in that house again. I fully expected that the kidnappers would return to trash the house, out of spite. The police said the possibility of such a scenario was high.

Life, liberty, and the pursuit of happiness, not clichés but precious entitlements, became abstractions. It took many years and tons of therapy to get my head straight again, but I did it. At some point during the recovery process, I adopted a new attitude: *if I can be kidnapped out of my own home in broad daylight and survive, what else can I do?* The point of the story is, no place in the world is immune from crime, and we all need to be attentive and reactive when a dangerous situation arises. The most important lesson I learned is that we can't surrender to the paralyzing effects of a negative experience. And even an experience like this—*any* experience—should never take travel off the table.

If there's one concept central to Stoicism, it's Stoic indifference: again, the ability to focus on beliefs that underlie our emotions and tease out their truth. After the kidnapping episode, one of the beliefs I clung to was that the kidnappers specifically targeted me. Because of how violated I felt, I blended my emotions with the facts of the event. At the trial I learned they'd kidnapped another woman the day before me and, using her credit cards, took her on a shopping spree. She was a realtor who had staged an open house just down the street, leaving the front door wide open. My front door was open, too, and they saw that as an opportunity. Nothing personal in that.

In his writings, Epictetus tells us how we are to deal with the semblance—the outward appearance—of things.

If we train ourselves in this manner we shall make improvement; for we shall never assent to anything but what the semblance itself includes, A son is dead. What then? A son is dead. Nothing more? Nothing. A ship is lost. What then? A ship is lost. He is carried to prison. What then? He is carried to prison. That he is unhappy is an addition which everyone must make for himself... Go out, man, and do not complain![17]

I was kidnapped. I escaped. Nothing more. My emotions around the event were added by me.

Epictetus has an imaginary conversation with Zeus, Greek god of the sky, thunder and lightning, law and order, and justice. Zeus speaks to Epictetus from the Olympian perspective: the "view from above."

I have given thee a certain portion of myself; this faculty of choosing and refusing, of desire and aversion, or, in a word, of making use of the appearances of things. Taking care of this, and making thine own to consist of this, thou wilt never be baffled, never hindered; thou wilt not groan, wilt not blame, wilt not flatter anyone. How, then? Do these advantages seem small to thee? Heaven forbid! Let them suffice thee, then, and thank the gods.[18]

Using Zeus as his mouthpiece, Epictetus promotes the idea that it's not things that happen to us that are upsetting, it's how we react to and judge them. Conditions change from moment to moment, and we need to manage our responses, recognizing the distinction between our own actions and thoughts and the external things that happen to us. Making use of the appearance of things, using the view from above to master Stoic indifference, is key.

The interplay of courage and caution is something else I learned from my kidnapping experience. In order to travel successfully and with purpose, balancing the two is essential. Epictetus writes that it's possible to be both courageous and cautious, even though caution seems contrary to courage. He compares people to deer that, when threatened by hunters (death), turn and run. They don't see that they're running toward nets the hunters have set up to ensnare them. The idea Epictetus is trying to convey is that we need discernment to judge what is truly threatening and what situations call for caution. He warns against caution turning us into timid deer full of fears and perturbations and also advises against courage causing us to act recklessly or confrontationally.

Seneca describes a state of anxiety with which we STOICs are intimately acquainted.

Weigh carefully your hopes as well as your fears, and whenever all the elements are in doubt, decide in your own favour; believe what you prefer. And if fear wins a majority of the votes, incline in the other direction anyhow, and cease to harass your soul, reflecting continually that most mortals, even when no troubles are actually at hand or are certainly to be expected in the future, become excited and disquieted. No one calls a halt on himself, when he begins to be urged ahead; nor does he regulate his alarm according to the truth. No one says; "The author of the story is a fool, and he who has believed it is a fool, as well as he who fabricated it." We let ourselves drift with every breeze; we are frightened at uncertainties, just as if they were certain... The slightest thing turns the scales and throws us forthwith into a panic.[19]

What better way to adapt ourselves to the present than by the moment-to-moment challenges of travel? Traveling solo is an excellent way to manage your obsessive, introverted, and compulsive symptoms. If you've ever had your scales turned and found yourself in a panic, then read on.

In the preface, I mentioned that fieldwork is vital to the STOIC traveler; no armchair traveling will do. You must coax the Chihuahua out from under the bed, and think full-immersion solo travel. Remember, Epictetus wrote that "We are eager and loquacious in the schools; but drag us into practice, and you will find us miserably shipwrecked."[4] Challenging one's STOIC self with Stoic philosophy and with travel helps you realize your inner hero. Make this your mantra: Roam-a-nation, not rumina-tion.

CHAPTER II

THE TYRANNY OF FEAR

Undue Influence

Some of your friends and family may try to persuade you that solo travel equals certain death. They are the ones who have never left the comfort and (imagined) security of their hometowns—or even their homes—and rely way too much on TV news for their information or on Internet sites with questionable credibility.

Here's an example. My niece's wedding in January 2009 was preceded by a bombing of the Taj Mahal Palace Hotel in Mumbai that occurred on November 26, 2008. The Taj is an icon of opulence and luxury, and for sixty hours, four heavily armed terrorists tried their best to raze the place and annihilate its occupants. In one of a dozen coordinated attacks, whole floors of the Taj were destroyed by explosives, hotel patrons were massacred, hostages were taken, and when it was over, 160 people had lost their lives. Horrific, to be sure. The wedding reception took place in the Fort Worth, Texas, version of an opulent and luxurious hotel. Had you been in attendance, you might have engaged in conversation with certain guests preoccupied with the Taj tragedy from two months earlier, in a place that's 8,800 miles to the west.

Virtù and I had planned trips to India leaving a week after the wedding; she to Jaipur, the capital of Rajasthan, to study sitar with a distinguished musical family, and me to Varanasi in eastern Uttar Pradesh to study sitar with a well known father/son duo. Jaipur is roughly seven hundred miles from Mumbai, and Varanasi is close to a thousand miles from Mumbai. Even so, the wedding guests who knew of our plans tried their best to dissuade us from going. To them, traveling anywhere in the subcontinent was suicide. They employed all manner of persuasion to raise our fear levels to their own, but nothing worked on either of us. We played along, but what they didn't know is that their words had no effect; it was what I was wearing that worried me at the moment. The kidnapping experience had left me with a new anxiety. Once you've been abducted in the middle of the day, interrupting your laser-focus on a writing project, you're *so* grateful you weren't still in your pajamas. Being an O-C, you re-think (repeatedly) how being in your pajamas would have added a deeper, more troubling meaning to the whole kidnapping experience. Being out in public in pajamas is analogous to dreams where you're standing at a lectern speaking to a group of peers and you've forgotten to put on pants, or you're dancing in the corps de ballet stark naked. Because everyone else at the reception was dressed to the nines, and I was— at best—a three, I had to remind myself that no, I wasn't wearing pajamas; they were back in the hotel room, freshly steamed and spread out on the bed.

The guests' concern for our safety was kind and thoughtful, but when you realize that being alive means vulnerability in all its many forms, your personal safety perspective changes forever. Life is fraught with inherent dangers, but you don't broadcast that bumper sticker sentiment to the world if you can help it. You choose either to accept that certainty and not let it limit your life, or you live with chronic fear and constraint. Fear generates a negative feedback loop; over time, your life can become—if you let it—more and more constricted and limited, and at some point, you realize travel is totally out of the question, even to a neighboring city. So after the first few encounters with hysterical wedding guests, we wearied of repeating our reasons for travel and our philosophical views on personal safety and just agreed with them. It's like what psychologists say to do when trying to converse with a relative suffering with Alzheimer's: inhabit their world. When they tell you that bombs are going off around them, you agree and say, "Yeah, I wish I had my noise-cancelling headphones right now" or "Let's hide under the table; that should make them stop." That approach worked well with the wedding guests, because what the relatives and friends really sought was validation of their fears so they could walk away from the conversation and say to themselves, "I was right; they're taking a huge risk, but whatever!" When you realize it's all about them, it's easy to resist taking on extra anxiety to add to your own. Of course you are anxious, but you don't admit it to anyone. You're a STOIC, and the obsessive-compulsive component means inherent anxiety.

Thou must be like a promontory of the sea, against which though the waves beat continually, yet it both itself stands, and about it are those swelling waves stilled and quieted.

—*Marcus Aurelius*[20]

Then there are the super smart friends who think through, even more thoroughly than you do, all the various negative scenarios that could befall a solo traveler and convey those to you. While in the planning stages of a trip to Ecuador, one of these friends sent, via text, a thirty-minute YouTube video of a pilot talking about the Quito airport and the difficulties of landing there. Commercial planes are not allowed to land anywhere over ten thousand feet, and Quito lies just under the limit at 9,730 feet. The runway is barely long enough, and, because of reduced air resistance at that elevation, planes needs more landing real estate than at sea level. Plus, the runway has a slightly curved, convex shape, so after first contact with the tarmac, the pilot has to pull up a few degrees to compensate for the curve. The more of the video I watched, the more I could feel my anxiety level gain in elevation, too, so I had to stop. Then I remembered that a shiny new international airport east of the city also serviced Quito, and the one in the video was in the center of town. Nervously I checked my itinerary and discovered that the flight was scheduled to land at the new airport.

The dangerous airport text was followed by one that said, "uh oh... hrm, according to Wikipedia, Quito is on top of a volcano... lol." On top of a volcano? You'd think I would have noticed that and rejected Ecuador as a travel destination. Frantically I Googled the volcanoes in/under

Quito and discovered that Ecuador boasts a corridor of thirty of 'em within a country the size of New Mexico, my current state of residence. Wikipedia states that Quito was built on the eastern slope of a volcano, not exactly on *top* of a volcano, but still this was disturbing. Most disturbing of all was a volcano called Cotopaxi that had entered an eruptive phase a few years before I was planning to be there, spewing ash and toxic gasses from its cone. I Googled "characteristic lava flows, Cotopaxi" and none of them had ever been a threat to Quito. But as mutual fund managers are required to tell investors that past performance is not indicative of future results, Cotopaxi's future eruptions aren't predictable by the patterns of past activity. Hawaii came to mind, a place with a volcano in continual eruption since 1983, and that thought helped compartmentalize my anxiety somewhat. Hawaii is a huge tourist destination, and nobody ever considers annihilation by volcano a travel deterrent.

Next my hand-wringing friend wrote, "Now I'm trying to see what the heat, insects, government, and crime situation is." I wrote back, "From what I've read, the temperature in Quito is even all year, 65° in the day and 60 at night. Mosquitoes live in the Amazonian part of E. and I don't know about other areas. Gov't is a republic. Just found out that firearms are illegal in Ecuador and even the police carry tasers only, no guns. E's currency is the USD." His reply: "I knew the USD was the currency but didn't know about the firearms. That said, I'm hearing from a Spanish-speaking colleague in TX to don't flash money or go outside at night… so hrm… not sure if that's straight info about crime. Starting to get a little worried about the lack of seasons and the insects/tropical diseases issue tho… still looking at that."

Clearly my friend suffers from travel anxiety that has plumbed great depths. He knows about effective insect deterrent chemicals and malaria prophylaxis and that you don't go out at night in unfamiliar places, not even in one's own city. And there are ways to carry money concealed, like in the travel underwear I use with the deep front pocket provided for that purpose. He was worrying about my destination as if the trip were a one-way ticket to a one-day, one-season time loop, a *Groundhog Day* circadian entrapment.

As you and I well know, the STOIC dark night of the soul can be attained without the help of others. Maybe if our family and friends understood this, they'd be more sensitive about over-sharing. Here's the short version of how it happens for me. Out of nowhere a feeling creeps into my brain, a premonition that the trip I've planned is my last. I'll never return to the safety and familiarity of my own bed, bathroom, and kitchen. Once I board the plane, I'll never see my family or friends ever again. STOIC dread will take me down—if I let it.

If you're like me, your anxiety infiltrates the deepest regions of your psyche, expressing itself through recurring airplane crash nightmares. Here are a few I've noted in my diaries:

Saturday, February 21, 2015
Had the recurring airplane dream. I was in a small plane taking off; it barely missed several power lines. The plane

flew so close to a house rooftop that my feet skimmed the roof. What were my feet doing outside the airplane?

Sunday, May 3, 2015
I had the airplane dream early this morning. This time I was in a commercial jet, and suddenly we lost significant altitude. I could feel it in my stomach. When the pilot gained control, we were only a few thousand feet above a verdant landscape. Then it happened again. A crash was certain, and somehow I knew the pilot was looking for a suitable place to land. I assumed the bending at the waist and tucking your head crash position, but no one else in the plane seemed concerned. A woman across the aisle lightly touched my leg to reassure me. We crashed, slammed into a mall, and slowly came to rest inside a Ross Dress for Less. I ran from the wreckage as fast as I could, covered in the latest summer arrivals.

Wednesday, June 7, 2017
I dreamed I was in a Cambodian detention camp masquerading as a spa. Under the pretense of getting a massage, a group of us detainees was ordered to strip. While we were waiting, I noticed we shared a runway with experimental, futuristic aircraft and missiles. One large airplane was flying back and forth across the sky, then it crashed nose-first into the ground. I hadn't taken my clothes off and rushed to the scene where I saw a field full of bodies covered in sheets. Vague about the rest of the dream, but there was a man assigned to watch me and it was hard to elude him. Three tall, blonde American tourists appeared, still clothed, and I tried joining the group so I could escape.

But I am a short brunette and the man looked at me like, "Really?"

Sunday, August 20, 2017

I had the airplane dream. Crashed into a grove of bamboo that then switched to a city with narrow streets. Susan M. was in the plane, too. I knew the crash wouldn't be fatal to anyone on board, and after the plane rolled to a stop, I stood up and looked back at her. She had this *I'm totally freaked out, I told you so* look on her face. We exited the plane. The pilot said we'd be taking off again in a few moments and we said, "Yeah, right." In the dream I told her, "I'm so glad this finally happened" (as if it were real life); "now it's over and I can stop having this dream."

These recurrent airplane crash dreams could have inspired a serious case of agoraphobia. I was in the grips of the tyranny of fear.

When you examine fear, you'll notice that it arises when you think harm will come to you, either physical or mental, and this perceived harm is the slippery slope that you think will lead to oblivion or, worse, annihilation. A mind in a state of fear is stuck in some future imagined event. According to the Stoics, to view life and death as tyrants and to develop indifference to both removes fear.

What makes a tyrant formidable? His guards, say you, and their swords; they who protect his bedchamber, and they who keep out intruders. Why, then, if you bring a child to him amidst these guards, is it not afraid? Is it because the child does not know what they mean? Suppose, then, that anyone knows what is meant by guards, and that they are armed with swords; and for that very reason comes in the tyrant's way, since, on account of some misfortune, he wishes to die, and seeks to die easily by the hand of another. Does such a man fear the guards? No; for he desires the very thing that makes them formidable. Well, then; if anyone, being without an absolute desire to live or die, but indifferent to it, comes in the way of a tyrant, what prevents his approaching him without fear? Nothing.

— *Epictetus*[21]

Epictetus and the Stoics illuminate many ideas about indifference; as I've written, it's actually the centerpiece of Stoic philosophy. They refer many times to the practice of facing one's fears by imagining the feared situations and the consequences of exposure to these situations, which is what modern exposure therapies are all about. Epictetus also encouraged us to use a distancing technique, stepping back from our thoughts and reminding ourselves that thoughts are our own sensory impressions and not literally "things." The Stoics tell us to cultivate an indifference to poverty, personal illness, the illnesses and deaths of our friends and relatives, and other of life's most profound challenges so that when the time comes that these events happen, we are equipped to deal with them in a more controlled, equanimous way. As mentioned in the introduction, this viewing from the Olympian perspective, or the view from above, considers things as if they were tiny and insignificant and transient—like being in an airplane and looking down on the city in which you're about to land. Houses look like real estate on a Monopoly board. Cars look like lines of ants traveling in tandem. Signs of poverty and decay blend with the occasional mansion and its bean-sized backyard pool.

Stoic philosophy tells us to remind ourselves repeatedly of the distinction between what happens to us and what happens because of us. It calls on you, when presented with conflict or faced with a person who is offending or upsetting you, to remember that his behavior seemed right to him even though it sets off alarms in you. The practice of these techniques creates Stoic indifference and helps maintain your equanimity.

If all of this is too hard to remember or to put into practice, consider these words from Seneca:

Let us prepare our minds as if we'd come to the very end of life. Let us postpone nothing. Let us balance life's books each day... The one who puts the finishing touches on their life each day is never short of time.[22]

Or something more direct and to the point from no nonsense Marc-A:

You will die, and shortly after, not even your name will be left. Both the longest lived and earliest to die suffer the same loss, the present, and if this is all he has, he cannot lose what he does not have. You should be content with your allocation of time. All that you see will perish, as will you—it is all the same whether you die before your time or in old age.[23]

The reason why travel is important to the O-C introvert is essentially this: travel forces you to live in the present. Wholly and deeply.

Anxiety Alters Your Sense of Time

STOICs, on the day before you leave on a trip, plan for the worst anxiety you've ever experienced. You can barely move; every task, regardless of how small, can seem herculean, and the tiniest irritation can catalyze a torrent of tears. You know you're living your last days, and you don't want to spend those precious remaining few hours cleaning the house to perfection. But if you don't, when you return, those dust bunnies accumulated in the corners of the living room will trigger a Category 5 O-C shitstorm and immediately reverse any chill you've achieved while away.

Hold on—you think you're going to die, but you're imagining dust bunnies in your future? What's going on is this: anxiety is robbing you of the ability to live in the present. Six months ago you planned your trip—some say planning is as fun as the trip itself—and tucked it away in the part of the brain under "things for later consideration." And you're imagining returning to a spotlessly clean house. Now that your departure date is upon you, what happened to the trip itself? In the interim it became a blurry, gray, featureless field of noise that time forgot, and you can't quite remember what prompted you to want to leave the comfort of your home in the first place. Recognize this for what it is. Anxiety is working behind the scenes, undermining your desire to travel independently and weakening your courage and resolve, trying really hard to make you call it quits. If you're not responding emotionally and mentally, anxiety will attack you physically. You may develop a fever, a toothache, a stomachache, heart palpitations, rosacea, diarrhea, experience hair loss. Anxiety may bring old trauma to mind.

As a five-year-old, I knew I was going to the hospital to have my tonsils removed, but the actual procedure was an abstract concept. The reward was all the ice cream I could eat afterward, a puzzling attitude reversal by my parents, who usually reprimanded me every day for eating too many sweets. I was incentivized. After the procedure, when I discovered that swallowing of any kind was something to be avoided, I understood the deception. Anxiety, like tonsil removal, is its own two-faced con. It fools you into imagining travel as an ice cream high, stimulating our reward system (the amygdala is partly to blame) with exciting new experiences. But it also makes you think of travel as something you endure and survive, and after a while, your life's equilibrium is restored. Anxiety has made you vulnerable and cowardly with such intensity that hourly you consider cancelling the whole thing, the trip you have poured hundreds of hours and thousands of non-refundable dollars into. Crawling under the covers with your phone, your computer, and your favorite stuffed animal feels like the only solution, but you know from experience that you take your anxiety with you wherever you go.

So strong and unconquerable a thing is human nature! For how can a vine have the properties not of a vine, but of an olive tree; or an olive tree not those of an olive tree, but of a vine? It is impossible. It is inconceivable.

—Epictetus[24]

The most insidious weapon in anxiety's arsenal, though, is its ability to alter your perception of time and your sense of being solidly ensconced in your own body. Time slows to a crawl, an experience similar to what is described by car crash survivors. The twenty-four hours before travel can seem like twenty-four days, and you just want the anticipation of the crash to resolve, the car to take its last roll and come to rest in a soft, green meadow. You're washing the dishes, a mindless activity that under normal circumstances is a good distraction, when suddenly the sink recedes precipitously into the distance. You look at your hands and they seem far away, too. Excess anxiety creates both temporal and spatial distortions mimicking certain recreational drugs. Anxiety is nothing but a bad trip and like any drug-induced bad trip must run its course. Remember this and bear it with patience and Stoic indifference.

Let not thy mind wander up and down, and heap together in her thoughts the many troubles and grievous calamities which thou art as subject unto as any other. But as everything in particular doth happen, put this question unto thyself, and say: What is it that in this present matter, seems unto thee so intolerable? For thou wilt be ashamed to confess it. Then upon this presently call to mind, that neither that which is future, nor that which is past can hurt thee; but that only which is present… and then check thy mind if for so little a while, (a mere instant), it cannot hold out with patience.
—*Marcus Aurelius*[25]

To help manage your anxiety, you may have considered acquiring an assistance dog for a travel companion, but that would disqualify you as a STOIC. Plus, assistance dogs always wear a uniform that says "service dog" or "comfort animal" or "working dog, do not pet," calling attention to *you* and broadcasting to the world that you are stricken with a mysterious and pitiable weakness. Assistance dogs create the ultimate in spotlight effects, meaning that whenever we're in public we think everyone is staring at us judgmentally. The dog makes onlookers curious about what kind of trauma their human charge has suffered.

Live as if you are in public view.
— *Seneca*[26]

STOICs, these unpleasant sensations and thoughts will stop if and only if you continue with your travel plans. The anxiety may lift on the way to the airport, it may happen when the doors to the departure area part and you enter, or it may happen at check-in. But it will happen. Time will snap back into place and you'll be brought back into your body, good spirits restored and excited about the adventures ahead.

What Not to Do before Traveling

If you live anywhere north of the fortieth parallel, your favorite time to travel may be during January. The holidays are over, the serious winter weather has set in, and flu season is in full swing. Because you're incentivized to escape to warmer climes, during this time of year and immediately before, you must vigilantly protect your health. Immune systems are compromised by the stress of the holidays, and yours may be extra stressed, being a STOIC. You may start to obsess about your pre-trip grooming and feel compelled to get a haircut or a mani-pedi. Or get that pneumonia inoculation your doctor prescribed the previous summer. Or work out more to insure stamina for long walks abroad. Or have lunch with friends since you may never see them again. Before you act on these impulses, think them through.

Because of holiday closures and pending New Year's resolutions, gym attendance may swell during the first half of December. It may also mean an increase of people who cough without covering their mouths and who neglect to disinfect exercise equipment after use, placing you at greater risk for exposure to germs. My advice is to cut way back on your gym schedule, but if your O-C won't let you, at least try to go when it's less busy. Nothing guarantees immunity while traveling, but this may reduce your chances of a problem.

I bring what not to do before traveling to your attention because I made the mistake of lunching with a friend with incipient stomach flu symptoms two days before a trip to Ecuador. My immune system is robust, but she was shedding viruses directly into my food for forty-five minutes. So I took precautions. To cover all the bases, I packed three different antibiotics, aspirin and Advil, Tums, Imodium, and electrolyte replacement options.

A week later, on the second night of a three-night stay at a cloud forest ecolodge, just after 11 p.m., it struck with a vengeance. Over the next four hours, fluid loss transformed me into a desiccated shell of a human being. We all know the feelings that signal an impending purge: profuse sweating, intense and inescapable pain of the GI tract, then after evacuation, uncontrollable chills. But this time was different. During round two, my vagus nerve, control central for the lungs, heart, and digestive tract, decided to render me unconscious. I woke up on the shower floor, a few feet away from where I'd been sitting moments before, my face in a puddle of water. Fortunately, I had minimal injuries, only bruises and scrapes; no broken bones and no concussion. The experience was an epiphany. What *not* to do before a trip can be as important as your most detailed preparations.

One of our strengths as a STOIC is that we manage solo illness quite well. No STOIC wants to throw up within sight or earshot of someone else; we abhor inconveniencing anyone else because of our infirmity, and because we practice STOIC indifference, we're able to objectify the illness and accept the outcome, whatever it might be. We thrive when our sense of humor transcends the terror of compromised health or body. Lying knocked out on the tile floor of a shower reminded me of my grandmother, a Stoic par excellence. She lived alone into her 90s, and when her neighborhood began to experience break-ins and burglaries, before going to bed at night she locked and barricaded the two doors that led to her bedroom. One night she got out of bed, fell, and broke her hip. She lay on the floor the rest of the night, waiting for morning to arrive so she could call my parents. (She never wanted to inconvenience anyone.) When daylight brightened the room, she dragged herself over to the phone. The EMTs arrived within a few minutes, but the house was so secure that there was no easy access to the bedroom. They removed a window and everyone crawled through, and when my parents saw her sprawled helplessly on the floor, they panicked. But grandma was calm and collected. She greeted everyone with a smile and by declaring, "it's been a long time since this many young men have been in my bedroom." Epictetus would have nodded in approval.

Oh Lord God, how shall I avoid anxiety!" Have you not hands, foolish man? Has not God made them for you? You might as well kneel and pray to be cured of your catarrh (mucus in the nose or throat). *Take care of your disease, rather, and wipe your nose. Well; and has he given you nothing in the present case? Has he not given you patience? Has he not given you magnanimity? Has he not given you fortitude? When you have such hands as these, do you still seek help in wiping your nose?*[27]

Don't forget, STOICs, that humor is a conduit to those gifts of courage, fortitude, and endurance. Self-pity is not our M.O.

CHAPTER III

PREPARING FOR YOUR TRIP

Planning Paralysis

The great thing about planning a trip is that you can accomplish most steps of the entire process from your smartphone—any time, any place, in your most introverted of moods and in your pajamas if you like. Where the planning paralysis enters is deciding where you want to go and why. When this happens, you could practice a literal version of the Stoic view from above. Give a globe a good spin, stop it with your finger, and make that abstracted place a real-life destination. Throw a dart at a world map. If you're an iPhone owner, give the emojis a swift swipe and stop in the flags section. But making travel decisions in these stochastic ways is not always recommended for STOICs. Even though I've been arguing for pushing ourselves outside of our comfort zones, STOICs have boundaries and M.O.s that must be respected. Some are more flexible than others; some completely inflexible.

No action should be undertaken without an aim.
—Marcus Aurelius[28]

I don't usually recommend travel as escape because you might end up in a situation eerily similar to the one you desperately wanted to flee. For example, if you've booked a week in Mexico to give yourself a much-needed break from the six relentlessly barking dogs living next door, you might want to reconsider that great Cancún deal. Dogs are just as popular in Mexico as in the U.S. and in most places around the world. If escaping barking dogs is your motivation for travel, then visit Saudi Arabia or Turkmenistan. Saudis customarily do not keep dogs as pets, and a past dictator of Turkmenistan banished dogs from the capital city, Ashgabat, because of their unappealing odor.

Closely examining your motivations for travel, in the context of your anxieties, is wise. The reasons don't need to be profound, but they do need to be clear and doable, whatever that means to you. Do you want to visit the Nazca Lines, those mysterious figures of animals and plants etched into the Peruvian desert, but are terrified of flying in a small airplane? Is the aurora borealis something you've wanted to experience for decades, but you hate cold weather? Want to go to the Edinburgh Festival Fringe, the world's largest celebration of the arts, but are afraid of crowds? Since you're a STOIC, knowing your comfort zones and boundaries is essential, but with the help of this book, you're going to push those limits.

In most areas of our lives we're overwhelmed with too much choice, and the same goes for travel. If the idea of organizing travel induces planning paralysis, you may have succumbed to anxiety overload. Start with a few modest trips and expand from there. Over time, you'll build confidence, and planning your trips will be a large part of the fun. Since planning isn't that big of a deal anymore, we can arrange all aspects of a trip—from modes of transportation to accommodations to tours and other ways to experience a place—and actually enjoy the O-C aspects of the process. Don't be alarmed by glitches that may happen along the way. The reason for taking modest trips is to sharpen those skills for the more challenging adventures. Get yourself out the door and into the world.

When planning your itinerary, include local tours, especially if you have limited time to spend in a place. You'll want to hit the highlights, and tours offer an efficient and often educational experience. Plus, as a STOIC, a fifteen-person tour bus gives you an opportunity to meet other travelers, some of whom may also be STOICs and want to bond over this fact. Or you can indulge your inner introvert and be silent; nobody will care and it's likely they'll be nice to you, regardless. Tours often combine two or more sites into one full day, including places far off the beaten path, like the dry, dusty, jungle back roads of the Yucatán that lead to a chain of hidden cenotes. You may be a great navigator with excellent intuition for place and direction, but you could waste way too much of your precious travel time trying to find those hidden cenotes yourself. So let go of that I-am-an-island inclination. Every person is a piece of the continent.

Packing Paralysis

You've made the big and brave decision to leave the house, get on a plane, and fly to a foreign country for two weeks. Being a STOIC, you're not sure any place but your hometown will have the things you need to sustain life when you arrive at your travel destination. To unpack this worry, my recommendation is to spend at least as much time as you intend to spend traveling examining your daily routine in great detail. Write everything down so that when you leave home, you'll have a clear understanding of what you do every day, how much time it takes, and what resources are required. Again, we're talking about the gap moments, the times and activities that to a non-STOIC are inconsequential, not even to be bothered with when it's the monuments, museums, music venues, and great restaurants you're going on vacation to experience. But when you *are* a STOIC, these gap moments can add up quickly, and three-quarters of the day can pass before you've done anything of consequence. Starting at the beginning, with the moment you open your eyes in the morning, you must calculate how long it takes to get out of bed, make the bed, eliminate (no delicate way of saying this), eat breakfast, take your vitamins, brush and floss your teeth, take a shower, get dressed, read and answer emails, and review your itinerary several obsessive times. That's a lot of activity that could take an inordinate amount of time to accomplish.

Let's examine the resources I'd need for those simple tasks mentioned above: toilet paper, a pot for heating water, coffee, a drip coffee filter cone and a paper filter, a coffee mug, oatmeal, blueberries, a bowl, a spoon, various supplements, a toothbrush, toothpaste, dental floss, soap, shampoo, conditioner, a razor, a washrag, at least one towel, Q-tips, tissue for nose-blowing, a comb and brush, a hairdryer and curler, undergarments, socks and shoes, a skirt or blue jeans, a blouse or sweater, earrings and other jewelry, makeup (at least four items here). That's already more than thirty items, most of which you'll be bringing with you on your travels and *more*. This simple inventory is the reason why I don't believe extreme minimalists who say they own only fifty or sixty things. It's simply not possible, at least if you're someone who observes good hygiene. However, as Epictetus wrote,

Encumbering ourselves with too many things burdens us.[29]

Practicing Stoic indifference, try to create a disconnect between you and your stuff and examine which of these items is essential to your survival. If this triggers confusion or plunges you into an obsessive loop from which you can't escape, stop. Take a deep breath, imagine a euphonious, iconic voice such as the late Alan Rickman's, and read the following to yourself:

To live happily is an inward power of the soul, when she is affected with indifferency, towards those things that are by their nature indifferent. To be thus affected she must consider all worldly objects both divided and whole: remembering withal that no object can of itself beget any opinion in us, neither can come to us, but stands with still and quiet; but that we ourselves beget, and as it were print in ourselves opinions concerning them. Now it is in our power, not to print them; and if they creep in and lurk in some corner, it is in our power to wipe them off.

—Marcus Aurelius[30]

Think about how this can apply to you and the essentials you need for your STOIC journey. Ask yourself, *Do I really need this item to maintain my personal ordered universe? What would happen if I needed it and didn't have it? If I don't have it, aren't there thousands upon thousands of alternate ordered universes in which these things exist?* Tell yourself, *Wherever I am in the world, I will intersect with a duplicate of the needed object left behind. And if I don't, I have the internal and external resources to get it, or to find a reasonable substitute.* With this in mind, when planning your journey, decide which items are absolutely essential, without which you cannot exist and which may not be available at your destination. Think *bare minimum.* Dog-ear this page so you can return to it, and to Marc-A's quote starting on the previous page, often.

Until we have begun to go without things, we fail to realize how unnecessary many things are.

—Seneca[31]

Appendix A is a list of every item I took on a trip to the Yucatán region of Mexico in January 2017, and Appendix B is a list from an around-the-world trip in May and June 2017. Lists like these are essential travel documents. What you will read represents two months' worth of the kind of research previously described, plus the anticipation of scenarios in which you might find yourself while traveling. The Mexico list represents a total of 124 items and the around-the-world list 136. Items on the around-the-world list were distributed among a cross body bag, a jacket, a camera case, and a roller carry-on bag. On both of those trips only one item was never put into service: a large, draping body scarf I thought I would need in Morocco to cover up. As I packed for these trips, I ticked off the item in the far-left column of the list. Note that I reduced the number of shirts I took to Mexico versus around the world from seven to four. Limiting clothes for travel precludes you from trying them on obsessively, an activity that short-circuits your decision-making capabilities and creates a time-eating vortex from which escape is exhausting.

Once you've identified all necessities required for your trip, next you must decide which things you'd be seriously compromised without, and those items go in the slash-proof, oversize, lightweight cross body bag you bought specifically for traveling. The next most important things go in your backpack or carry-on. Everything else, the easily replaceables, goes in your suitcase or other checked luggage.

If you've read Appendix A by now and noticed "empty lip balm with $20," let me explain. Either use depleted lip balm tubes already on hand, or visit your local dollar store and buy a three-pack of the cheapest generic brand. Remove the lip balm (I did it with a fingernail file), fold a twenty-dollar bill in half, roll it up, and insert it inside the tube. Put one of the tubes in a pants pocket, another in your travel jacket with the dozen secret compartments (again, see Appendix A), and hide the third one in your carry-on. That way, if your purse is stolen, you still have a little cash on you elsewhere.

By the way, the list doesn't include what I wore for the plane ride to Mexico, which was a nice white shirt, my nicest blue jeans, the black travel jacket with secret compartments, and tan Ecco lace-ups. On the plane to England, my first stop around the world, I wore black quick-dry pants, a navy quick-dry shirt, a beige cardigan sweater, a scarf, the Ecco shoes, and the black jacket. And for those of you who read Appendix A and wondered about this, Celestún is a beautiful bioreserve on the northern coast of the Yucatán peninsula, a lagoon replete with flamingoes and mangrove forests.

I forgot to take something very important on the Yucatán trip and, being a STOIC myself, I was surprised to realize—at the moment I needed it—what it was. I wonder if you read Appendix A and mentally added essentials of your own to the list. More on that later.

How much did all that stuff weigh, you might ask? This brings up another crucial issue.

Weights and Measures

Weights and dimensions of individual items are important because they add up fast. Here's an example. For breakfast every single day I eat a specific brand of oatmeal with blueberries. The oatmeal box, containing ten individually wrapped packets, measures 7.5"×6"×2" and weighs one pound, three ounces. Only one object out of a possible fifty or more, and already that's a huge amount of weight and space in a small piece of luggage. So consider leaving oatmeal, or something of comparable size and weight, behind; oatmeal is sold in other countries. Because they can be difficult to find elsewhere, I lower my blueberry expectations unless I'm traveling to Chile, where you may land in a place where you can pick them right off the bush. Travel forces many diet modifications, so you're going to have to adjust.

A Grayl water purification system is essential for anywhere I travel outside my home. The Grayl is like a French press for water, but instead of starting with pure, clear water, pressing the center post down until you have a delicious dark cup of coffee, you start with dingy, sketchy water, press down, and the purification system turns the sludge into crystal clear H_2O. The Grayl cylinder is nine inches tall by three inches in diameter, while the aluminum water bottle into which I pour the purified water is also nine by three. Those two bottles alone take up a lot of carry-on real estate, but both are lightweight and are perhaps the two most important items you'll take on your trip.

These two things are tempting to pack, but you must resist: no heavy books (likely downloadable on your Kindle or other reading device) and no big packs of makeup remover. We all get lazy and at the end of the day want to swipe our faces with a makeup-removing cloth instead of properly cleansing and moisturizing, but these packs are big and heavy and, as I discovered on a domestic flight, leak when compressed and decompressed during takeoff and landing. The effluvium from these packs soaked into a favorite hat and reminded me of the heavy syrup from a can of cling peaches.

You ought to consider your whole body as a useful ass, with a pack-saddle on, so long as possible, so long as is allowed… And since you are thus to regard even the body itself, think what remains to do concerning things to be provided for the sake of the body. If that be an ass, the rest are but bridles, pack-saddles, shoes, oats, hay for him. Let these go too. Quit them yet more easily and expeditiously.

—Epictetus[32]

Without belaboring the point, go through your lists item by item and ask yourself these questions:

- What is the particular merit of this object, and is it essential?
- What are its dimensions, and how much does it weigh?
- If I leave it at home and discover while abroad that I need it, will I be able to find and purchase it or its equivalent?
- If I need to bring it, can I reduce the size of the item by repackaging it in a ziplock?

In the process of packing my suitcase for Mérida, Mexico, I decided I wanted to take a box of green tea containing sixteen individually wrapped tea bags. I intended to re-package the tea bags in a ziplock, but when I opened the box, I saw that they were squeezed in like sardines already, so I didn't see the point. You might be thinking, *Couldn't she buy green tea in Mexico?* At 4.25"×3"×2.75", a tea box consumes a lot of room, but bringing the box was a good call because I never did find green tea in Mérida or even a great cup of coffee. I know, first world problems. I congratulated myself on the excellent decision, and you should, too, if you have a similar experience. Note: Many countries have food import restrictions and customs may require a declaration of food items. I really don't want to go on record advising you to lie, but if you've packed food and you're next in line at customs, wear your best poker face and think about something other than getting caught.

An item on the list you might think is unnecessary is laundry detergent. Think again. Don't we all have a favorite detergent because it smells good, or doesn't have a smell, or is environmentally friendly, or comes in clever packaging, or has other redeeming qualities? Have you ever been in a country that sells an off-brand version of a beloved powder detergent? In India, Tide sells a product called Jasmine and Rose with Dirt Magnets, a substance that exudes a sweet, flowery smell to disguise the fact that it's really some awful chemical. There were no laundromats anywhere I visited in India, so I washed my clothes in plastic buckets filled with water and Jasmine and Rose with Dirt Magnets. The product didn't dissolve, it just floated around in clumps, making dirty bubbles on the surface of the water, emitting such an awful odor that I had to turn my head and squeeze my eyes shut while washing my clothes. The smell lingered for days, causing all kinds of allergic reactions and other discomforts, and I so regretted not packing the product from home, which comes in a convenient, single-use travel size.

Another product you might be tempted to bring is a big roll of your favorite toilet paper. Note in Appendix A that I included a travel-size Charmin To Go in the backpack, transferred to my cross body bag once I reached my destination. CTG is an essential item and needs no explanation.

But leave the big roll behind. It measures a whopping 5.5"
in diameter by 4" in height and takes up way too much
space. You'll be happy to read that India boasts an excellent brand of toilet paper called Spruce Up, and Mérida's
toilet paper was good at sprucing yourself up, too. When
needed, you can replenish the travel-size Charmin To Go
with the local offering.

It's worth noting that drugs, even those requiring a pre-
scription in the U.S., are easy to find and buy in India. If
you're traveling through the subcontinent for any amount
of time, it's likely you'll experiment with many of them. An
excellent product called Dabur Pudin Hara Pearls is an
herbal digestive, soothing to the inevitable angry stomach
aches that arise from eating too much spicy food. And if
you need serious pain relief, Crocin painkiller will do the
trick. It's paracetamol (acetaminophen), and each caplet is
500 milligrams. A typical dose of acetaminophen in the
States is about half that. In addition, the pharmacy across
the street from where I stayed in Varanasi sold Cipro for
the asking, but I was afraid to take the Indian version and
later developed an allergy to it on a trip to Brazil.

Now that you've determined which products are indis-
pensable for your trip, you should establish how much of a
product you will need for the duration. This research must
begin at least as many weeks before your trip as you plan to
spend away from home. For example, if you'll be gone for
a month, you start your research at least a month before
you leave, better to go out six weeks or two months if
you're seriously O-C. Take your dental floss, write today's
date on the plastic packaging, and note how long it takes
you to use up the floss. Simple math will disclose how

many packages of floss to bring. Of course, sometimes re-dundancy is a good idea, and like laundry detergent, I'm sure you have a favorite floss and don't want to risk being without, so throw in an extra for good measure. If you brush twice per day, those little tubes of travel toothpaste last two weeks. Go through this process with all your ex-pendables and you'll be happy you did. To maximize your sightseeing and adventure-seeking time, deconstruct how long your daily routines take to accomplish. Time these activities: showering with and without washing your hair, drying and styling your hair, brushing your teeth, cutting fingernails and toenails, eating, getting ready for bed, and so on, then add up these times for the result.

Practice yourself in little things, for heaven's sake, and thence proceed to greater.

—*Epictetus*[33]

A note about the toiletry bag, if you have the luxury of the space to accommodate it. Ideally, it's one of those hanging, multi-compartment, "flat" ones, named by a per-son on whom eighth grade euclidean plane geometry made no impression. Selecting the right toiletry bag is extremely important, and the first thing to consider is: *Will it fit in both my backpack and a small suitcase?* This is where flat is good. If you're smallish like me, you have purchased a backpack that conforms to your size and weight, and my choice was the Osprey Ozone Travel Pack 35 Ultralight in black. I absolutely adore this backpack. Once you've de-termined, through multiple measuring of the backpack and suitcase's interiors, that the toiletry bag you want to order will fit inside, you need to consider its compartments and whether they'll hold the necessary products. This is so difficult to verify in advance that my advice is to go for it and order the one that speaks to you. (Remember, you can always return it.) When it arrives a few days later, first make sure it fits into both the backpack and the suitcase. If it passes the fit test, then it's time to stop obsessing over this fact and get into the guts of the thing. But wait until the next morning when you're slogging through your routine. Congratulate yourself for possibly choosing the right bag, and try not to let the deferred product test interrupt a good night's sleep.

It's morning. You're in the shower. You take an inventory of the products you're using. Soap, face cleanser, shampoo, conditioner, shaving cream, a razor, exfoliating scrub, a washrag. If you can get by without the exfoliating scrub and washrag, you're up to six essentials already. Even though one of my mantras is "you can buy it at your destination," as an O-C you have likely spent years, sometimes decades, experimenting with various shampoos and conditioners on the market, plus hundreds of other beauty products, to discern which ones are perfect for your face, body, and hair. This represents a huge expenditure of time, money, and effort, and the toiletry bag is command central for these products. Therefore, it's essential you choose the correct bag for your needs, and ideally you carry it with you in the backpack or carry-on rather than check it on an airplane. There's simply no replacing those essential items if a checked suitcase is lost or stolen in, say, Ulaanbaatar (the capital of Mongolia), even though it's a city of 1.3 million persons and probably has a CVS. The entire trip could be shot to hell.

When you first opened the toiletry bag the night before, you may have thought, *How in the world am I going to get everything I need into this flat bag? My products are so 3-D.* Take a deep breath; you've only completed the first step of your morning routine. The next step involves the application of sunscreens, lotions, and possibly makeup. If you're like me, you use two moisturizing sunscreens on your face and a completely different one for your neck, chest, and arms— and yet another lotion for the rest of your body. So that's four sunscreens/lotions right there, and none of the ones I prefer are sold in travel size. Only available in a glass bottle, my makeup foundation requires a sponge pad to apply. Pre-bedtime, I use makeup removing wipes to undo everything I did earlier in the day, but as already discussed, the bulky makeup remover packet stays behind. Keep the panic under control and consider accepting a more natural look for your trip.

And here thou must remember, that thy carriage in every business must be according to the worth and due proportion of it, for so shalt thou not easily be tired out and vexed, if thou shalt not dwell upon small matters longer than is fitting.

—*Marcus Aurelius*[34]

The toiletry bag I bought is 9.5"×15" (no depth dimension). One of the three compartments expands an extra inch, and another compartment is lined with plastic to manage liquid eruptions. These compartments flank the middle section, which measures 9.5"×7". The flap that zips all this up has a mesh pocket with 4"×4.5" of useable area. Organizing your bag carefully is critical, so let's discuss what goes in the bag and where, moving from left to right and starting with the plastic-lined compartment, the one for liquids.

This compartment, the one I call "skin care," is not the expandable one, in my view a big design goof. However, since it's lined, it's the only logical place for liquids because, as I mentioned, my preferred sunscreens are not sold in travel size and they tend to explode when flown. Three sunscreens wouldn't fit, though, so I had to leave one behind. The logical choice was the one formulated with human adipose stem cells, expensive and not worth the explosion risk. The compartment to the right of skin care I call "face and head." That's where liquid makeup, the sponge makeup pad, blush, Q-tips, mascara, an eyelash curler, and a shower cap goes. The middle compartment is for whatever won't fit into the three smaller ones. To its right is "teeth, hair, and nails": toothbrush, a small tube of toothpaste, floss, nail clippers, a nail file, a small comb, hair ties, and a few hair clips if they'll fit. To contextualize all this detail, Conair makes a 230-piece kit for emergency hair fixes, and we're talking twenty to thirty items, tops. Note that TSA security personnel may consider your nail file a dangerous weapon and confiscate it, demonstrating a potential scenario with sharp, stabbing motions, so consider packing it in your small suitcase. Travel size shampoo and conditioner, in a ziplock, and your large styling brush and travel-size hair curling iron will have to go in there, too.

STOICs make great museum archivists and conservators, librarians, brain surgeons, and certified public accountants; we excel at anything that requires high standards of organization and pathological attention to detail. It's because we can't tolerate thinking about where everything is and obsessively wondering if it's okay. Organization is essential so that when traveling you can pursue the purpose of your trip without this encumbrance. Although the chaos of your products can seem overwhelming, once you make your final *bare minimum* decisions, stick to them. Start using the toiletry bag and consider living out of your suitcase for a few weeks prior to your trip. You could realize an added benefit: you may be inspired to toss those decades-old, partially used bottles of shampoo under the bathroom sink and to reduce the contents of your closet. Invoke Stoic indifference for inspiration.

The happy life depends on very little.
—*Marcus Aurelius*[35]

A final word about ziplock bags. Whenever you need additional layers of organization, ziplocks of all sizes are the ultimate in utility. If you can find a large, high tensile strength ziplock, you can use it to wash your clothes if a sink or bucket isn't available. Even the most imagination-challenged person can dream up hundreds of uses for ziplocks.

CHAPTER IV

DEALING WITH OBSTACLES

Keys and Locks

If you drove yourself to the airport, your car key has created an O-C problem. Loss and/or theft is a worry, so STOICs will check obsessively to see if it's still in a front pocket or a purse. Please obviate this worry either by asking a friend to take you to the airport or by taking a train, shuttle, or cab. If, like in New Mexico's capital Santa Fe, your city no longer offers cab service, there's Uber or Lyft. Most Spanish and Portuguese-speaking countries have Cabify. Other countries may have additional options.

I agree with the general wisdom that it's not a good idea to arrive at your destination after dark, especially in a city to which you have never traveled. Sometimes, though, that great travel deal is available only if you leave at a time of day that makes your arrival at the other end late at night. This is what happened on a trip to Mérida. I couldn't pass up the $350 round-trip from Albuquerque that became available two months prior to the trip. I'd read that Mérida is the safest city in Mexico, so I went for it.

When the cab driver deposited me in front of the Airbnb, a spectacular hacienda, at about 9 p.m., suddenly I was standing at a huge old wooden door, locked. I looked around for a buzzer and didn't see one. I was already on notice that my phone didn't work in Mexico, so there was nothing else to do but pound on the door. After a few minutes had elapsed, a most congenial young woman appeared, and I stepped into an alternate universe from an earlier century. The hacienda was huge and meandering and had a smell of old books, hinting at how the Mérida elite lived in more prosperous times. High ceilings supported by elegant porticoes framed interior courtyards planted with bougainvillea and palms. Plaster walls were painted in the colors of our sandstone deserts in New Mexico: deep ochres, taupes, and manzanita red. The floors were its most outstanding feature, laid in "pasta" tiles, handmade tiles of colored concrete poured into elaborately designed metal molds. The place felt happy and welcoming, I bonded instantly with my host, and serotonin flooded my brain.

She escorted me to a room with the most charming old wooden door like the one at the entrance. Covered in numerous layers of paint and varnish, it resembled old doors I'd seen in homes of New Mexico's wealthy, repurposed as a table or hung on a wall as decoration. Aesthetics aside, I knew this door would spell trouble for me. I have a history of incompetence to the extreme when it comes to keys and locks.

Whatever your destination, you will be followed by your failings.
—*Seneca*[36]

Many times in the past I have either not been able to unlock a door or have been locked inside a room unable to escape. On two occasions door knobs have come off in my hand, once inside a hotel bathroom in Cancún, the other time inside a tiny basement room in Brooklyn where no one could hear me. I've been trapped inside a Starbucks bathroom in São Paulo by a lock that spun in circles. I've forgotten the code for the TSA-approved locks on my luggage, lost the key to the locker at the gym, you name it. So when I saw the simple, antique cast-iron key and the corresponding teeny hole cut into the door into which the key would be inserted to access or to secure my room, my amygdala gained the upper hand.

Especially difficult for the STOIC is being knocked off one's routine, affecting the carefully planned schedule the traveler has spent a lot of time perfecting. Routines rule the O-C's life—routines that have been in place for years—and being severed from the home environment will challenge you to make adjustments to those ways of negotiating the world that are habitual. Based on experiences of your new, unfamiliar environment, you must alter your routines not only to survive but also to maximize the time you enjoy your trip. But as it is back home, any change in the steps in which a task is completed can throw you into a panic.

Here's an example relating to keys and locks. You're in your room standing in the best location for optimal Wi-Fi signal. You arrange an Uber for a ride across town and the driver will arrive in three minutes. You gather your stuff and exit the room, laying everything on a sofa on the veranda outside so you can devote your complete attention to locking the door. Most carefully you insert the key into the lock and encounter resistance. You jiggle the key, remove it and try again; it slides into the hole, but the hole rotates when you turn the key. Nothing you do makes it work, and now this ticking bomb situation has made you panicky. Two minutes to Uber. You give up and run to the host's quarters, and luckily she's available to help. One minute to Uber. As the two of you return to your room, you are self-deprecating and jokey to show her how nonchalant you are about this slight inconvenience. Fortunately, she locked the door on the first try, you thank her profusely and bolt, exiting the front door of the hacienda just as your driver arrives. Crisis averted!

However, this incident alters your routine. The original sequence of steps to perform before leaving the room placed the "schedule Uber" step *before* the "lock up" step; now they are muddled because Uber arrived uncomfortably close to achieving lock up. As a STOIC, you may have to revise many carefully planned routines to accommodate unforeseen hijacks of this nature.

Metal keys in Indian hotels have an added function. In contrast to the slender, antique key at the hacienda, Indian keys can be big and bulky and an inconvenience to carry. But when the key is inserted into a metal slot on the wall near the door, the electricity activates. At a hotel in Jodhpur, I fumbled around in the dark for a long time before realizing this. Once I recovered from the irritation and anxiety, I found it quite ingenious and particularly great for people who are always misplacing their keys. No key, no electricity. End of story.

A STOIC's life would improve greatly in the absence of all keys and locks. Seneca would agree, but for a different reason.

Keys and bolts are signs of greed.[37]

Annoying LED Lights

Annoying, blinking LED lights are a fixture of the twenty-first century. We've all experienced checking into a hotel for the night, watching a little TV, and turning off the bedside table lamp only to be tormented by intense red, green, and blue pulsating points of light. The TV itself usually accounts for two of the light sources, the cable/internet modem is often a row of blue blinking lights, the carbon monoxide detector on the ceiling has a blinking red light, and the air conditioning/heating controls have red lights. Some hotels still have in-room phones with a large, maddening "message waiting" blinking red light. These photonic incursions can deprive you of a good night's sleep, and if you're not comfortable wearing a light-blocking eye mask, don't worry. Your black socks and underwear can cover these offending lights. Bring some duct tape so you'll be able to affix the sock or underwear onto a vertical surface such as the TV. Wrap about six inches of tape around the shaft of a pen or pencil and throw it in your purse or bag. If the idea of wearing socks and underwear that have been draped over a germy surface makes you queasy, light blocking stickers and sheets are also available. Short of spray-painting the LED on the ceiling-mounted carbon monoxide detector black, there's really nothing to be done about that. Sleep on your side.

An enigmatic object was installed in my room in the Mérida hacienda. Eight inches in diameter, this plastic circle of blinking, blue LEDs, attached to a wall near a desk, resembled a small alien aircraft. It must have been the Wi-Fi device. When I turned the lights off to go to sleep, the thing lit up the entire room with a nauseating blue glow. Three black socks did not cover the device completely, so instead, I grabbed a dark-colored t-shirt, still on its hanger, and draped it off the desk to block the light. Every hotel room, Airbnb, or other accommodation will involve this kind of improvising; just be sure you've packed plenty of black. Hint: You may want to remove the socks and underwear in the morning and pack them away before housekeeping arrives. STOICs are uncomfortable drawing attention to ourselves even with the cleaning staff—people you'll probably never lay eyes on.

The many ways in which travel O-C may manifest in your accommodations include:

- Must use the toilet paper down to the last sheet that's stuck to the cardboard tube.
- Must clean the toilet so it looks like no one has used it.
- Must clean any tooth brushing/flossing spray off the bathroom mirror.
- Must wipe the bathroom sink faucet of all splashes.
- Must clear any hair from all drains and collect it from the floor manually.

- Must hang all towels so their edges are straight and even.
- Must make the bed so the housekeeper won't think I'm messy.
- Must repack any stray items lying on tables and chairs and lock suitcase.
- Before leaving the room for the day, must arrange the money in my wallet in numerical order, with all the presidents'/royals'/tyrants' portraits facing the same way.
- Must check to see that all items are in their correct zip pockets in my cross body bag; otherwise I might have to resort to rummaging in public, which signals "tourist".

If you've resisted the introvert's urge to nest and you're able to leave the room by 9 a.m. or earlier, congratulate yourself on a well-managed morning.

The Issue of Wearing a Hat

If your genetic predecessors cursed you with vulnerable, pale, papery-thin Northern European skin, then at the first rays of dawn you probably apply sunscreen head to toe to ward off damaging photons. High-SPF, long-acting super emollient sunscreen, applied once in the morning, will likely provide protection all day long. If you have room to pack the expensive stuff, the formula that includes human adipose stem cells, and if cabin pressure doesn't extrude most of it into your carry-on, all the better. Regardless, taking that precaution might not be sufficient to keep your skin from burning to a crisp.

This raises the issue of wearing a hat. Not many STO-ICs want to wear a hat because not many practical hats meet our high standard of cool. Wearing a wide-brim floppy hat, especially those with a lower face cover that hooks over the ears, is not a fashion statement and signals "tourist" more than anything else. Since STOICs live in an almost continuous state of self-consciousness, we suffer from the spotlight effect which means, as I've said, whenever we're in public we think everyone is staring at us judgmentally. Since the floppy hat is a definite *no*, and we've applied the expensive, high-SPF sunscreen, kick your protection strategy up a notch and walk on the shady side of the street whenever possible.

Perhaps a self-evident observation, city streets have a shady side and a sunny side. Common sense tells you to walk on the shady side of the street when possible; that is, if you care about the health and look of your skin. However, STOICs are bothered by not walking on the same side of the street as our destination. For example, that great breakfast place is only three blocks away from the hacienda, and it's illuminated in blinding morning sun. You know you should cross the street and walk in the shade, but your O-C says no. For the sake of your skin, you must try very hard to repress this aversion to crossing the street unnecessarily and remember that every drop of sunlight that falls on your skin potentially triggers cancer and certainly causes wrinkles. Prioritization is key. If you can't stand to walk on the "wrong" side of the street, you can always wear the stupid-looking wide-brim floppy hat and face cover. But safety is also an issue. The more you cross the street, the more chances you have of being struck by a driver who's also contending with the blinding morning sun. You won't need to worry about skin cancer or your nagging O-C if you're dead. Please be extra cautious.

Study your impulses to act or not act so they are obedient to reason.
—*Epictetus*[38]

Visiting monuments or ruins, usually sited in full sun, presents a different situation. Under these conditions absolutely you must wear a hat and just not care about how you look. Many other visitors will be wearing hats like yours, so the site becomes an ugly hat safe zone. Your self-consciousness will take a back seat.

Umbrellas are sometimes necessary, and some STOICs prefer them to the ugly hat. The problem with umbrellas is that they require a hand to hold them. Hands-free umbrella hat options are available, but a STOIC would only use an umbrella hat to complement a Halloween costume, in the pool, or to wear in the hot tub when it's raining. The rainbow umbrella hat, the kind that golfers, mail carriers, and parking lot attendants sometimes wear, is never an option. Places where you definitely need a hat or an umbrella, and preferably a sun-reflecting one, include any monument, museum, or attraction where you're outside standing in line near a building in temperatures over 80°F. Both the building and the sidewalk will reflect light and heat onto your body, and even an umbrella doesn't provide enough comfort and protection in these situations. To help mitigate the heat, someone needs to invent a travel umbrella that emits a fine mist from its brim. I'm working the problem myself.

Managing Minor Injuries

While visiting the ancient Mayan site of Uxmal, about an hour-and-a-half drive south of Mérida, desperate for more shade than my hat provided, I wandered into the jungle to cool off and to enjoy a more solo traveler experience. The Yucatán was in its dry season and the trees were parched. Brittle sticks shed from the trees littered the trail leading into the jungle. The sticks snapped and crumbled under my feet, but one of the sturdier ones launched into the air when I stepped on it, and on its trajectory gave me a nasty scratch on the left ankle. I had Band-Aids, of course, in my cross body bag, but when I pulled out the ziploc, I saw that the only shapes left were dots. I had depleted my supply of the bigger rectangular-shaped ones on blisters rubbed while breaking in a pair of new shoes (a traveling no-no; *never* wear new shoes on a trip if tons of walking is part of the plan). And I realized I'd made a huge planning error referenced earlier (see Appendix A list). *I had neglected to bring an antibacterial ointment.* I washed the area with drinking water, let it air-dry, and when the wound started bleeding again, applied two of the dot Band-Aids. I wasn't going to let this minor injury put a halt to exploring the jungle, but the scratch wouldn't stop bleeding and the dots weren't doing their job. So I headed back to Uxmal's entrance, leaving a trail of blood behind me and invoking Stoic indifference.

Whatever happens was bound to happen, so refrain from railing at nature.

—*Seneca*[39]

When entering Uxmal, as with most monuments worldwide, first you are herded past several gift shops that, in addition to souvenirs, offer a variety of overpriced provisions and emergency supplies like headache remedies, antacids, Band-Aids, and antibacterial wipes. I was confident I could take care of the problem, thanks to one of these shops, and be back in the jungle in a few minutes. As the gift shops came into view, I saw a bare-legged elderly man sitting on a bench. His skin was as white as mine and his legs were covered in long red scratches, some of them dripping blood: in that instant, trivializing my single little scratch. Regardless, I wanted to take care of it as soon and as quickly as possible. Looking at him created a mirror effect, and if he'd had an amputated leg, I would have believed I did, too. I felt a wash of panic. Stoic indifference wasn't working. A friend I'd made back at the hacienda in Mérida had relayed a story about a teeny scratch of hers turning into blood poisoning, and I couldn't shove that possibility out of my mind.

Desolation comes when we are bereft of help.
—*Epictetus*[40]

A Stoically indifferent response would go something like this: I'm still alive, my life is not immediately threatened, and blood poisoning is not the reality I'm experiencing. My inner Seneca spoke up:

Let us face up to the blows of circumstance and be aware that whatever happens is never as serious as worry makes it out to be.[41]

The more I stole glances at the elderly man with the julienned legs, the more Stoic indifference lost its grip. Soon Alan Rickman overwhelmed Seneca and shouted, "YOU'RE GOING TO GET BLOOD POISONING, DO SOMETHING!" I tried my best to respond rationally, and Seneca made a brief reappearance.

This prompts me to marvel at our madness in cleaving with great affection to such a fleeting thing as the body, and in fearing lest some day we may die, when every instant means the death of our previous condition.[42]

Not surprising, STOICs can be germ- and injury-phobic. I'm mostly not that way, but blood poisoning seems particularly disagreeable. It can be easy to acquire, like from a hair that gets stuck under a fingernail or an ingrown toenail that's trimmed too severely. Or it can happen from the inside-out, like from a small bone fracture. Sinister! Surprisingly, the two gift shops stocked no emergency essentials, only the usual touristy coffee cups, t-shirts, and mini monuments. Exiting the second gift shop, I scanned the area for other options. The man with the scratched legs was still sitting on the bench. Across from him and nestled in between a tourist information office and a place to buy bottled water was the narrow entrance to a first aid station. I wondered why he didn't avail himself of their services and wondered if he silently scorned me for doing so. I made "the worst rarely happens in actuality" my mantra for the moment. I tried my hardest not to catastrophize. The panic subsided, but only a little.

The entrance to the first aid station opened into a large room fully equipped to handle any Uxmal emergency: defibrillators, splints to set broken bones of people who have tumbled down the pyramids' narrow stairways, an ominous-looking gurney for things more serious, a dated x-ray machine—a mix of old medical equipment and new technology. The room was painted a bilious green color reminding me of the doctors' offices of my childhood. A friendly receptionist greeted me, and a handsome medic named Luis immediately came to my aid. I sat on a padded table, also bilious green, covered with white crepe paper, the kind that sticks to the backs of your legs and rustles loudly every time you shift around. Reminiscent of the sounds of the leaves in the dry Yucatán forest.

To call attention to my trivial injury and to use precious resources when the man outside appeared to be bleeding to death reddened my face. On the other hand, I was excited by the opportunity to apply one of my Five Essential Phrases (which I describe in detail a bit later; see "Using a New Language") to communicate an apology for the trouble. *Lo siento mucho.* I added "mucho" for emphasis. Eyes lowered, Luis either ignored the remark or was stifling a laugh because of my bad pronunciation. He treated me as if I were a delicate flower that any swift move or too much pressure would crush. He spent a good thirty seconds examining the scratch from all angles (more embarrassment), gently palpated the ankle for swelling, pondered it for a while longer, then produced three ancient-looking glass jars containing cotton ball-soaked substances. He cleaned the wound with what smelled like alcohol, applied what I think was iodine, then liberally applied a gooey substance I assume was an antibacterial. He covered the scratch with a big, thick Band-Aid and a long, wide piece of sticky white tape to keep out moisture. Total overkill.

When the procedure was finished, I felt that opened-floodgate release of tension that happens when you realize you've dodged another bullet and everything's going to be okay. Serenity restored, momentarily. Then I remembered I was short on cash and asked the receptionist, "*¿Cuanto cuesta?*" Number three on the Five Essential Phrases list: "How much does this cost?" She gave me a funny look and said, "*Nada.*" All I needed to do was to sign a paper saying I'd been treated by Luis, and I was on my way. That was it.

Upon every accident, remember to turn towards yourself and inquire what faculty you have to deal with it. If you encounter a handsome person, you will find continence the faculty needed; if pain, then forti-tude; if reviling, then patience. And when thus habituated, the phenomena of existence will not overwhelm you.

—Epictetus[43]

Bus Challenges

Sometimes dumb luck works in your favor but, unless you have a history as a successful gambler, don't rely on it. A few hours earlier I'd bought a second-class bus ticket to Uxmal, and second class equals no bathroom. Knowing how slowly buses, planes, and other cattle car–types of mass transportation board, I decided I'd visit the bus station bathroom at the last minute. A five-minute window to complete the task and return to the bus seemed like plenty of time. When the bus began to board and tourist confusion kicked in, I headed for the *baños*. And what's this? You have to pay five pesos and go through a heavy security turnstile to access the bathroom? Twenty minutes earlier I'd bought a bag of mini croissants at the bus station *tienda*, and the change from that purchase amounted to a single coin sitting in my left pocket. The coin could have been a five-, ten-, twenty-, or fifty-centavo piece or a one-, two-, five-, ten-, or twenty-peso coin. The chance of it being a five-peso coin was one in nine—pretty bad odds. A little panicky, I fished for the coin and pulled it out. Amazingly, it was five pesos, the price of admission to the bathroom. I would have been out of luck otherwise—no time to go buy something else to get change, visit the bathroom, and board the bus. I would have been in agony for an hour and a half. Lesson learned: always carry a pocketful of change of various denominations, two of each at least, wherever you go. You may not like the extra weight, but you may find yourself in a situation where you're congratulating yourself for your STOIC smarts.

Yucatecan buses always leave on time from their point of origin, so don't think you have a window of time to get to the bus station for that 6 a.m. departure; you'll miss the bus. However, returning is a different story altogether. I learned this while waiting for the 5 p.m. bus from Chichén Itzá, another ancient Mayan ruin, back to Mérida. The Fascist era–like efficiency of the buses running on time made me anxious about missing the last bus of the evening, so I was in the parking lot at 4:45. At least a dozen buses were waiting for their passengers, and I was sure that the ADO first-class bus to Mérida was among them (my prepaid ticket was with ADO). I walked the gauntlet of buses and saw not a single ADO bus, but several second-class buses displayed the word "Mérida" on their electronic signs. I approached one driver and showed him my ticket, and he said the ADO bus would be along shortly. Several large groups of tourists bound for Cancún and Playa del Carmen appeared and boarded their buses, leaving the parking lot thinned out. The remaining confused-looking tourists assembled under the only shade tree available, so I decided to join the group. Collectively we agreed we hadn't missed the bus. The 5 p.m. bus appeared at 6:30, and seats were available for everyone.

The bus made one brief stop in the city of Valladolid, and everyone except me disembarked to visit the bathroom and to buy snacks. I stayed on board for fear of experiencing what could have happened in the Mérida bus station and to enjoy some introvert time. For the ten minutes everyone else was away, a window washer appeared with his ladder and cleaning equipment and began scrubbing the windshield with great concentration and meticulous technique. Cleaning glass of any kind is a favorite activity of the O-C person, and watching his process was both satisfying and stimulating. He had attached a child's pink shoe, possibly outgrown and discarded by one of his children, to one of the spreader bars of the ladder. Maybe the shoe was a kind of talisman or a reminder of his family that helped him get through the day.

The return bus from Uxmal to Mérida was predictably late, and waiting by the side of the road in the hot sun lulled everyone into a stupor. The bus stop was located near a complex of buildings that included an upscale hotel, a chocolate museum called Choco-Story Uxmal, a grove of calabash trees, and an exhibit of agave plants, one of the varieties used in mezcal production. I'd memorized the text on a sign next to the calabash trees explaining how maracas are made from its fruit. I'd visited the excellent Choco-Story but couldn't focus on the exhibits for worrying about missing the bus. I'd silently admired, in an O-C way, the perfectly symmetrical forms of the spiky agaves planted in neat rows.

The mind spent viewing variety, majesty, and sublimity in things around us never succumbs to ennui. Ennui is a result of idle and in-active leisure.

—*Seneca*[44]

I noted how much trash previous inconsiderate visitors discarded in the most desirable waiting area under a big shade tree. I felt compelled to pick up as much of it as I could but resisted the urge because there was nowhere to deposit it. More and more tourists arrived, and after an hour had passed, the group grew into a swarm. Everyone was anxious about getting a seat on the bus.

Like at Chichén Itzá, the bus arrived an hour and a half late, kicking up clouds of dust as it coasted to a stop on the side of the road. In an instant, the isolation and ennui of waiting surrendered to mob mentality, and it was conta-gious. Conventional behavioral norms collapsed and the communal limbic brain kicked in, triggered by the thought of being left behind. Another long wait for the next bus was not an option. We made a frenzied, desperate dash to the door as it opened.

Avoid the massed crowd—it will impart vice, and you will become more selfish, self-seeking, and self-indulgent.
—Seneca[45]

As the crowd pushed and shoved, I sensed that the driver intended to include everyone. I hung back so I could be one of the last people to board, to avoid being crushed somewhere in the middle for the hour-and-a-half ride back to Mérida. The bus was already near capacity, so no one had a chance in hell of finding a seat, but at least no one had to resort to climbing on top. Still, it was dangerously loaded with at least twice as many people as a bus can comfortably accommodate, but it was either that or wait for a situation that may not be better—and obsess about whether the bus would show up at all.

I was one of the last three people to board the bus, and I squeezed in right behind the driver. I was witness to everything he did, which included many things not related to driving a bus safely. As he pulled into the road, his forearms lay on the large and nearly horizontal steering wheel while he sorted and counted the day's pink bus tickets and stuffed them into a small pouch. Frequently he wiped his forehead and eyes with a dirty cloth, sometimes covering his eyes for seconds at a time, playing chicken with the road. Next, he gave himself a manicure, tearing the nails off between his upper and lower incisors. His head bobbed and eyelids drooped, and the bus drifted to the wrong side of the yellow line.

A constant backdrop to these activities was a game he played with the bus's high-frequency, high-decibel alarm system. When the driver exceeded the fifty-nine-miles-per-hour speed limit, the alarm emitted a shrill, eardrum-rupturing blast, the kind that either makes you want to run away or curl up in a fetal position, and neither were an option. He tried keeping the speed as close to fifty-nine as much of the time as he could, and since a bus is neither a precision instrument nor a machine that responds to sub-tlety, the effect was nearly constant no-touch torture. Enjoying any thoughts of my own, other than wanting to disable the bus speaker system in the most destructive way possible, was futile. I understood how relentless, high-decibel sound could make someone want to confess mili-tary secrets they had no idea they knew. Anything to make it stop. It occurred to me that Mexican bus alarms could be an effective addition to the CIA's well-known torture playlist (Barney the Dinosaur's "I Love You" song, the Meow Mix jingle, and "These Boots Are Made for Walk-ing"). I opened my mouth in a silent scream; I imagined blood trickling out of my ears.

Your distress has some external cause; it is not the thing itself that troubles you but your own judgment of it.
—Marcus Aurelius[46]

Even though my distress did have a troubling external cause, I let the sound bother me way beyond reason. I had let my Stoic guard down. Entering the outlying urban are-as of Mérida and their thirty-miles-per-hour speed limit filled me, instantly, with peace and gratitude.

Using an Unfamiliar Language

For travel, the Five Essential Phrases are:
1. Hello, and its variants: good morning, afternoon, night.
2. Can you take me to…
3. How much does it cost? (You must know numbers to comprehend the answer.)
4. Where is the bathroom? (essential especially for older, incontinent travelers)
5. I'm sorry.

Asking for food did not make the list; when you're a STOIC, you say "I'm sorry" much more than you ask for sustenance. We always think we're doing something wrong.

If you're feeling linguistically ambitious, in addition to the Five Essential Phrases you could try to learn some idioms and slang from the host language. Here are a few idioms to use while in Brazil:

If you have a problem, say *estou frito* ("I am deep fried").

If you're "letting your hair down," you *soltar a franga* ("release the chicken").

If you want to tell someone to get lost, say *catar coquinho* ("go pick coconuts").

And if something is really expensive, you say *custar os olhos da cara* ("it costs the eyes on your face," like the American English "costing an arm and a leg").

Here are some useful slang expressions:
Foi mal! = My bad!
Arrasar = Nailed it!
Legal = Cool!

Note that the "r" in Portuguese is pronounced like "h," "d" often is pronounced "gee," and words are commonly eliminated altogether. So Rio de Janeiro is pronounced "HEE-oh ja-NAY-hoo". Just "HEE-oh" will suffice.

In Brazil you'll see the words *puxe* and *empurrar* on every door of every business. *Puxe* (pronounced "POOSH-ee") means pull, the opposite of what you expect. It takes a lot of walking in and out of places to get this right.

Translation apps are useful, but a lot of them can't contextualize. Words that are both nouns and verbs, like "brush" or "watch" or "rear," are a type of homonym and confuse the algorithm. If a Portuguese speaker looks up the English word for *relógio*, what pops up are several meanings, including "clock," "watch," "timepiece," and "ticker." "Ticker" also translates as *coração*, which means "heart" in English. Therefore, the Portuguese speaker may think that "clock" and "ticker" are interchangeable words for "heart" and declare to a person with whom he or she has become smitten, "You have stolen my clock."

Riding the open-air tourist train to the Argentina side of Iguaçu Falls, two Brazilian tour guides discussed the Spanish word *coger* ("co-HAIR;" "to pick up") and how it traditionally means to pick up someone in the car or to pick up a book, but in other Spanish-speaking countries it can mean to have sex with someone. I thought of the word *boquete*, the name of a popular expat town in Panama, which means "gap" in Spanish and "blow job" in Portuguese. I reflected on the three years I studied Mandarin Chinese and the scary things you could say by messing up your pronunciation. By mispronouncing one of Mandarin's four tones, you could ask someone for a blow job when you really wanted to tell her she had a piece of noodle dangling from her lip. In Mandarin, "blow job" is "kǒu jiāo"; "kòu jiǎo" means "to hand over" or "garnish" (as in wages), and "kǒu jiǎo" means "the corner of the mouth."

Here are a few tricky words to be aware of and to be careful to translate correctly when you need to use one of their variants: "ball," "bear," "box," "date," "duck," "kid," "lead," "light," "long," "mean," "member," "mind," "mug," "object," "palm," "pound," "rear," "rock," "stalk," "stick," "tender," "tip," and "trip." "Ball": a round object, a dance, or a slang word for intercourse? "Date": a time at which an event occurs, or a fruit? "Rear": bringing up your children, a horse standing on its hind legs, or someone's behind? "Tip": to push something over, the top of a pointy object, or what you leave the waiter as a gratuity? Or advice on which horse will win the race?

When you're feeling overwhelmed by these linguistic issues, and you discover that slogging through those years of high school language study did nothing to prepare you for communication in the country you're visiting, a few simple practices will facilitate an increase in your vocabulary and comprehension.

You're on a bus driving through a city. Signs are everywhere, and you'll begin to notice a lot of repetition in the texts. Advertisers commonly use many of these words worldwide, a clue that you can figure out some of them on your own. When you're in Mexico, you'll see the word *calidad* on signs, a lot. *Calidad* means "quality." *Calidad* food. *Calidad* cars. *Calidad* service. There are even *Calidad* Inns in Mexico. You see the word *ahorro* a lot, too, which means "saving," and *aval*, which means "guarantee." When you want to ship something back home that you don't want to schlep around, you look for the word *envois* ("shipments") on a place of business. *Zona escolar* is a school zone; *señales* means "signals" or "signs." Again, you see these words with such frequency that they become part of your everyday experience, and what follows after enough exposure is that the veil of strangeness lifts. These words become a part of your vocabulary, reminiscent of how you learned new words as a child and how they insinuated themselves into your native language. That tight, imprisoned feeling that arises in your brain when you can't think of how to express yourself will relax.

Riding in a bus also offers a great opportunity to see lots of frequently used words in a short time. Carry a small notebook and write down words you can look up on your phone's translation app—or type it right into the app if there's time and if the ride isn't too bumpy. When you're driving on a highway, you'll see signs such as:

Si Toma No Maneje = If you drink, do not drive.

Prohibido el Paso = No trespassing.

Con Lluvia Disminuya Su Velocidad = With rain, decrease your speed.

No Maneje Cansada Evite Accidentes = Do not drive tired; avoid accidents.

And here's my favorite, a meaningless, self-referential command: *Obedezca Las Señales* = Obey the signs.

Visiting a museum gives you plenty of opportunity to improve your vocabulary and at your own pace. This is where the translation app on your phone is invaluable. As you stroll through the museum looking at objects and reading the labels next to them, you'll see words that both help with the interpretation of objects and that are useful in the outside world. In the Museo Regional de Antropología in Mérida, I entered:

cuadro = picture

ollas = pots

cazadores de venado = deer hunters

mitos = myths

escultura = sculpture

símbolo fálico = phallic symbol

sacrificio humano = human sacrifice

príncipe de los demonios = prince of the devils

guerra endémica = endemic war

One last language tip. It's a good idea to learn a single joke in the language in which you will be trying to communicate. Learning a joke and delivering it well will endear you to (most of) the people you encounter. Taxi drivers and museum guards toil at repetitive jobs and the work can be demanding for that reason, so a little comic relief will endear you to them. Plus, museum guards are required to stand for long periods of time, sometimes in a confined space, so if you can rouse a laugh that gets their bodies moving you've done your good deed for the day.

In New Mexico, we have a joke that goes like this: New Mexico: not really new, and not really Mexico. It makes a great bumper sticker. It also translates well into Spanish: *Nuevo México no es realmente nuevo y no es realmente México.* It's easy to remember, and *Méxicanos* understand the humor. Contrary to what seems logical, New Mexico got its name before Mexico was known as Mexico. When Spanish explorers first arrived in New Mexico in 1563 and documented the region, they incorrectly believed that the area was populated with wealthy Mexica Indian cultures who were descendents of the ancient Aztecs. Even though the area had no connection to Mexico or to the Mexica tribes, the name New Mexico stuck. Here's where the confusion enters. Old Mexico wasn't called Mexico back in the 1500s; it was called New Spain. It wasn't until 1821 that New Spain won independence from Old Spain and started calling itself Mexico. So New Mexico had its name over 250 years *before* Mexico was called Mexico. For the twenty-seven years between 1821 and 1848, Mexico annexed New Mexico but then ceded it to the United States. New Mexico officially became the forty-seventh state of the U.S. in 1912. So not really new, and not really Mexico.

CHAPTER V

EVERYONE'S HAVING MORE FUN
THAN YOU

A cenote is a deep, spring-fed pool of crystal clear water exposed when surface limestone collapses. Over six thousand cenotes spread over a seventy-six-thousand-square-mile area give the Yucatán peninsula its Swiss cheese character. The ancient Maya used cenotes for ritual human sacrifice; today, swimming in a cenote is touted as a rite of passage, a transformative spiritual experience compared to surviving clinical death. With their vaulted ceilings, cavernous spaces, and mystical light, cenotes convey solemn, sacred, otherworldly qualities. Swimming in one is a baptism into the realm of the divine.

Having seen the famous cenote at Chichén Itzá clogged with algae, opaque and stagnant, I had my doubts about an all-day cenote swim tour as mystical transformation. But I booked a tour regardless. I hoped at least one of the cenotes was what I'd seen in travel books and on websites, an enchanted pool of sapphire blue illuminated by golden shafts of light. Over-thinking the logistics of the experience, the STOIC in me had resisted the call.

These were the problems. No changing cabanas are available in the middle of the jungle, so STOIC women are forced to wear a one-piece swimsuit all day (for the sake of modesty, bikinis and their variants are not recommended). For protection from the sun and insects, a long-sleeve shirt and either long pants or shorts that reach the knees are mandatory. The problem with this outfit becomes obvious the first time you visit the bathroom. You attempt to pull the crotch area of your bathing suit to one side to pee, but you realize you'll just pee your hand and probably one of your legs, too. You must completely disrobe, exposing yourself to mosquitoes. Your anxiety spikes thinking that someone may open the bathroom stall door.

What is unlooked for is most crushing—put your thoughts ahead of every eventuality. Rehearse them in your mind.
—Seneca[47]

Here's where another problem arises. Some designers of bathroom stalls forget that functionality is important and fail to include a hook on which to hang your things. In my experience, hookless stalls outnumber stalls with hooks. In a hookless stall, after disrobing you're forced to toss your clothes over the top of the door, a place that may have been accumulating dust for a while. A piece of clothing might slip off onto a dirty, wet floor. Someone might walk past and swipe your clothes. None of these scenarios is acceptable, so you may want to include an over-the-door hook with your bare essentials. Make room for it in your luggage because its size and weight can throw off your carefully curated bag/backpack combo.

Another issue concerns airport bathroom stalls primarily, although I've experienced this inconvenience in plenty of other types of bathrooms around the world. I'm always incredulous when the stall door opens to the inside. Houston's Intercontinental Airport, Denver's International Airport, and Chicago's O'Hare are all offenders. If you're traveling with a roller bag carry-on and a cross body bag, and maybe a shopping bag full of souvenirs and possibly a hat, or if it's just you and you're pregnant or generously proportioned, it's supremely difficult to maneuver you/you plus your stuff into a bathroom stall with an inward-opening door. You can hijack the handicapped stall, but you risk the wrath and scorn of other patrons, trigger the spotlight effect, and create another layer of unneeded anxiety for yourself by doing so (*What if a* real *handicapped person needs the stall and I'm in it?*) I often wonder if this design feature represents a passive-aggressive act on the parts of designers and airport officials, devised to make the traveler's already challenging experience even worse. I'm proud to report that New Mexico's own Albuquerque International Sunport's bathroom doors open outward, only one of the many *calidad* designs found throughout this excellent facility.

Back to the Mexican stall. You've disrobed and tossed your clothes over the top of the door. If you can't manage to pee with your bag around your neck, it sits on the floor near a puddle of you-know-what. You prepare to sit down, but wait; there's no seat on the toilet. Yucatecan toilets often have no seats even though the toilets have attachment holes. The first time I faced this situation I was wearing jeans and couldn't pull them down far enough on my legs without the jeans brushing the wet floor. So when I squatted over the seatless toilet, I couldn't crouch or separate my legs enough to direct the pee to its intended place and ended up with wet jeans from the waistband to about mid-leg, a great learning experience.

Except for your shoes, you are totally naked and about to negotiate the seatless toilet. When you sit down, if you're small like me, you brace yourself with your hands on either side of the toilet so you don't fall in. When you're finished, you are courteous to the next patron and wipe the perimeter of the seat. Getting dressed can take five minutes. The entire process may take ten or fifteen.

Make the best of what is in your power, and take the rest as it occurs.
—*Epictetus*[48]

When we arrived at the first cenote, Sambulá, I followed a young man into a small, dark hole in the ground, descending an ominous wooden staircase into the gloom. Like Dante following Virgil into hell. When my eyes adjusted to the darkness, I saw that the cave was larger than its entrance suggested but not much bigger than a two-car garage. The hemispherical shape of the cave's ceiling amplified the laughter and talking and splashing around of scores of people enjoying their swim. No lifeguards are on duty at cenotes. Clothes, shoes, and bags were scattered everywhere. Here's where I encountered the next problem. Where do you put your stuff and not worry about it disappearing? Back in the States, I pre-worried this problem a lot. Would the tour guide accompany us into the cave to watch everyone's things? Not likely. Would lockers and a lock be provided, with a big safety-pin to secure the key to your swim suit? Even less likely. What was everybody else doing? Not worrying about it and having fun.

When you set about any action, remind yourself of what nature the action is. If you are going to bathe, represent to yourself the incidents usual in the bath—some persons splashing, others jostling, others scolding, others stealing. And thus you will more safely go about this action, if you say to yourself, "I will now go to bathe, and keep my own will in harmony with nature." And so with regard to every other action. For thus, if any impediment arises in bathing, you will be able to say, "It was not only to bathe that I desired, but to keep my will in harmony with nature; and I shall not keep it thus, if I am out of humor at things that happen.

—*Epictetus*[49]

I undressed down to my swimsuit, hung my bag on one of the staircase's posts, and concealed the bag with my clothes. I stepped into the water, hoping to drown the chiggers I was sure had attached themselves to my ankles during the walk to the cenote. The water was rust-colored and murky, reminding me of institutional iced tea, and the slimy, rocky bottom was hard to negotiate. The quantity of people in this tiny space made me nervous, but I tried to maintain a smile and my *alegría de vivir*. I thought about the waterproof pouch I'd purchased for my iPhone so I could take underwater photos and how irrelevant it was. STOIC self-consciousness activated the spotlight effect. I stayed in the cenote long enough to signal I was enjoying myself and having fun but was heading up the ladder within fifteen minutes.

Quit the game when it no longer pleases you, and depart.
                                                —*Epictetus*[50]

Emerging into the upper world was a relief, and I quickly understood why no one, including myself, had a towel. In the hot and sunny Yucatecan dry season, water evaporates from wet swim suits in a matter of seconds. The jungle trees had dropped most of their leaves, and the only place to sit in the shade was under a simple pole building with a thatched roof. A man stood under the structure next to a large cooler of drinks sitting on a table. I thought perhaps he was selling them, but my introversion prevented me from asking. I sat on a bench next to the table and surveyed the dry landscape when a powerful gust of wind blew through the trees, the sound of shifting piles of thick, crisp leaves so loud that I jumped. A family emerged from the cenote, the kids' teeth chattering (in the 90°F weather) as they ran toward the man, who I realized must be their father. Their mom opened another cooler full of ham sandwiches and the kids peeled oranges. I was mortified that I'd crashed their picnic. *¡Lo siento mucho!*

Dzonbakal was our second stop. This cenote was much bigger and not as claustrophobic, the water an indigo blue at the deep end. I conquered my reluctance to get in and swim, doing my best to suppress a rush of intrusive thoughts about what non-human creatures might be in the cenote with me. I kept my head above water and my mouth slammed shut. After a few moments dog paddling in the indigo water, I could feel myself relaxing and enjoying the experience.

Happy is the one who can adjust and shape his own personality.
—*Seneca*[51]

Saving the best for last, Xbatún cenote was the largest of the three and more like a pond sheltered by a limestone overhang than an underground cave. A huge strangler fig was its centerpiece, and water lilies floated in turquoise-colored water. Gnarled roots cascading over the limestone cliff created intimate enclosed spaces that kids hid behind to escape their parents and teenagers used for make-out sessions. The strangler fig's more delicate feeder roots re-sembled a cascade of hair undulating in the water. Clinging to the edge of the overhang, the tree that the strangler fig had colonized and overwhelmed was magnificent: a Mexi-can tree of life from which this microcosm had emerged, now having the last bit of vitality squeezed out of it. I swam to the far end of the cenote to position myself directly un-der the tree. My eyes followed the trunk up into its canopy, its leaves still vibrant and shimmering. I had emerged from the underworld to this vision of paradise. I thanked the universe for bringing me to this pure, Stoic moment and for everything that participated in making it be.

Whatsoever is now present, and from day to day hath its existence; all objects of memories, and the minds and memories themselves, inces-santly consider, all things that are, have their being by change and alteration. Use thyself therefore often to meditate upon this, that the nature of the universe delights in nothing more, than in altering those things that are, and in making others like unto them. So that we may say, that whatsoever is, is but as it were the seed of that which shall be.

—*Marcus Aurelius*[52]

I have a suggestion. Don't spend too much time before your trip obsessing over photos of the places you intend to visit. You may develop an unrealistic idea of a place or create expectations that might not be met. I obsessed over photos of cathedral-like cenotes and was surprised to be delivered to a small hole in the ground. Maybe a camera isn't so much a tool for stealing the soul but a fun house mirror that distorts reality: a photograph a shape-shifting trickster that fools you into thinking that representation is equal to essence. If you can approach a new place with the freshest possible vision and without preconceived notions, the better your experience and the more open you will be to its special magic.

CHAPTER VI

THE UNEXPECTED

Driving with Strangers

Think about how many times you enter strangers' vehicles when you're traveling, and consider how remarkable it is that you think nothing of it. Your first point of contact in a country, not counting customs, may be a taxi driver or a bus driver, someone you think of as a public servant of sorts—but in reality, they're not that at all. They're just some guy or gal whose job it is to take you to your destination, and they may not be invested in the job the way you assume they are, or care about your safety. You already know one bus driver who fits this description, who kicked back and gave himself a long-overdue manicure on company time. Plus, many people become Uber drivers to supplement their incomes doing who knows what, and standards of professionalism may be lax. So, at times, public transportation can be a little sketchy. Be assured, though, if you are in the backseat of an auto rickshaw in Delhi, you are in the expert hands of a finely-tuned driving machine, and I mean the man, not the rickshaw. (Auto rickshaws are three-wheeled open-air vehicles with a canopy, a bench seat, and handrails; they're also known as tuk-tuks.) Your first tuk-tuk ride through Delhi may trigger an intense flight or freeze response, so be forewarned. You may be shocked by the density and amount of traffic, the speed at which you are traveling, the close calls that happen with regularity, and the chaotic sound of the drivers honking at each other. This sensory overload may be too much for the STOIC, but when you parse the cacophony and understand what's really going on, you'll be able to relax and enjoy the ride.

Think of how bats echolocate. From their megaphone-shaped nostrils they emit high-frequency clicking sounds that reflect off objects, letting the bat know with great precision, and in real time, direction, size, and distance of objects in their environs and whether an obstacle is in their path. This is exactly what Indian drivers are doing, but with the added advantage of excellent vision. The constant honking functions as a kind of bat-inspired GPS to let other drivers know your coordinates, from where you are entering their space, and how quickly; split-second computations in the brain parsing the sounds relevant to positioning. These drivers are so skilled that routinely they come within inches of one another on all sides, and the occasional collision is the exception, not the norm. As a passenger you must keep your head, hands, and feet inside the vehicle, and as long as you invest your unconditional trust in the driver, you will arrive at a destination safely. I say "a" destination because it may not be your intended destination, but don't worry, you'll get there, eventually.

Say you've agreed on a price for the driver to take you to Dilli Haat market in Delhi and you've climbed into the back seat of his tuk-tuk. The driver shifts into gear, and off you go. You head toward Dilli Haat, but suddenly the driver takes a "wrong" turn down a side street. At first you think he knows a great shortcut, and you congratulate yourself for choosing such a savvy driver. But then you realize you're way off course and ask the driver where you're going, while contemplating how you can jump out and run away the next time he stops. He answers, "I am taking you to a place *better* than Dilli Haat," giving you a radiant smile and a jiggle of the head. You reply, "But I want to go to Dilli Haat." He says, "Don't worry, better than Dilli Haat." You go back and forth like this until you have arrived at the place better than Dilli Haat, which is more upscale and way more expensive. You're struck by the exquisite rugs and fabrics hanging outside the entrance and the driver says, "Just try, if you don't like then I'm taking you to Dilli Haat." Essentially you've been held hostage, but you don't mind so much. Delhi is a huge, congested city of nineteen million people that is difficult and time-consuming to navigate, and the driver is providing a new shopping experience that you would have never discovered on your own. Reluctantly you enter the store, the owner hands you an Indian Coke with a hint of betel, and before long you're wearing a stunning indigo *shalwar kameez* with golden threads, custom fit. You also buy a small marble jewelry box inlaid with semiprecious stones in the image of the Taj Mahal and several silver ankle bracelets for yourself and as gifts. The tuk-tuk driver is richer by five percent of your purchase price. You've spent more money than your budget allows, so you ask the driver to take you back to the hotel.

While in Udaipur during another trip to India, I was eating breakfast in the hotel rooftop restaurant. The restaurant overlooked a wetland that flowed into Udaipur lake with its famous "floating" palace. For the prior three days, every morning an elephant and his caretaker appeared at the same time at the ghat (steps) on the far side of the wetland. A huge tree was shedding its branches, and they were collecting them. The man stood on the elephant's head, the elephant picked up branches with his trunk and slowly passed them back to the man, and the man arranged the branches in a pile on the elephant's rump. The elephant needed no prompting and, like old friends completely accustomed to each other, they made a perfect team.

By that point in the trip I had full-blown Indian turista and felt lousy much of the time. A couple at breakfast had adopted me and were raving about a magnificent city near the Pakistan border called Jaisalmer and how I needed to see it. I was already thinking about hiring a driver to take me to a hill station called Mount Abu and to Jodhpur, and Jaisalmer was only another 130 miles to the west. But the thought of being out in the middle of nowhere, driving with a stranger and having to hurl, had held me back.

Sickness is an impediment to the body, but not to the will, unless itself pleases. Lameness is an impediment to the leg, but not to the will; and say this to yourself with regard to everything that happens.

For you will find it to be an impediment to something else, but not truly to yourself.

—Epictetus[53]

Their enthusiasm was persuasive. A few hours later I hired a car and driver from a local travel agency, and we embarked on a three day tour of western Rajasthan. Khan, the driver, was tall, fortyish, and fashion-conscious: he wore white pants and white slip-on patent leather shoes, a patterned silk shirt unbuttoned to his navel, and a thick gold rope chain. He had a chill manner and a beautiful, broad smile framing flawless teeth. He spoke perfect English.

In a fever we should have principles ready as relate to fever; and not, as soon as we are taken ill, forget all…Some way or other I must depart and take care of this frail body whether a fever comes or not.

—Epictetus[54]

Part of the package included stops at two amazing sites that anyone traveling in western Rajasthan must see: Kumbhalgarh Fort and a Jain temple called Ranakpur. We arrived at both places without gastric incident, but I did have to stop twice by the side of the road to pee. On the first occasion, I crouched behind a wall that screened me from the road and the second time hid behind a large mango tree. It occurred to me that he could abscond with my possessions—my passport, bag, and my brand-new sitar—and leave me squatting in the Thar Desert. But Khan was a good, honest man and nothing worrisome happened. Before entering the Jain temple, he said I needed to remove my watch because it had a leather strap, and a leather purse I was carrying had to stay in the car. The Jains are deeply committed to non-violence—they're the ones who wear face masks to prevent tiny creatures from being inhaled—so no products derived from slain cows are permitted. When I returned to the car, nothing had been touched in my absence.

The dishonest man is not better off because he has lost respect.
—Epictetus[55]

On the road between Jodhpur and Jaisalmer, long convoys of army vehicles and small missile launchers clogged the road, holding up traffic. Khan explained that because of western Rajasthan's proximity to Pakistan, the army shuffled their gear around regularly in that part of India. It amounted to so much posturing and chest-thumping and wasn't a threat. Stoic indifference was easy in his company.

We arrived in Jaisalmer to see its golden sandstone buildings blaze in the afternoon sun. Jaisalmer's Golden Fort looms over the city, its parapet walls reminiscent of the lower jaw of a giant camel with its flat, rounded teeth. One of Jaisalmer's most striking architectural features is the *haveli*, ornate townhouses constructed during the early nineteenth century for the rich merchant classes who lived in the area. During the twentieth century many havelis were converted into museums or hotels, and I stayed at one called the Mandir Palace, an architectural marvel inhabited by Jaisalmer's elite for over two centuries. Jaisalmer's locals adorn themselves with outlandish, colorful clothing dripping in pompoms and with jewelry that rivals the royal bling of any monarch. Their camels' thick fur coats are often shaved in intricate patterns echoing the detailed stonework seen on the buildings' façades.

The next morning Khan and I made the long drive from Jaisalmer to Mount Abu, a hill station near the border of Rajasthan and Gujarat, used for centuries as a popular retreat from the heat of the desert. The eight-hour drive gave us lots of time to become further acquainted, and I discovered that he was a film buff, preferring vampire movies, James Bond, and Mr. Bean. We arrived in time for sunset, an event in Mount Abu where most of the town's population makes the trek up the mountain to pay their respects to the sun. Tribal men wearing bright red turbans hauled people in tiny carts up the winding road, or for a few rupees you could ride one of their horses—slender, piebald creatures with long legs and pointy ears that curled in a spiral. Vendors at the top of the mountain sold corn on the cob, peanuts (which they pronounced "penis"), soap bubbles, and plastic Slinkys. Everyone was laughing and having fun, except for two dour German women sitting on a rock plotting a route to their next destination. It seemed like they could use some help from the Stoics, but clearly they did not want to interact. As the sun descended, the revelers (me included) took turns photographing each other pretending to hold the sun between a thumb and forefinger, as if it were a juicy clementine we could pluck from the sky and pop into our mouths.

· · · · ·

A few entries in *Travel for STOICs* are not strictly about solo travel but have important STOIC messages to impart. So I'm bending the rules and including them.

My first time to visit São Paulo, Brazil, was to see Virtù and to experience Rio's *Carnaval*, the world's most extravagant party. I also wanted to visit two colleagues I'd met in the States a year earlier. Native Brazilians, they'd been long-time Miami residents and had relocated to the mountains near the sea port village of Mangaratiba (pronounced "Mahn-gar-a-CHEE-ba") in Rio de Janeiro state. Virtù was getting around São Paulo without a car, which is a bit like living in Los Angeles and relying on public transportation—only São Paulo has four times the population of Los Angeles while occupying approximately the same area of land. The bus from São Paulo to Rio made stops in Paraty ("Pat-a-CHEE") and Mangaratiba, so we bought our tickets.

This coastal route meanders through some of the last remaining stands of original Atlantic Forest. Decimated by resource-hungry colonizers of past centuries and by our contemporaries in the cattle industry, it's humbling to see these hardy survivors in today's world. The coastal forest is only a narrow strip of land, and to the north lie vast ranches on rolling hills where native trees are considered intruders. Stands of non-native eucalyptus are planted, for erosion control, in uniform rows on the tops of these hills and look strangely out of place. From a distance, they resemble giant matchsticks poked into the landscape, foregrounded by a bright green ocean of grass populated with thousands of giant termite mounds.

Halfway between São Paulo and Rio, Paraty is a historic coastal town with a sketchy colonial past. In the seventeenth and eighteenth centuries the Portuguese absconded with hordes of gold mined by African slave labor, decamping to Portugal from the port of Paraty. A 745-mile handmade stone road from Paraty to the state of Minas Gerais leads to what were the world's richest gold mines in the late 1600s, and today the Gold Trail is a tourist destination. As if 745 miles weren't enough, the town is paved in cobblestone streets, and once a month on the full moon, Paraty becomes a little Venice. At high tide, water rushes onto the cobblestones from holes in the seawall and recedes again with the tide. Lush mountains replete with wildlife and waterfalls rise to the immediate north of Paraty.

The height of summer in Brazil is February, the month of my visit. The bus from São Paulo to Rio was advertised as air conditioned, which I learned meant that it was possible to open some of the windows. By the time we arrived in Paraty, a hot, sticky, and relentless wind had deposited a layer of grime on our faces, and we were desperate for a jump into one of the area's ice-cold waterfalls.

At the Paraty bus station, the driver told us that the bus continued directly to Rio with no stop in Mangaratiba. Or rather he told Virtù, because the only words I knew in Portuguese were *obrigada* ("thank you"), *com licença* ("excuse me"), and of course, *eu sinto muito* ("I'm very sorry"). Had we misunderstood when we bought our tickets? He suggested we get off at one of several undesignated road-side bus stops along the route to Mangaratiba and our friends could pick us up there. Brazil's cellular infrastructure was seriously bad in those days, so back in São Paulo we had arranged a meeting location and time in Mangaratiba with my colleagues. It was a good STOIC move because as soon as São Paulo was in our rear view mirror, our cell phones were useless. Their cell phones didn't work in the mountains, so there was no way to communicate a change of plans. Regardless, being dropped off on the side of the road after dark, with impenetrable jungle on either side in a GPS no-man's-land, was nonnegotiable. We had only one option: to rent a car.

In the late afternoon heat and humidity everyone seemed to be moving in slow motion through sludge. The misting umbrella would be popular in Paraty. Or simple pole buildings where you could relax in a hammock with a block of ice underneath. Fans blowing on the ice would evaporate the water, cooling you off. Crossing the street from the bus station to the car rental company was like walking across hot coals.

Virtù and an employee discussed the details of the rental, none of which I understood; an ancient printer produced a multi-page document of inscrutable complexity. Virtù read the document patiently, and it turned out to be a standard car rental agreement. A five-hundred dollar USD temporary deposit was required to cover potential damage to the car; again, standard, but a little pricey. The employee handed me a pen for my signature. Finally all the arrangements were made, and I expected to be handed a set of keys and off we'd go. But outside there was no lot full of shiny new air-conditioned Chevrolets and Chryslers. The employee explained to Virtù that a driver was bringing a car from another location. They were closing for the day, and we were locked out of the building. After another twenty minutes had elapsed, we wondered if we'd been scammed.

Finally a beat-up white Toyota Corolla pulled up, and the driver got out and introduced himself. Again, I expected to be handed the keys and off we'd go, but he said he'd be driving us to Mangaratiba. I had just signed a document declaring my responsibility for the car, so this new development created a problem. Via Virtù's translation, I told him no way would I be responsible for a rental car that somebody else was driving. We began to argue, with Virtù interpreting and trying to match both party's emotions, gesturing wildly and in my face when interpreting for him; lowering her posture and avoiding eye contact when interpreting for me. The guy was volatile and wouldn't back down.

Anger is not manly. Rather a gentle calm is more human and virile. It shows strength, sinew and courage—not the indignant and complaining. Anger is a sign of weakness.
—Marcus Aurelius[56]

A woman with a baby appeared and approached the car. She opened the back door and got in, as if the car were hers. In fact, it was. She was his wife, and they were driving to Mangaratiba to visit relatives on my dime. He agreed to amend the contract to read that I wasn't responsible in case something happened to the car.

Virtù sat in the front seat with the driver; the wife, the baby, and I huddled together in the back seat. Our adopted family was sick with bad colds. As we entered the coastal highway to Rio, the driver began arguing with his wife, screaming who knows what into the back seat. She stared out the window and said nothing, her eyes brimming with tears. Brave Virtù confronted him and demanded that he stop being abusive. He became sullen and silent, and his anger assumed a more dangerous form. The highway between São Paulo and Rio is narrow and winding, and his fast, reckless driving inspired thoughts of regret for the O-C and introverted ways in which I'd squandered my time on Earth. I grieved for Virtù and the very real possibility that her life would be cut short by this lunatic kidiot.

What would you like to be doing when you're overtaken by death?...
It makes no difference how we die because we must.
—Epictetus[57]

Rehearse death. It is a very good thing to familiarize oneself with
death.
—Seneca[58]

This is how we passed the next two and a half hours. When anxious, I worry a special place on my chin that mitigates anxiety, and it felt bruised and raw. The road was populated with crumbling, unmarked bus drop-offs choked with vines and covered in gang graffiti, and in spite of the peril we faced with the angry, abusive driver, it seemed like we'd made the correct lesser-of-two- evils decision. When the lights of Mangaratiba appeared in the distance, Virtù, the wife, the baby, and I breathed a communal sigh of relief. Virtù unfolded the crumpled, sweaty directions to our rendezvous point and read them to the driver. Still furious, his driving prowess affronted, he refused to listen. "*Eu sei para onde vou!*" ("I know where I'm going!") At a split in the road he hesitated, went the wrong direction, and came to a screeching halt. He snatched the directions from Virtù's hand, read them for a few seconds, and hit the accelerator without checking to see if the road was clear.

See to it that nothing comes by surprise.
—Seneca[59]

Taking the same split in the road that we had, it would have been impossible for the other car to avoid the accident. We collided, but no one was injured. For an instant, I allowed myself to feel triumphant for anticipating this scenario and insisting on the contract modification back in Paraty. Not very Stoic to gloat about someone else's misfortune, though; and if Marc-A had been crammed in the back seat with us, not a single aspect of our journey would have fazed him. Plus, things could have attained a greater degree of sideways than they did. We successfully rendezvoused with my colleagues and left our dysfunctional family behind.

On paper I was indemnified for damage to the car, but the company still had my five-hundred-dollar deposit. When the accident was explained back at headquarters, they promised a refund, but I had pretty much kissed that money goodbye. A few weeks passed, I went online to check the charges on my credit card and, to my surprise, the deposit had been removed.

Because we STOICs fall somewhere on the forbearance/acceptance spectrum, being a STOIC can place you at an advantage when negotiating challenging situations and anticipating outcomes. Embrace the STOIC in you and use these qualities to your benefit!

Seek at once, therefore, to be able to say to every unpleasant semblance, "You are but a semblance and by no means the real thing." And then examine it by those rules which you have…whether it concerns the things which are within our own power, or those which are not; and if it concerns anything beyond our power, be prepared to say that it is nothing to you.
—Epictetus[60]

Actually, Explosions Are Common in India

The Fort Worth wedding guests would feel vindicated if they could experience the wedding season in Varanasi. Explosions abound, usually harmless but not always. Wedding season in Varanasi meant that every night large parties of people came parading down the streets of the city banging on makeshift drums and metal containers; playing trumpets, trombones, and tubas, and setting off fireworks. The first time I heard this racket my amygdala lit up, misinterpreting the sound as a riot that had erupted in the street below. To escape the claustrophobic, closet-sized room I'd rented, I was sitting on the music school rooftop where a gentle evening breeze moderated the oppressive heat. During our briefing at the school, the teachers told us we'd be hearing a lot of the same in the coming weeks, late into the night. Citizens of Varanasi would find a Fort Worth wedding tame by comparison.

Like in many places around the world, celebrations of the end of winter and the beginning of spring are numerous in India. One of those celebrations, Vasant Panchami, is in part a tribute to the Hindu goddess Saraswati, the goddess of wisdom, learning, truth, and purity who plays an instrument called the vina, a cousin to the sitar. The color yellow is important to this celebration, signifying the sun, the vibrancy of life, and the beauty of nature, and people wear bright yellow clothing in honor of the occasion. Another important spring festivity is Holi, a total free-for-all where celebrants wear white from head to toe and become living canvases for colored powders that everyone slings on each other. People also carry squirt guns and water balloons filled with colored water, both very effective delivery systems. These colors don't just wash out when the party's over; they stain your hair and skin, get under your fingernails and toenails, and stain your tongue and teeth. After our mini Holi celebration at the music school, we scrubbed the white marble floors for hours to remove deposits of electric blue, yellow, and red. Fireworks and other explosions are integral to all of these celebrations, and if you're from the U.S. and/or are conditioned to think that terrorism and the potential for gun violence lurks in every shadow and around every corner (and in every school), this can take some getting used to.

The soul becomes dyed with the color of its thoughts.
—Marcus Aurelius[61]

Once you've been in India for a week or so, and explosions become a predictable part of every evening, your amygdala adjusts to non-threatened status. The joy of these occasions will mediate your introversion, so you may feel compelled to seek out opportunities to participate in the festivities.

Another practice involving explosions took place at the Varanasi train station. Since cows freely roam the streets, the highways, and pretty much wherever they please, this created potentially dangerous conditions for arriving and departing trains. Cowherds weren't on the Ministry of Railways's payroll, so to keep the animals from wandering onto the tracks, maverick citizens took the matter into their own hands. Crude cluster bombs covered in molasses, salt, and cement—salt licks with a lethal punch—were placed near the tracks to attract and dispatch the animals. The local press reported that the extermination plot was hatched not out of concern for trains and passengers but as an excuse to kill cows for their coveted skins. The spiritual capital of India, over three million Hindus live in Varanasi; that's three million souls with a special reverence for cows. But the citizens of Varanasi looked the other way.

The train station offered a reliable supply of animals. Many explosions happened during the two months I lived in Varanasi, endangering hordes of passengers waiting on platforms, but the only casualty had been a single dog. Bombs left out to dry after an application of salt and molasses had been found on the platforms. Bags of bombs, too, just sitting there. How could it be that in a place where the cow was considered sacred, there was no display of public outcry? Were the hit men paying everyone off to keep them quiet?

Tearing of the flesh is a pleasure of habit where cruelty was formed.
—*Seneca*[62]

Solo Camping in the Middle of Nowhere, New Mexico

Around the world, the International Dark-Sky Association has established officially designated dark sky areas, and a location in southwestern New Mexico received the first designation ever in the U.S. Called the Cosmic Campground, the closest source of light pollution is twenty-four miles away in Reserve, New Mexico, population 276 at last count. A star party is planned for two days every October, and astronomy buffs from all over North America schlep huge, heavy telescopes to the Cosmic Campground for unobstructed views of celestial phenomenon. Photos on the website of previous star parties showed smiling people outfitted with the latest in optical viewing technology, with lanyards around their necks holding astronomy-friendly red light flashlights, standing in front of the latest model RVs and next to tables spread with mouthwatering picnic lunches. The dry and desolate southwestern New Mexico landscape in the background was an incongruous setting for all this high-tech gear and gourmet food. I'd forgotten my advice to myself after visiting the Yucatecan cenotes. *Don't spend too much time before your trip obsessing over photos of the places you intend to visit. You may develop an unrealistic idea of a place or create expectations that might not be met.* Incentivized, I decided to make the five-hour Santa Fe–to–Cosmic Campground drive to experience it. Before leaving Santa Fe, I'd checked the weather for temperature and wind and both were within my range of tolerance. There was no chance of precipitation.

The drive itself was astonishingly beautiful, meandering through mountains, forests, flatland desert, the grounds of the Very Large Array, and decaying but cute little towns. I was enjoying the journey and glad I'd decided to go. Before I left Santa Fe, I'd Googled gas stations in the area, and at the final turnoff to the campground, there sat the combination gas station and convenience store I'd found online. Since Reserve was the last vestige of civilization for twenty-four miles, I availed myself of their bathroom and provisioned myself with an Almond Joy. A weathered rancher who could have been Bill Murray's older, craggier brother ran the cash register. The store's interior was festooned with elk antlers installed along the perimeter of the ceiling.

The more distance I put between me and the convenience store, the more my anxiety increased. What if no campsites were available because of the crush of star partiers? Since the Cosmic Campground is so famously dark, the event would be hugely popular. But as the campground came into view, only one lone tent was visible and the camper's car was elsewhere. It was close to four o'clock, maybe too early in the day for the serious astronomers to arrive since night sky viewing was at least five hours into the future. The campground was about as primitive as they get: no water, no shade, no shelters, no friendly retired couple camp hosts, only two hole-in-the-ground toilet facilities—but, amazingly, a strong Wi-Fi signal. The temperature on my phone read 65°F and the wind had increased to twenty-five miles per hour, shifting from the west to the northeast. A cold front was blowing in.

Setting up my tent was like struggling with a sail in a squall, and it took almost an hour to get everything tied down. I'd secure one corner, run to the next, and the wind would undo what I'd just accomplished. I'd wait for a moment of calm and work frantically before another gust. I was relieved that the star party folks hadn't arrived yet to witness this travesty of amateur tent camping. Regardless, a STOIC can feel totally embarrassed in the presence of only him- or herself.

After a previous experience tent camping on bare ground, enduring temperatures in the high 20s, I'd bought a sleeping bag with a temperature rating of +20°F and an inflatable mattress. Promising the comforts of a bed by means of a "unique wave beam construction," this single miracle mattress would eliminate all awareness of any rocks or bumps. Plus a flocked surface guaranteed to keep the bedding from slipping off. I'd also bought a liner for my sleeping bag, adding 20° of "extra toasty warmth for those unexpected chilly nights," the tag read.

I pulled the mattress out of its box, plugged the mattress pump into the car's cigarette lighter, and flipped the switch. Since I hadn't used it in a year, I'd forgotten the pump had an internal rechargeable battery, and it was dead. I read the fine print: "Charge for eight hours prior to use." My inner critic went ballistic. I realized the pump could have been charging on the drive down, and now I was going to be sleeping on hard, rocky ground again. My STOIC self fought back. *I will embrace this situation; I will wish this to happen as it does happen.* Marc-A was standing by.

When in agreement with nature, we are flexible to circumstances; we adapt easily.[63]

And Epictetus chimed in.

When you get angry, you should know that you aren't guilty of an isolated lapse, you've encouraged a trend and thrown fuel on the fire.[64]

He added:
The bare ground is the softest bed.[65]

I know he meant that as metaphor, but I desperately wanted its literal meaning to be true. I set the flaccid mattress inside the tent and lay down on it, hoping that I'd cleared the area under me sufficiently before staking the tent. I wasn't up for another hour-long struggle in case I had to start over, but a ten-hour night of lying on a bed of rocks wasn't going to work either.

Does what's happened keep you from acting with justice, generosity, self-control, sanity, prudence, honesty, humility, straightforwardness, and all other qualities that allow a person's nature to fulfill itself? So remember this principle when something threatens to cause you pain: the thing itself was no misfortune at all; to endure it and prevail is great good fortune.
—Marcus Aurelius[66]

An hour of daylight remained, and I was still by myself at the campground. I plugged the pump back into the cigarette lighter and turned on the car. Maybe a partial charge would be enough to inflate the mattress? The noise and pollution of internal combustion engines was something I'd wanted to escape, but without hesitation I'd compromised my ideals. So much for primitive camping in the pristine wilderness, away from the annoyances of urban life. I could have turned the ignition key to the accessory position to activate the electronics, leaving the engine turned off, but a drained car battery would leave me stranded in the desert wasteland. Socorro (Spanish for "help") was the nearest largish city, and it was 150 miles away. I had plenty of gas and kept the car running for thirty minutes, worrying the entire time that it would overheat. But the car delivered enough of a charge to the air pump to inflate the mattress successfully. Crisis averted again.

As I mentioned, another tent was set up at the Cosmic Campground. For the two hours I'd been grappling with camping challenges there'd been no activity at the other tent and no vehicle present. Only the wind assaulting the tent, snapping the flysheet like a locker room smack with a wet towel. The sun was going down, and it was getting cold. I was in the middle of nowhere with only bear spray for protection, and I started imagining grisly scenarios of another kind involving the other tent's occupant. Since STOICs can be superior catastrophizers, we excel at making anything seem ominous. I imagined a Unabomber-inspired loner (Bill Murray's sketchy brother from the convenience store?) living in the tent and in the middle of the night delivering a bomb package to me, tiptoeing back to his tent and dispassionately detonating it remotely. Or, in a crouched position, using the wind as a sound mask and his knowledge of stealth, creeping over to my tent with an elk antler and bludgeoning me to death in my sleep. I remembered a long-ago group trip to Paris to study the decorative arts at the Louvre. In our *chambre d'hôte*, my roommate insisted on sleeping with the windows open, and I was afraid of vampires. For dinner most nights I ate the iconic French dish Chicken with Forty Cloves of Garlic; I slept with a scarf wound around my neck and a cross in my hand. Contemplating my vulnerability kept me awake most of the night.

What if someone should attack me when I am alone and murder me?
Fool, not murder you *but your trivial body.*
—*Epictetus*[67]

I thought I was crashing the star party, but where was everyone? Was I having fun? We STOICs pre-worry nearly everything, and I'd spent the entire day before my camping adventure in a state of anticipatory anxiety. Now that I was ensconced in a teeny tent with no view of the outside world, with the wind doing its best to dislodge the tent and flysheet from their moorings, I realized that I could just as well be home in the living room with a couple of big fans blasting air at the tent and a cricket soundtrack playing in the background. I'd forgotten how much I loathe the crinkly sound of the flysheet rubbing against the tent, although it's not as bad as the sound of a crisp plastic bag from the grocery store or a cellophane candy wrapper at the movies. Instead of wanting to flee to escape these annoyances, I was paralyzed with anxiety and cold. Around 10 p.m. I had to force myself to vacate the tent. I'd almost forgotten why I was there.

The night sky was magnificent. I was my five-year-old self again, sitting in the small plaster dome planetarium of my childhood and watching, in time-lapse, the sun sink behind a silhouetted horizon. The red-orange color so intense that your eyes water. The color fading from orange to green to indigo to a deep violet; not a sunset you usually see from the ground but from an airplane at thirty thousand feet. Then the first celestial bodies appear—Venus, the Big Dipper, Orion—and soon the entire dome becomes a mass of stars so luminous that their light dispatches thousands of tiny beams directly into your brain. This is how the sky looked at the Cosmic Campground. The Milky Way was a colossal, glowing, curved handle attached to Earth, as if a celestial giant could come along, pick Earth up, and deposit it over in the next galaxy. The Big Dipper, Draco, Pegasus, and other autumn constellations were unambiguously defined in a sky teeming with billions of other stars, stars we never see if we're anywhere near a city. All that was missing was Alan Rickman, explaining the names and mythologies of the stars and constellations, rotating the sky at will and identifying celestial objects with his laser pointer. I felt safe and happy.

To look about, and with the eyes to follow the course of the stars and planets as though thou wouldst run with them; and to mind perpetually the several changes of the elements one into another. For such fancies and imaginations, help much to purge away the dross and filth of this our earthly life.

—Marcus Aurelius[68]

Back in the tent it took forever to fall asleep, which was sometime around midnight. My brain had finally given up trying to parse the strange sounds produced by the crinkly flysheet, convincing itself that those alarming sounds were merely fabric on fabric and not a family of black bears or feral hogs encircling the tent. Friction between my inflatable camping pillow and the sleeping bag created the most annoying sound of all, mainly because of its subtlety. My brain told me it was the sound of a small animal outside shuffling and scratching in the dirt, maybe digging a hole—nothing alarming, but repetitive and relentless. A few times during the night my eyes popped open from a tentative sleep. I unzipped the tent just enough to stick my head through the opening and catch the critter by surprise, but nothing was there, not even footprints or scat. Was this a case of the "spooky action at a distance" paradox, in which the appearance of my head made the critter disappear at the same instant, like some crazy quantum entanglement? Had I watched too many Road Runner and Wile E. Coyote cartoons as a child?

By 2 a.m. the moon appeared at the horizon, its light flooding the tent like truck headlights on high beam. By 3 a.m. I was shivering uncontrollably. Even though I was wearing a knit hat, long underwear, a thick T-shirt, a ski jacket, jeans, and wool socks and I was inside the sleeping bag with the extra warmth-producing liner, nothing could ward off the penetrating cold that had hijacked the tent. But it wasn't as if I were stranded with Sir Ernest Shackleton and his men after their ship was crushed by Antarctic pack ice. This wasn't an ill-fated expedition to the summit of Everest or the depths of an Arctic winter. I got a grip.

Who is not himself the cause of his own unrest?
—*Marcus Aurelius*[69]

I'd positioned the tent on an east-west axis so that I could see the sunrise on the morning of the next day, and by 5 a.m. I was desperate for the sun's rays to warm me. I began staring at a section of tent just past my feet, as if I could coax the sun to rise faster, like the time-lapse sunrise at the planetarium signaling the end of the star show. The flysheet was orange, so at the first hint of daylight, at about 6 a.m., a faint orange color became visible. Over the next hour, the tent's interior brightened incrementally. By 7 a.m. sunlight made a direct hit, bathing me and the other contents of the tent in an intense, soothing orange glow. I knew heat was to follow, and my mood was back on track. The relief I felt after Luis the medic treated my scratched ankle in Mexico was how I felt in that moment.

Accept comforts without pride or apology, with no routine acceptance of their presence or regret in their absence.
—*Marcus Aurelius*[70]

By 8 a.m., while still inside the tent, I packed up the sleeping bag and liner, deflated the mattress, and looked forward to a steaming cup of coffee. As I exited the tent, I saw a car parked beside the other tent, a modest, nerdy car, not a heap like the Unabomber might have driven in his pre-Luddite days. The winds had calmed during the early morning but with sunrise increased in force again. Making a fire, even with my single-burner propane stove, was out of the question, and suddenly a good cup of coffee was 150 miles away in Socorro. Sleep- and caffeine-deprived, I finished packing up and left.

STOICs, solo tent camping under ideal conditions may be the only option for us: temperatures no higher than 80°F during the day and no lower than 50°F at night; no sustained gale-force winds, no insects, snakes, bears, or feral hogs, and the campground ideally equipped with a bathroom and shower, not too crowded or too close to a road or a major city, with some kind of shelter from inclement weather, and with a Wi-Fi hotspot (the Cosmic Campground gets a huge thumbs-up for this). There should also be a store with provisions and good coffee within a few miles of the site.

Please let me know if you've ever found such a place.

In every affair consider what precedes and follows, and then undertake it. Otherwise you will begin with spirit indeed, careless of the consequences, and when these are developed, you will shamefully desist… But consider what precedes and follows, and then, if it be for your advantage, engage in the affair…When you have reckoned up all this, if your inclination still holds, set about (doing it in earnest).

—Epictetus[71]

As a solo Cosmic Campground tent camper, Seneca may have expressed a different viewpoint.

There is pleasure in having endured something unpleasant. When it comes to an end, we should be glad.[72]

So what happened to the star party? I'd read the date on the website incorrectly and missed the event by a year.

CHAPTER VII

STOIC LONELINESS

Are You Traveling Solo?

When visiting the country America's president had described as a breeding ground for rapists and murderers, you may feel compelled to stop people in the streets and apologize for the lunacy of the United States's leadership. I was in Mérida, Mexico, on Trump's inauguration day, and I wanted to assure my kind and gentle hosts that most Americans share an anti-Trump point of view and agree the election was a corrupt, rigged affair. I considered modifying a cereal box costume to make it look like a wall, painting a big red verboten symbol on it, and pinning a sign on the back that read "*No es mi presidente.*" A goodwill ambassador representing American's sane, I would march proudly around the city. When I reflected on the reasons why this seemed like a good idea, I realized I was lonely and Trump provided common ground for conversations with strangers. If carried out, my protest fantasy would have resulted in more attention than any STOIC can handle comfortably. Feeling lonely intensifies introversion and couples with the suspicion that everyone knows it and is watching for you to burst into tears or curl up in a fetal position on a park bench. An unintentional spotlight effect could end in disaster. When you're traveling solo and suffering from a bout of loneliness, remember the words of Seneca:

"What progress, you ask, have I made? I have begun to be a friend to myself." That was indeed a great benefit; such a person can never be alone. You may be sure that such a man is a friend to all mankind.[73]

Sometimes it feels utterly beyond our power to control loneliness, but try to connect with the world outside your head. Smile at people so they may think not all Americans are self-important narcissists who regard the people and country hosting them with contempt. If you're on a bus, force yourself to say a few words to the person sitting next to you. On the trip back from Chichén Itzá, my water bottle fell from the luggage rack onto the head of a Mayan man and was a great conversation starter, but more gentle approaches are recommended. If your travel destination doesn't have an indoor skydiving place or a mega mall for retail therapy, find a museum and go there to be reminded of the beauty and timelessness of the best of humanity's creative output. Give a few pesos to the tiny grandmothers who flank the entrance to the bank on your street, like the lions that guard the entrance to the New York Public Library. (The lions are allegories for patience and truth, two qualities both Stoics and STOICs embrace.) Pursue the blind street guitarist, the guy you see every day in different locations with his guide at his elbow, enjoy his music, and contribute to his support. Or the young, expert musician I heard from a distance and mistook for Herb Alpert and the drummer from the Tijuana Brass. With his wife and small child, they circled Mérida's grand zocalo. He played one-handed trumpet while beating a drum with the other, and she collected donations in a Panama-style hat while pushing the baby in a heavily used stroller. If you're anywhere in Mexico, buy yourself an orange, remove the peel, and bite into it. You'll begin salivating as soon as the peel is breached and the orange's fresh smell stimulates your olfactory receptors. On that first bite your brain will flood with dopamine. Loneliness interrupted.

One Saturday night I walked to the grand zocalo to listen to live music, and half of Mérida's population was there, too. You could hear so much laughter I began to wonder, *Is Mérida the epicenter of the world's joie de vivre? What's wrong with us sullen, angst-ridden, and anxious Americans?* I sat on a bench next to a mother, her daughter, and the daughter's infant and reflected on the fact that the number of strangers who greeted me on the streets that day exceeded the number of friends I'd made in twelve years of living in Santa Fe. I tried to imagine this scenario happening back in the States and realized there was no equivalent. The kinds of assemblies we stage are often motivated by negativity, discontent, and inequality: assembling for the purpose of protesting our president. White supremacists rallies. Calling attention to the fact that women, minorities, and members of the LGBTQ communities still do not enjoy equal status with America's mainstream and primarily male members. If we assemble to be educated or entertained, an embittered, smoldering misfit may exact his revenge on us with an AR-15 semiautomatic rifle. In 2017, an estimated fifteen million of them were registered to Americans. Even at the neighborhood level, we are policed and controlled by home owners' associations (HOAs), small groups of sometimes-rogue people harboring special interests and making decisions for the entire group. HOAs surveil their constituents, assess fines for infractions of the rules, and impose liens on homes when a few quarterly HOA payments are missed. We do not celebrate life in the healthy, humanistic ways of our Mexican neighbors.

The young mother sitting next to me laughed so often and robustly, shaking the rickety wooden bench, that we were on the verge of collapsing in a heap. I tried to sneak looks at this happy family, but I thought they'd feel stalked or judged. The young mother caught me in the act, though, and instead of averting my gaze, I smiled at her and she gave me a big, beautiful smile in return. For an instant I was a contributing member of the great human collective.

Life is to be happy—free from hindrance and restraint.
— Epictetus[74]

When you're out in public by yourself, everyone you meet asks if you're traveling solo. Travel sites often warn never to reveal your solo travel status, and if asked, lie and say your partner is back at the hotel. Depending on the culture and the context, you will either be believed or not. It's difficult to prove your couple status if you're on the Trans-Siberian Railway in the middle of Mongolia and your partner is always somewhere else. You can say he or she is back in the room with a bad cold, but s/he's gotta come out sometime during the six-thousand-mile trip, and people will be watching. You can try to deflect solo travel questions by wearing a sham wedding ring, but this strategy hasn't worked well for me. I use a modest silver Claddagh to that purpose, and perhaps only the Irish understand the symbolism. (Worn on the ring finger of the left hand with the hands, heart, and crown pointing toward the wrist signifies marriage.) I've worn the Claddagh every time I've traveled, and not a single person has ever asked if I'm married. But wearing it fools *me* into thinking I'm married and my husband is waiting back in the room with a bottle of champagne and a box of truffles. I've even caught myself behaving as if I were married, nagging myself about that second glass of wine or agreeing to an activity I have no interest in. Wearing a ring doesn't mean you'll have the same experience, but it's a strategy to consider. Maybe a simple silver band would communicate more effectively. You can also proudly declare your solo traveler status where appropriate. Use your own discretion.

Many truths appear paradoxical to the ignorant.
—Epictetus[75]

It's important to know that solo women travelers aren't welcome in certain establishments. In Riyadh, Saudi Arabia, women without an escort are banned from Dunkin' Donuts and Starbucks. Women can enter one of the minarets in Old Delhi's Jama Masjid but only accompanied by a man. Originally known as the Mosque Commanding the View of the World, the view from the top of one of its minarets is definitely spectacular. Even with a man in tow, women should be on guard against teenagers and boys who lurk along the dark, narrow, spiral staircase to feel women up as they pass. Female travelers should skip Muslim cemeteries, where it's a grievous sin for a woman to pass near the grave of a male Muslim saint. Women are not allowed in Iranian football stadiums, but if we were, would you really want to risk it? Have you ever been carded for being of menstruating age? If you're a female between the ages of ten and fifty, you can expect this when visiting certain sacred mountains, monasteries, and temples.

Happily there are places in the world where lying about solo travel or fudging your menstruating status is unnecessary. Nobody cares and no one will threaten you. When traveling in the Yucatán, for example, it's likely you're riding in a first- or second-class bus or in a tour group with an international clientele. Either situation encourages camaraderie, especially the luxury fifteen-passenger vans with ice-cold air conditioning. Even introverts make friends and by the end of the excursion are exchanging email addresses and invitations to visit other countries. In Mérida I felt perfectly safe on the streets and enjoyed a calm contentedness walking back to the hacienda from nightly festivities at the neighborhood zocalo. You can carry the fun and happiness you were recently a part of, and contributing to, with you all the way back to your bed.

I want to assure you these are not the uninformed ramblings of a naïve traveler. I've been a STOIC or a semi-STOIC for a long time, and in many situations, I've both witnessed and been involved in sketchy circumstances. In 1997 I flew to Hong Kong to make a film about the reuni-

fication of Hong Kong with mainland China. The afternoon before the July 1 festivities I spent a few moments at
a pier overlooking the South China Sea. A beautiful young
British woman stood next to me also enjoying the view.
Suddenly a much older Chinese man approached her and
started chatting her up, and within ten minutes she took
off with him, ostensibly to tour the city. I was incredulous.
I would have invented not only a Big Strong American
Husband on his way, at that moment, to join me, but also
an entire extended family watching televised Chinese opera
back at the hotel and waiting for our return. I hope everything worked out well for her.

During my sophomore year at college, every few weeks
I drove solo to Manhattan from Providence, Rhode Island,
to film random events in Times Square. Inspired by the
great documentarians Dziga Vertov and Robert Flaherty
and the television show Candid Camera, cinéma vérité was
my thing. In those days, a huge billboard face loomed over
Times Square— the face of the Marlboro Man blowing
smoke rings that pulsed out of a round hole in his mouth.
I'd park the car right in Times Square, illegally I'm sure,
and set up an ensemble of heavy video equipment on the
sidewalk, including a wooden tripod and a two-piece cam-
era/recorder unit called the Portapak. (The black-and-
white camera's imaging device, known as the Vidicon tube,
was notoriously sensitive to bright light. If you were careless and pointed it at a reflective surface, such as a glint off
a car bumper, or worse, at the sun, the tube was toast,
permanently. A black streak or, more seriously, a big black
hole in the center of the image would appear. The Vidicon
was the macular degeneration of video cameras. The reel-

to-reel recorder had to be held absolutely still while re-
cording if you desired image stability, and the wooden
tripod was as heavy as the small tree it was in its previous
existence.) I drew attention to myself with this ensemble,
and a friendly Times Square resident attached himself to
me and would not leave my side. He pestered me for a ride
in my car, only for a spin around the block. By the time I'd
finished filming and was ready to move on, I had no
qualms about hanging out with this chatty, charismatic
guy—so I agreed to give him a ride. But the moment he
entered the car an important boundary was breached—the
implied boundary between you, your car, and everything
else—and I was sure I'd made a horrible mistake. I did my
best to hide my panic, but it intensified over the twenty
minutes he was my passenger. I'd been in control, relinquished it to a stranger, and hadn't considered the
consequences.

*What is quite unlooked for is more crushing in its effect, and unex-
pectedness adds to the weight of a disaster... This is a reason for
ensuring that nothing ever takes us by surprise. We should project our
thoughts ahead of us at every turn and have in mind every possible
eventuality instead of only the usual course of events.*
            —Seneca[76]

  Nothing awful happened. I learned my lesson, but it only partially stuck. Many years later, the panicked feeling
returned when I picked up a Navajo mother and daughter
on the road to Chaco Canyon in New Mexico. Again,
nothing happened; they simply wanted a ride and weren't
in the mood for chitchat. I tried making conversation, and

they were utterly silent. An act of generosity quickly turned catastrophic for me. I was certain mother and daughter hid knives under their skirts and intended to steal the car, leaving me disemboweled on the side of the road.

With lack of practice, we worry and fancy things graver than they are.
  —*Epictetus*[77]

Though lacking in drama, the Hong Kong, Times Square, and Navajo mother and daughter incidents all had their teaching moments. Experiences like these are good for practicing Stoic negative visualization and for helping you react appropriately to perceived threats. With the Navajo mother and daughter, the menace was more imagined than real, and I was able to power down the panic spectacularly fast. Even when a situation enters the zone of truly threatening, Stoic practices help defuse additional, unexpected anxiety that multiplies the anxiety that's already there.

On another occasion I was hitchhiking from Arizona to Texas (not solo) and my companion and I were picked up by a truck driver in a station wagon. His destination was a truck stop where he was connecting with a job. A hot, dry wind blew through the windows of the station wagon; I sat in the passenger side of the front seat and my companion sat in the back (we should have observed the "boys in the front, girls in the back rule"). The driver looked at me and said, "If I find you a ride to Texas, will you talk to me?" I enthusiastically answered, "Of course!" The shocked expression on his face told me that "talk" was not the verb he had used at all. We arrived at the truck stop, I excused myself to go to the bathroom, and it being a large, busy, public place, I waited a sufficient amount of time in the bathroom until I felt certain he'd lost interest and left.

Be silent for the most part; or speak merely what is needful and in few words. We may, however, enter sparingly into discourse sometimes, when occasion calls for it; but let it not run on any of the common subjects, as gladiators, or horse races, or athletic champions, or food, or drink—the vulgar topics of conversation; and especially do not talk about people, so as either to blame, or praise, or make comparisons. If you are able, then by your own conversation, bring over that of your company to proper subjects; but if you happen to find yourself among strangers, be silent.

—Epictetus[78]

I think you can understand why I say if anyone should be fearful of solo travel, it would be me. The stockpile of experiences that could have gone south take a toll that's cumulative if you allow it to be. Fifteen years have passed since the kidnapping incident, the situation that *could* have ended badly, and I'm still vulnerable to amygdala hijack and emotional incontinence. The triggers will always be lurking, but I know what they are and can compartmentalize them pretty well. I'm so grateful for the help I received to restore my sense of calm and autonomy. Sometimes it's an effort to avoid a tumble into the abyss, but it was never an effort to resist the xenophobic and racist camps, unfairly blaming huge swaths of people for the random act of violence with which I intersected. I forgave my kidnappers. So be assured that if I can manage solo travel as a STOIC and as a victim of a major crime and a bunch of near-misses that could have transformed me into a career agoraphobic, you can too!

When You're Not Traveling Solo

Getting sick in India is a given. The preparations and precautions you've taken are necessary and good, but situations arise that are beyond your control. You must either accept this or stay home, and I recommend the former. Yes, India is dirty and chaotic and polluted and noisy, but it's also replete with exquisite architecture; an exceptional musical, art, literary, linguistic, and spiritual tradition; and some of the best sweets on the planet, including apple pie like your mother used to make.

As I've written, I lived in Varanasi for two months at a music school, studying sitar and exploring this three-thousand-year-old city in between practice sessions. The population density of Varanasi is roughly 38,000 people per square mile, more than twenty times that of my home city of Santa Fe (1,800 people per square mile), and depending on the place and the time of day, Varanasi can be as crowded as a Rolling Stones concert or the crush when Pope Francis delivers a speech from his balcony at the Vatican. In Varanasi, city residents gather every night to observe a fire ceremony called Ganga Aarti, or putting the river to bed, and this ceremony is so crowded yet so moving that even though introverts do not blend well with crowds, nor do we often take part in collective actions or submit to crowd contagion, I was a regular attendee. Young priests dressed in saffron robes each occupy a small stage covered in exquisite rugs. A low table holds ceremonial objects including a conch shell, hand bells, incense, and marigold petals. Prayers and songs to Shiva and to Mother Ganga are chanted and sung, and in synchronization to the sounds, the priests describe wide circles of light with tiered, conical-shaped candelabras. Hundreds of devotees float a single ghee-fueled tea light surrounded by marigolds onto the Ganga, creating a mass of twinkling lights. The ceremony was transfixing, even on Holi when children took advantage of the crowded conditions and persisted in throwing colored powders on the foreigners. I felt tranquil and connected to my fellow human beings. Even so, I hung to the edges of the crowd in case I had to make a quick exit.

Peace will come to the mind that can provide its own seclusion amongst a crowd.

—*Seneca*[79]

In Varanasi, the only sure way to grab some quality introvert time was to escape to the roof of the music school. I could see into the neighbors' outdoor cooking and washing areas undetected or watch the flow of life in the street below. If it was late in the afternoon, children home from school were on their roofs laughing and flying colorful kites. A thick layer of dust covered the broad leaves of the bodhi trees after four months with no rain.

The day I arrived at the music school, along with a few others from the U.S. and Europe, Guruji told us only to eat food prepared by the school's cook. He knew getting sick was on the minds of the foreigners. For the first week we took his advice to heart, and the cook's very capable hands produced delicious North Indian fare. But by week two dissent was brewing. Someone had discovered a charming little bistro owned by a French expat couple, and by then we were desperate for an espresso or a cappuccino—so one by one we defected. By week three, all of us went to the bistro for breakfast and ate lunch and dinner back at the school.

After breakfast I'd return to the school via a long, narrow street where the locals applied water buffalo patties to adobe walls. The locals used the patties for fuel, and these long, smooth walls offered a convenient place to slap the wet dung, shaped like thick pancakes, to desiccate. By exposing myself to this gauntlet of shit, I was giving my immune system something to do.

I remember the moment that it happened. I'd ordered my usual breakfast: cappuccino, toast, and a hard-boiled egg. A few moments passed, and the kind and overly obsequious waiter emerged from the kitchen with the cappuccino and toast. He had forgotten the egg. Feeling STOIC empathy, I hesitated to mention the missing egg. I knew how embarrassed and apologetic he would be. But eggs had been my sole source of protein in India, so I decided I needed to bring it to his attention. Of course, I prefaced it with, "I'm sorry, but…" He rushed back into the kitchen and came out with a peeled egg cradled in dripping wet hands. I wanted to ask for another egg still in the shell, but I didn't want to insinuate that his hands were dirty. Chances were that the water they'd been in had come from the tap, so I should have accepted the egg with a smile, taken it with me, and fed it to one of the mangy neighborhood dogs. Instead I ate it myself.

A few days later I began to regret that decision. Chills, intense stomach cramps, and nausea overtook me in waves. I could only eat rice mush and apple pie. Whatever had colonized me would lay me flat for twenty-four hours, then I'd be fine, off and on, for the next several days. The worst part was its unpredictability. Thinking I'd be okay for a few hours, I'd strike off to explore a Hindu temple or tour a palace and out of nowhere feel intensely bad. Bathrooms were never close enough. A round of cipro had no effect, but over-the-counter Pudin Hara Pearls (the little green, minty balls for upset stomachs) were the only remedy that brought relief. After four weeks of this, I realized that something was seriously wrong.

Traveling back to the U.S. from India seemed like an insurmountable challenge. By then a bathroom could be no more than ten steps away, and if there was a line, I cut queue without hesitation. I made the long flight to Amsterdam without incident, but the nausea returned while waiting in the terminal for the connecting flight to the U.S. An unsympathetic flight attendant refused to let me change seats on the plane so I'd be closer to a bathroom. She said, "Don't get on the flight. Stay in the airport until you feel better." I took eight Imodium and boarded the plane.

I had acquired an unintended passenger called *cryptosporidium*, a one-cell protozoan parasite that had multiplied by the thousands in my gut, rivaling the population of Varanasi itself. This is what they do. *Cryptosporidium* parasites settle into the walls of your intestines, reproduce, and shed in massive quantities into your poo, where they are highly contagious. In the process they create an inhospitable environment for most foods and do their best to upend travel plans. By the end of my stay, Indian apple pie was the only ingestible that agreed with me. *Cryptosporidia* defy diagnosis ("crypto" derives from the Greek word for "hidden") and do not respond to conventional treatment. Because they're encased in a hard, ellipsoidal shell like an egg, they're resistant to chlorine but not to strychnine, which is what I took in diluted form for three days to eradicate the little demons.

STOICs, don't let this story discourage you from a pilgrimage to India. *Cryptosporidium* is a parasite living in your own backyard. In 1993, Milwaukee, Wisconsin, experienced the largest waterborne disease outbreak ever documented in U.S. history. Yep, it was our guy. Following a sewage system leak that infected the city water supply, the cryptos passed through the filtration system of one of the city's water treatment plants, and two weeks later, over four hundred thousand of the 1.6 million residents of Milwaukee were infected and sick. Since 1993, infected public swimming pools have spawned hundreds of crypto outbreaks in the U.S., and this is how it happens. The average swimmer contributes about a quarter of a gram of fecal matter to pool water within the first fifteen minutes of entering, plus one in five Americans admit to peeing in public pools. Use your STOIC common sense and stay away from these cesspools of filth. Go to India and take precautions, and don't accept a hard-boiled egg from the dripping wet hands of anyone, regardless of how much empathy you may feel for the person.

"I am ill here," said one of the scholars. "I will return home." Were you never ill at home, then? Do you not know that both illness and death must overtake us? No matter what we are doing? The husbandman at his plow, the sailor on his voyage. What do you wish to be doing when you are taken? For no matter what you do you will have to be overtaken by death. If there is any better employment at which you can be taken, follow that. For my own part, I would be found engaged in nothing but in the regulation of my own will; how to make it undisturbed, unrestrained, uncompelled, free.

—Epictetus[80]

Managing Your Personal Space

You're traveling through an insanely busy airport in Southeast Asia, riding the up escalator to the departure area. The escalator is packed with other travelers and their oversize luggage that should have been transported via elevator. The person in front of you struggles with two of these bags. He gets to the top, successfully steps off the escalator with his bags, and stops. You scramble not to trip over the bags and fall on your face while you're trying to manage your bag, and other travelers behind you are piling up. A similar thing happens with the general flow of pedestrian traffic through any airport. Travelers walking briskly along, with no warning, will suddenly stop. If you're not paying close attention, you crash into their carry-ons. In the majority of airports I've passed through this has happened, and up to now I've been able to avoid slamming into someone and knocking us both to the concourse floor. It's the adult version of roller skating outdoors as a kid, coasting down your driveway and hitting a pebble that halts your forward momentum, creating a pile-up with friends skating behind you. But in crowded airports, solo travel offers advantages for managing your personal space. When you travel solo you have a much better chance of avoiding collisions of this sort than if you were walking side-by-side or in tandem with a friend, which is doubling your chances of catastrophe.

People hate what stands in their way.
> *—Epictetus*[81]

Then there are times when I feel like the Invisible Woman, but not in a superpower kind of way. It's as if I don't exist at all. Someone will stroll over to the bench where I've parked myself and my carry-on and practically sit in my lap, roll over my foot with their cart full of luggage, turn away from their friends to cough in my face, cut in front of me in the queue, completely block the international best sellers aisle in the bookstore with both a backpack and a front pack, or steal a taxi right out from under me. This aspect of solo travel is not much fun for a STOIC because we play by the rules and these types of people aren't even thinking "rules." Even though we desperately wish they were.

To desire things impossible is the part of a mad man. But it is a thing impossible, that wicked men should not commit some such things... As for the things themselves, they touch not the soul, neither can they have any access unto it: neither can they of themselves any ways either affect it, or move it. For she herself alone can affect and move herself, and according as the dogmata and opinions are, which she doth vouchsafe herself; so are those things which, as accessories, have any co-existence with her.

—Marcus Aurelius[82]

As an introvert and a person quick to apologize for taking up space in the world and even for breathing its air, it's difficult to stand your ground. Before you travel you must decide between either putting up with others' rude behaviors or calling them out. If you don't, you will find yourself cursing at them under your breath and wishing them ill, and a host of other passive-aggressive feelings will arise in your being that you may someday act on and regret. I'm not saying you'll be driven to purchase the AR-15 semiautomatic rifle and ridiculous amounts of ammunition and start mowing people down, but you may resort to insidious, aggressive acts that in the long run will cause you more suffering than the person to whom they are directed. For example, with your luggage-laden cart you may slightly nudge the back of the ankles of the guy who cut in front of you in the "goods to declare" line. Or you might pocket a ten-dollar bill you saw a businessman drop, the same man who cut in front of a whole slew of people in the security line because he was in a hurry to board the flight we were all destined to share. Or you might implicate the entitled rich traveler as a suspected terrorist because she left a huge discharge of pee on the toilet seat for you to clean up.

Betimes in the morning say to thyself, This day I shalt have to do with an idle curious man, with an unthankful man, a railer, a crafty, false, or an envious man; an unsociable uncharitable man. All these ill qualities have happened unto them, through ignorance of that which is truly good and truly bad. But I that understand the nature of that which is good, that it only is to be desired, and of that which is bad, that it only is truly odious and shameful: who know moreover, that this transgressor, whosoever he be, is my kinsman, not by the same blood and seed, but by participation of the same reason, and of the same divine particle; How can I either be hurt by any of those, since it is not in their power to make me incur anything that is truly reproachful? Or angry, and ill affected towards him, who by nature is so near unto me? For we are all born to be fellow-workers, as the feet, the hands, and the eyelids; as the rows of the upper and under teeth: for such therefore to be in opposition, is against nature; and what is it to chafe at, and to be averse from, but to be in opposition?

—*Marcus Aurelius*[83]

The indignities are plentiful, but on the positive side, most airport experiences are short lived—split-second even, like the young man who slams you with his backpack as he passes or the person who leaps into the bus transport that ferries passengers from the terminal to the airplane, taking the last available slot.

Another widely experienced personal-space management issue is something I call the "inter-adipose dilemma." It's when you're relegated to a middle seat in the plane and you're squeezed in between two generously sized people. Their ample legs and laps and torsos spill over into your seventeen-inch-wide space. Forget about ever having the opportunity to use either armrest. Fortunately, most of the time this happens only on domestic flights in the U.S.; the rest of the world tends to be more modestly proportioned.

CHAPTER VIII

READY AND CONFIDENT

After ten months of planning an around-the-world trip, the day of departure arrived. My brain stuffed with Stoic wisdom, and with plenty of solo travel practice under my belt, I was ready and confident, but only for a few moments at a time. For a STOIC, organizing travel this complicated creates a bottomless pit of anxiety. You live in a chronic state of O-C, worried about what tasks you've forgotten to do or what situations you've failed to anticipate. Up to the last minute, it's as if you're the boatswain of Columbus's expedition to the New World, preparing to sail uncharted waters and expecting to fall off the edge of the Earth.

But paralyzing anxiety can lead to helpful ideas. As part of my preparations for the trip, I referenced the Mars One astronaut training program for insight and found it extremely helpful, modifying the program for solo travel on Earth. The training consists of three phases: technical, personal, and group. During the technical phase, astronauts learn how to be proficient in the use and repair of all equipment. For me, that meant memorizing the code for my TSA-approved suitcase lock, practicing how to insert a microscopic SIM card into my phone, familiarizing myself with electrical service in other countries and having the correct adapters, practicing how to switch lenses on the new camera I bought and understanding other operational features. Repair of equipment would always exceed my competence, but I wrapped a length of duct tape around a pencil for any gross repairs that might arise, like the sole of my shoe detaching, the latches on my carry-on breaking, or my plastic raincoat ripping. Astronauts receive extensive medical training, and again, I fell short in this department, although I'm certified in CPR. I assembled a simple emergency medical kit but forgot the antibacterial ointment, as you know.

A phase one training also includes a study of the topography of Mars, a brilliant idea for terrestrial travelers here on Earth to adopt. Here's where Google Maps and Google Earth become invaluable resources. If you're driving from one place to another and Google Maps says it takes three hours to drive twenty miles, you can assume you'll be negotiating either some difficult terrain or horrendous traffic. When you know it's a schlep from the metro to your Airbnb, you can either reference topological maps or look at actual street views to see if you'll be walking up and down hills to get there. You can note the conditions of the streets, too, to see if your carry-on wheels will likely survive any challenges, like cobblestones or granite setts. Curiously, the text of the phase one training includes this statement: one crew member "will gain expertise in exobiology, which is the biology of alien life."[84] Isn't that admitting the existence of alien life forms and revealing that there are individuals on Earth who have studied them?

Phase two of the training consists of developing an astronaut's ability to adapt—a tall order on Mars, and a lot easier on Earth. I felt confident that I'd reached a certain level of proficiency in that department already. I'd resigned myself to the unlikely availability of blueberries for breakfast and to the idea of using public transportation everywhere. My water collection and purification system is state of the art, and I always carry two different antibiotics to cover bacterial challenges my body can't resolve on its own. For communication in other languages, I carry basic phrases written in a six-by-nine-inch, top-opening, spiral-bound writing pad. I never assume my iPhone will work outside of the U.S., so I create analog redundancy of information normally stored and retrieved on the phone: important email addresses and phone numbers, some passwords. Phase two training also includes a psychological component. "Since these individuals will be unable to speak to friends and family on Earth face-to-face, a certain amount of coping skills are essential."[85] For a STOIC, this is largely a nonissue. We *like* solo; it's one of the conditions that define us as STOIC.

It is in thy power whenever thou shalt choose to retire into thyself. For nowhere either with more quiet or more freedom from trouble does a man retire than into his own soul.
—Marcus Aurelius[86]

Phase three's training is all about simulated missions, immersing astronauts in situations that prepare them for the real mission to Mars. I think I'll write the Mars One team and suggest southwestern New Mexico, including the Cosmic Campground, as the ideal training ground. Blowing dust, huge temperature swings, lack of water, high-elevation hikes, and Hatch chiles are all available to the astronaut trainee. Why are chiles important? Astronauts report cravings for hot sauce in space, and scientists believe it results from a loss of smell that occurs in zero gravity. Since smell and the ability to discern flavors are connected, hot sauce, not freeze-dried space ice cream, is the astronaut go-to. Plus, hot sauce increases receptivity to other flavors, and the burning sensation on the tongue releases endorphins. Any New Mexico hot sauce emporium would be pleased to help a future astronaut decide which product he or she prefers. Pinch your nostrils together and taste. Don't launch without your preferred hot sauce on board.

Phase three participants are required to take part in Mars simulations for a few months out of every year. Like the astronaut in training, a STOIC must train for STOIC experiences. We have to maintain our solo travel chops, and the best way to do that is with practice. To prepare for a Big Trip, as I've written, take modest ones here and there and challenge yourself in meaningful ways. Remember,

With lack of practice, we worry and fancy things graver than they are.
—Epictetus[87]

. . . . .

Twelve hours before the first flight for my around-the-world trip, I realized I hadn't recorded the reservation confirmation number anywhere—an oversight that could have been catastrophic. Would I really need this, though? Swiping one's credit card at any airline kiosk causes the confirmation number to appear in nine-hundred-point bold Helvetica. If you ask a ticket agent for the number, before you finish saying your full name, she's got it. But what about the airports in Lisbon, Marrakesh, or Phnom Penh? Would they have the sophistication of big U.S. airports and be multilingual, or would their computer screens display information only in Portuguese, Arabic, or Khmer? Should I manually record the confirmation number in several places? The answer was "yes."

People of a certain generation who are well-traveled still can't quite commit to the digital age and don't feel secure without analog backup (print on paper). If you're traveling the world with only a carry-on, like I was, all this paper can take up precious space that could otherwise be occupied by a favorite shirt or some extra black socks and underwear. STOICs, opt for the paper. I brought printouts of my complete itinerary, a calendar with flight and accommodations info plus all activities I'd booked in advance, copies of: tickets and receipts for those activities, my passport and immunization record, my Trusted Traveler and Global Entry cards, my credit and ATM cards, my travel insurance policy, a military time conversion chart, a list of anticipated expenses for each country, and printouts of Google Earth street views and directions to accommodations (more on this later). I managed these reams of paper by arranging them according to country and placed the papers in five separate envelopes, one for each of the countries I planned to visit. A sixth envelope held miscellaneous items. When I left a place, I shed the paper no longer needed, soothing my O-C in such a satisfying way.

This was my itinerary: Albuquerque to Chicago to London; in England for six and a half days; Lisbon for three and a half days; Morocco for nine and a half days; Cambodia for six and a half days; and Australia for eight days. I lost a day traveling to Cambodia and gained it back flying from Sydney to Los Angeles. I know, not nearly enough time in any one place, but cash was the limiting factor. My airline ticket was free. No frequent flier miles were used, and no cash exchanged hands. Free. I did the entire thirty-five-day trip for under thirty-five hundred dollars, booking Airbnbs and eating on the cheap.

Every day of the three months before departure was challenging in the same way. I knew this trip was going to do me in, and, irrational as it was, I couldn't get the thought out of my mind. My anxiety reached unexpected heights even though I wasn't admitting it to myself or to anyone else. Maybe those non-traveling guests at my niece's wedding were right and I should just stay put and resign myself to the agoraphobia closet. None of the routines that kept things in balance for me were effective, not even my frenetic workout at the gym. I'd come home, shower, get into bed, and not be able to find a comfortable position to lie in because of my pounding heart. I was miserably shipwrecked before ever setting sail. When this went on day after day and still I wasn't acknowledging the anxiety, I'd run through a list of possible causes. Was it coffee, chocolate, Indian food, too much salt? Was it living at seven thousand feet elevation? I was stuck in a negative feedback loop that was spiking my cortisol. I scheduled an appointment with a local cardiologist but canceled the day before the appointment, sparing myself the embarrassment of being outed as a hypochondriac. I tried evoking Stoic indifference, but nothing worked.

Temper your fear with hope. There is nothing so certain among these objects of fear that it is not more certain still that things we dread sink into nothing and that things we hope for mock us. Accordingly, weigh carefully your hopes as well as your fears, and whenever all the elements are in doubt, decide in your own favour; believe what you prefer. And if fear wins a majority of the votes, incline in the other direction anyhow.

—*Seneca*[88]

When the root of your distress lies in anticipating the future, sometimes relief comes only when that worrisome future becomes the immediate present. And that's exactly what happened. The way to relieve the anxiety was to leave home and start the journey. During the drive from Santa Fe to Albuquerque, my mind kept cycling through the contents of my carry-on and wondering what crucial item I'd forgotten to bring. But when the Albuquerque Sunport came into view with its faux adobe architecture, beautiful landscaping, and Native American–inspired public art, months of anxiety shifted to genuine excitement and confidence. I knew I could do this; what was the big deal? I remembered that even though I'm an introvert, I have the ability to feel at home just about anywhere.

What should anyone do but, like Socrates, when he was asked from what country he came, never to say that he was an Athenian, or a Corinthian, but a citizen of the universe?
  —*Epictetus*[89]

Aesthetically, one of the world's best airports is the Albuquerque Sunport. The Southwest–Native American theme is repeated throughout. It's like a typical Santa Fe hacienda on a huge scale: adobe walls painted in earth tones, high ceilings with decorative wooden vigas (beams), faux brick floors that the wheels of your roller bag interact with in a pleasing, musical way, suggesting excitement and momentum. The airport lighting makes you look good instead of ghastly. A special nod goes to the ambience of the bathrooms. Instead of setting the bags under your eyes in high relief, giving you that exhausted traveler look and spotlighting the fact that you haven't colored your hair in weeks, you look fresh and rested. And as you know, the bathroom doors open outward and the doors have a hook. The entire airport facility is spotless; TSA is cordial. As I walked to the departure gate, I felt a familiar twinge of sadness and nostalgia that arises when you're about to leave something beloved behind.

Devoid of the folksiness of ABQ, Chicago's O'Hare is the fourth busiest airport in the world and known for delayed flights. But the airport has good public art, good restaurants, the world's largest dinosaur skeleton in terminal one, and a World War II fighter plane suspended from the ceiling in terminal two. While I waited for the (delayed) flight to London from O'Hare, a young United Airlines employee stood three feet away from me shouting,

"Eunuch, eunuch!" She looked far into the distance, searching for harried, running, castrated passengers. After a few minutes a fellow employee joined her; both sets of eyes trained on a sprinting traveler. He said, "He must be our last passenger to Munich." I wondered if Munich eunuchs, if there are any, are relentlessly teased. A musician sitting at a baby grand at the piano bar across the corridor played his Bach repertoire on what sounded like a high school practice room upright while a TSA announcement repeated the grammatically incorrect three-one-one rule every five minutes. After listening to the announcement repeat for half an hour, I still didn't understand what "three-one-one" meant. "Liquids, gels, aerosols in three-ounce or less containers that must all be collected in a quart ziplock." Isn't it "three-ounce or *fewer*"? My liquids fit into a gallon ziplock (if barely), and thanks to a Trusted Traveler designation, I strolled through TSA unexamined. I wondered, why this announcement to us passengers who had already gone through security?

CHAPTER IX

ANXIOUS IN ENGLAND

A Bungee Jump into the Abyss

Even with earplugs attenuating the noise by a hundred decibels, the roar of the wing-mounted engines immediately outside my window was relentless and deafening. Seats that were eighteen inches wide in the '70s seemed now to be reduced to only twelve. I couldn't know for sure because the tape measure I usually carry (not an essential travel item) was back in Santa Fe. Paradoxically, Americans' girths are expanding, not shrinking, so seat size sends an unkind message to those who are generously proportioned. Sitting next to the curved wall of the plane reduces available seating volume, so the window seat puts its passenger at a disadvantage. Even at five feet five inches and 115 pounds, my body felt straight-jacketed. Curled up in a fetal position, Seneca tapped me on the shoulder.

There is a pleasure in being in one's own company as long as possible, when a man has made himself worth enjoying.[90]

I could think of better ways to pass time in my own company, but I was stuck with myself for eight confining hours. The best way to avert full-blown airplane panic, after you've exhausted the movie selection, is to try to bond with the passenger seated next to you. If you're lucky, the person isn't a relentless bloviator who sizes you up as an introvert and takes advantage of the fact that you can't run away. In my case, he was a nineteen-year-old from Idaho and his parents, with whom I also bonded, were sitting across the aisle from us. We talked about near-death experiences, a great topic for a trans-Atlantic flight. After disembarking at Heathrow, we kept running into each other. It's comforting to sort of know someone in an unfamiliar place.

Heathrow was where I encountered the first glitch of the trip, and Heathrow was where I realized the wisdom of bringing all that paper with me. After exchanging one hundred dollars USD for British pounds, I headed for the SIM card counter to connect my phone to the local network. Back home, three different employees of my cell phone provider assured me that using the phone with SIM cards would work anywhere in the world. But England proved them wrong. After wrestling with the nanoscale thing to install it in its slot (oops, forgot the tweezers and the magnifying glass) and snapping the card carrier shut, a message appeared that said "the phone is not unlocked." The helpful woman at the SIM card counter confirmed that yes, the phone must be unlocked to operate a non-U.S. SIM card, and I didn't have the key. This precipitated the Big Challenge of the trip, which was finding my accommodations without the availability of online maps and without being able to call or text internationally. I'm sure you can imagine a few situations where this might be inconvenient.

In a place like London, Airbnb is much more affordable than a hotel. But most important, booking a room in someone's home or flat creates the option for contact with others, essential if you're prone to ST (solo traveler) panic. I'm not one of these travelers, but lack of phone connectivity has pushed me over the edge more than once. Clearly you're a tourist, and a potential target for exploitation, when you've just emerged from the Tube, the metro, or the train and you're walking the streets with your rollerbag, overstuffed cross-body bag, and camera, looking lost and traversing the same area trying to connect to the wormhole that leads to your flat.

A person bereft of help is exposed to those who would injure them.
—*Epictetus*[91]

A Holiday Inn was within walking distance of my designated Tube stop, and after thirty minutes of random wandering, I was inside talking to the concierge, who so kindly offered to print a map of the area. Another twenty minutes and I found the Airbnb; a grocery was right across the street and a Turkish restaurant was on the opposite corner. Perfect!

The flat situation was a little inscrutable; after a few days in residence I still couldn't figure out who were the permanent occupants. For certain it was owned by a Latvian mother and daughter, and a Latvian friend visited every afternoon with her toddler, pre-verbal but with an earsplitting scream. A Rastafarian occupied another bedroom, and at first I thought he was a boyfriend but later learned he was a fellow traveler from Austin, Texas. So at minimum, four people shared the flat's single bathroom. These kinds of details are rarely included in Airbnb descriptions, and by the time you discover something that tweaks your O-C or disrupts your need for introversion, it's too late to cancel. Hosts never share that they are hoarders or horrible housekeepers or love to cook foods that emit putrid odors. You never know if you'll be sharing the flat with fifteen feral cats, or that a hot shower isn't included, or that your host likes to bring home one-night stands, or that a crowing rooster lives next door, or that you will be greeted at the gate by a pack of snarling dogs.

The flat I'd booked, in Canning Town east of central London, had been my second choice. My first choice was in a neighborhood called Shadwell Gardens, also east of central London and closer to the city's main attractions. On my second day in London I rode an above-ground train that passed through Shadwell Gardens, a cluster of sooty, red brick, mid-rise "projects," as we call them in the U.S., with laundry hanging on most balconies and gang graffiti everywhere else. I gasped and congratulated myself on my good instincts. The hosts of this Airbnb were terrible communicators, so I had cancelled. When a red flag is raised and waving, you simply must pay attention.

Little is needed, merely a small deviation from reason, to destroy and upset all. A pilot does not need so much apparatus to overturn a ship as to save it; but if he heads too much into the wind, it is lost; even if he should not do it purposely, but only because he is thinking of some-

thing else for a moment, it is lost. Such is the case in life, too. If you do but nod a little, all that you have hitherto accomplished is gone. Take heed, then, to the appearances of things. Watch over them.

—Epictetus[92]

After settling in to London Airbnb number two, I indulged in a favorite travel pastime, perusing the local market and checking out the names of domestic products. I was surprised to learn that England surpasses India for the funniest product names, and I challenge the rest of the world to outdo the cleverness of the Brits. As mentioned, India's version of Tide, called Jasmine and Rose with Dirt Magnets, describes a product that both smells like a cheap, blended version of those two fragrances and that sucks the negatively charged dirt out of one's clothes. But the names with which the Brits endow their products surpass the merely descriptive. I found a shampoo called Knackered Cow, "knackered" meaning "exhausted," and a product like Drain-O called Drain and Able. And the cookies: Hobnobs, digestives, Nik Naks, and Discos. For a "guilt-free delight!" a raw fruit-and-nut concoction called Posh Bits delivers elitist appeal: elegant, stylish, high class. It's as if the Royal British Brand Name Association collaborated with Monty Python, based on their enthusiasm for Spam. For flavor, texture, and a great name, though, nothing beats Australia's Tim Tams. But I jump ahead.

Another favorite travel pastime involves locating the highest point of a city and getting to the top of it. I'm not sure how to describe the appeal of this activity, since I don't feel the compulsion to scale mountains, an analogous exploit. On Hong Kong Island, the highest point of the city is Victoria Peak, accessible via the world's longest covered outdoor escalator, and riding the 2,624-foot escalator was reason enough to seek the peak's summit. (Visit travelforstoics.com to see a photo of the world's shortest escalator, at only seven steps, in Minas Gerais, Brazil.) In Sydney it's the 1,016-foot-tall Sydney Tower, whose only self-referential function is to take tourists to the top. Before boarding the elevators, perky young Australians coerce you to stand in front of a green screen and make funny, frightened faces. While you're up top, they're at work Photoshopping your face onto a Sydney background, as seen from the viewing platform, and on your way out they bully you into buying a package of these photos. The biggest thrill at Sydney Tower is ascending nineteen floors into the air at nearly twenty-three feet per second to stand on a glass platform and look down at the street where you'd been walking ten minutes earlier. A notable exception was a visit to Mount Everest during a trip to Nepal. I'd bought a seat on a tiny plane that flew tourists up to its peak and discovered I liked viewing its 29,029 feet of grandeur from the ground better than from the air. When you're flying at 29,000 feet and the peak of the mountain protrudes from the clouds, it's like seeing the tip of an iceberg and knowing the bulk of it is under water. It's all about point of view.

I set off for the Shard, also 1,016 feet; London's tallest building. True to its name, it looks like a shard of glass— perhaps a splinter that fell from Mount Olympus and stuck in the ground when Hera threw a rock at Zeus and missed, shattering the windowpane behind him. I've read that when the weather's not cloudy and gloomy, which it was on the day I visited, the Shard offers great views of the city. London's amount of annual sunshine is measured in hours.

Something I didn't expect to see on my way to the Shard, because we Americans think the Brits are superior to us culturally and developmentally, was people huddled over their phones. Everywhere. As much as Americans are in relationship with their phones. Routine travel on the Tube presented an opportunity to scroll through selfies, and engaging with the phone was an acceptable way to avoid uncomfortable eye contact. Walking the sidewalks, in the British Museum, waiting for the changing of the guard at Buckingham Palace, in Westminster Abbey, hanging out in Trafalgar Square, few people's eyes were facing forward. As a visitor, those behaviors inspire a greater sense of security for one's person and things when out in public. Why would a thief target a hyper-vigilant tourist, grasping her cross-body bag with clenched arms, when twenty of his compatriots are not paying attention, wallets bulging in back pockets or purse straps precariously sitting on slippery shoulders? This low-hanging fruit was ripe for the picking, and let's face it, human beings are basically lazy, so that's what pickpockets will go for.

What, then, is to be done? To make the best of what is in our power, and take the rest as it occurs.

—Epictetus[93]

Even if someone managed to separate me from my anti-theft travel purse, they'd be pretty disappointed to see what was inside. If only they knew the effort I put into formulating a cash concealment plan. For the cautious traveler, there are book safes, fake rocks, Ajax cleanser safes, permanent marker pens, fake D cell batteries, a car cigarette lighter, a fruit cocktail can, a water bottle with a fake bottom, and even a hairbrush where you can stash your valuables. Weeks of searching Amazon, ordering products almost daily and experimenting with various concealment schemes, ended when I found the perfect underpants. A company called Stashitware makes the same stretchy, black, mid-rise underwear I've worn for decades, but with a deep front pocket in which to hide whatever you see fit. To demonstrate just how large an object could fit into the man's version of this underwear, the manufacturers placed a two-liter soda bottle in the front pocket and posted the photo on Amazon. When I first saw it I thought, *This man probably has huge feet to match.* I could stuff a thousand dollars and my passport into the underwear pocket, wear tight leggings, and no one could tell the difference. Nothing fell out when you went to the loo, which was my big fear. Pulling my knickers down and having it all cascade into the toilet was never an issue.

When the phone-obsessed weren't looking down at their screens they were looking up and smiling at their devices attached to selfie sticks. The monument, place, or event of significance was relegated to the background. This global phenomenon underscores the question, *What is the purpose of tourist travel?* Do people spend gobs of money to travel to a place just to crowd in front of St. Paul's Cathedral, the Eiffel Tower, the Taj Mahal, the Great Wall of China, the Statue of Liberty, the Coliseum, and so on to take a selfie and post it on Facebook? On another crowded Tube car I stood behind a young woman, clearly a tourist, looking at her phone. She scrolled through hundreds of selfies, all close-ups, so the locations weren't identifiable. There wasn't a single photo of something other than her face. Surely there's more meaning in travel for the selfie-seeker than using the world as a backdrop. Stunned, I began to question my own intentions. As we travel around the world, I'll explain the reasons for my choices of destination. Here's what Seneca had to say:

Travel and change of place impart new vigor to the mind.[94]

Probing an Enigma

So why was I in England? To go to London Dungeon, to say I'd crossed Abbey Road, to visit a wax version of Queen Elizabeth at Madame Tussauds? Yes, I wanted to do a few touristy things in London, but two small towns north of the city, called Steeple Morden and Duxford, were the focus of the trip.

When a person is following a track, there is an eventual end to it somewhere, but with wandering at large there is no limit. So give up pointless, empty journeys, and whenever you want to know whether the desire aroused in you by something you are pursuing is natural or quite unseeing, ask yourself whether it is capable of coming to rest at any point…

—*Seneca*[95]

Three years earlier, I'd learned that my biological father had flown reconnaissance missions during World War II as a member of Steeple Morden's 355th Fighter Squadron. I'd also discovered a 355th Yahoo group, so I emailed one of its few remaining contributors, hoping he knew Dad and would be willing to share a few stories with me.

Dear Jack,

The 355th Fighter Group Association, and your name, were mentioned in Gene G.'s obituary in 2006, and I felt like perhaps enough time had passed that I could contact you and learn a few things about Gene's history. There is no easy way of approaching this complicated and difficult topic of my connection to Gene, but he and his wife, Connie, gave me up for adoption. I suspect you must be feeling an uncomfortable mix of emotions right now, but I don't intend to cause you or anyone else distress. Ever since I knew I was adopted, I had wanted to know my biological mother and father, not from any deficiency in my adoptive family, but because I felt that an important piece of my identity was missing. I know that compelling and sometimes untenable situations drive the decision to give up a child for adoption, and I have never presumed to understand their reasons or to judge them for it.

After I gained access to my original birth records, I located Connie and Gene in Dallas and sought contact. They declined, but what developed next was a several-years-long correspondence with Connie, which I cherish. She seldom wrote about personal matters; however, I learned she was an equestrienne and an accomplished musician, and when I was a young woman I, too, was an equestrienne and played piano. Toward the end of our correspondence, Connie sent me a cassette tape of an organ performance of hers, and in no way did I approach the caliber of musician that she was.

I hope you will understand my desire to learn what I can about my biological parents. Perhaps you're close to someone in a situation similar to mine. I would love to know more about Gene, but no pressure if you've come to the end of these specific memories. Please know I am always open to hearing more stories, seeing more photographs, and learning about your experiences, too, if you'd like to share them.

Best regards,
Eva

To my surprise, Jack wrote back immediately.

Dear Eva:

Yes, I knew your dad quite well. We flew many missions together. He was a comrade you could count on. Steady and true. And a soft-spoken, modest, courteous, elegant gentleman... with a deadpan sense of humor. I enjoyed his company immensely, as did the rest of our 355th Squadron.

I would like to hear more about you. Please forgive me, but I did not know your dad had a daughter. I am very glad to hear about you.

With all best wishes.

Jack

PS: Welcome to the 355th Fighter Group Association. Since the messages in this Yahoo group were readable by everyone in the group, I also received a communication from a couple named Linda and Jonathan who lived in Steeple Morden during the years Gene was there.

Eva,

I saw your email on the 355th Yahoo group. My father was the head crew chief for the 2nd Scouting Force with your dad. Jonathan, my husband, was the organizer of the U.K. reunions for many years and the one who, with my cousins, built the 355th Fighter Group Memorial in Steeple Morden. We currently live part-time in Steeple Morden and part-time in California.

If you wish, I'd love to connect with you.

Linda

Three years later I was riding a train to Royston, a town near Steeple Morden, to meet Jonathan. We planned to visit the American Air Museum in Duxford; Jonathan and Linda knew the museum had accessioned my father's Air Force jacket for their collection of American objects. Flying five thousand miles to see it seemed like a worthwhile thing to do.

Jonathan was six years old when twenty-year-old Gene hit town in 1944. He and Linda swore they had memories of Gene from those years, and maybe they did. In 1944, three hundred people lived in Duxford, and overnight the village was overwhelmed by two thousand American troops. Dozens of new pubs opened within days. Barracks were established in huge Quonset huts and officers' quarters in small brick buildings that after the war were assimilated into the American Air Museum. Dad's jacket was stored in one of those brick buildings.

The 355th Fighter Group flew P-47 Thunderbolts and P-51 Mustangs, aircraft that looked like thirty-two-foot cruiser yachts with wings. The "P" stood for "pursuit." With these fast and maneuverable planes, the pilots pioneered ground strafing techniques, the practice of attacking ground targets at low altitude with aircraft-mounted automatic weapons. Gene was a reconnaissance pilot, identifying targets for the bombers to destroy. Thunderbolts and Mustangs were each flown by a crew of one.

I never met my biological parents, although after decades of searching they finally turned up only a few miles away from the house in which the three of us would have lived had they raised me. Wanting to establish contact, I wrote them a carefully composed letter and sent it off, hoping it would be well received and I'd be welcomed into their lives. But it was anything but that. "Obviously you were not part of our plans." Ouch. *So why did I want to see his World War II jacket?* I asked myself that question a lot.

Jonathan and I connected with the curator in charge of the objects collection, a young and enthusiastic woman named Sarah, and when we arrived at the small brick building that housed the jacket, I wasn't prepared for the shock. When we opened the door, the jacket was draped on a half-mannequin form sitting on a white table in a white room. Seeing it felt like seeing Dad, only in the form of a corpse or a ghost. Standing next to the jacket, with the bearing of an undertaker, was the museum's head of conservation, wearing a sympathetic look and white gloves on hands clasped over his crotch. As the unacknowledged daughter of an esteemed serviceman, the conservator treated me with the utmost respect. He removed the jacket from the mannequin with deliberate, methodical movements and laid it on the table as if it were Winston Churchill's favorite bowler. With the same fascination one experiences when seeing something strange or unexpected, I photographed the jacket in every way possible. I was allowed to touch the jacket but not to put it on. I tried to imagine the man wearing the jacket and looked for signs of wear that would provide clues to his physicality. The collar lining was worn and the lining of the armpits torn and stained. The cuffs were frayed. I smelled the leather in various places, trying to detect a hint of his odor. But after seventy-plus years, the possibility of any lingering smell, even at very low concentrations, approached zero.

Finally I knew the answer to why I wanted to see the jacket. I hoped the experience would awaken primitive memories, either visual or olfactory, but the jacket remained stubbornly inert and inscrutable, just like its former owner. I examined the interiors of the front pockets, fantasizing about finding a long-lost correspondence to his relinquished daughter, an apology and a declaration of fatherly love.

Thirty minutes or so with the jacket had elapsed, and Jonathan and Sarah were chatting merrily in another part of the room. I noticed I felt impatient, sad, angry. Shaped by his body, this object, battered and torn, protected him from harm on scouting missions and kept him warm, and represented what I desired from him but could never have. The jacket conveyed an indifference to me, and I wanted to take it by the shoulders and shake some sense into it. I wanted to treat it not as a precious object but throw it to the ground and kick it around and toss it into the trash— the way its owner had done to me. I'd show it a thing or two; teach that man a lesson for giving his daughter away.

Not even a sheep, or a wolf, deserts its offspring; and shall man? What would you have—that we be as silly as sheep? Yet even these do not desert their offspring. Or as savage as wolves? Neither do these desert them. Pray, who would mind you, if he saw his child fallen upon the ground and crying? For my part, I am of the opinion that your father and mother… would not have thrown you away.
                                            —Epictetus[96]

But of course in 1944 Gene had no idea he would be facing a tough decision nearly a decade into the future and that he would have a daughter who cared about him even though he rejected her, not once but twice. The man who wore the jacket had the free world to defend.

For the remainder of the day Jonathan drove me around Duxford and Cambridge, showing me the sites, and everyone we encountered knew him. Everyone knew my story, too, and they all said the same thing. "I just don't understand how someone could do that…" Neither did I.

The next day I took the train back to London and was by myself again. I had time to reflect. I was embarrassed that I had allowed the jacket to become an object of semiotically charged importance. In conflating Dad with the jacket, I had let my Stoic guard down.

Seek in all things your own highest good; and for the rest, be content to take simply what has been given you, in so far as you can make a rational use of it, contented with this alone. Otherwise you will be unfortunate, disappointed, restrained, hindered. These are the established laws, these the statutes. Of these laws one ought to be an expositor.

—Epictetus[97]

Encounters with Critters

Dear Old England. So story book, even in the twenty-first century. On my third day there, I was part of a group of a hundred tourists loaded up in a bus and headed for Windsor Castle, Queen Elizabeth's weekend pied-à-terre. Early May is not exactly the high season for tourists, but we encountered an inexplicably bad traffic jam close to the entrance. The progress of our bus was reduced to a crawl. Police vehicles pushed through the traffic, sounding their augmented-fourth sirens made famous in James Bond movies (British sirens were used to help us remember that interval from a long-ago music theory class). Eventually the cause of the traffic jam was revealed. Britain's version of *Make Way for Ducklings* was going on right outside the bus window. A huge swan, with feet the size of scuba fins, was standing next to one of Windsor's finest right in the middle of the road. The policeman encircled the swan's neck with his left arm, as if they were best buddies headed for the pub, as he cautiously coaxed it across the road. His right hand was on his baton, just in case the swan got crazy on him.

In all of nature, danger lurks in the beautiful. Rose bushes have their thorns; huge tree limbs can detach from their trunks at any moment and without warning crush your skull. Calla lilies are poisonous; digitalis, or what we call foxglove, is also known as "dead man's bells;" and the lovely angel's trumpets flower can literally make you lose your mind. Enough crocuses, ingested, can cause a heart attack. Kew Gardens has all of these and more, including its own population of fowl not to be disrespected.

After entering Kew through Victoria Gate and making your way through the gift shop, you emerge into the Garden. The Palm House Parterre and the Conservatory create a grand vision in the distance, but like Dorothy and friends following the yellow brick road to the Emerald City, you have to navigate a dangerous, thorny path to reach your destination. The most direct route takes you past a large pond populated with loons, ducks, and geese on the east side of the parterre. Loons, one of the lower-IQ bird among the avians, have been known to use their dagger-like bills to kill people mistaken for predators, striking them right through the heart. Ducks aren't an issue, but geese are vile, aggressive creatures that will chase you unprovoked and, if they catch you, will wrestle you to the ground and bite off your fingers. When I saw one go after a tiny boy's bag of crisps, or potato chips as we say, I gave the geese a wide berth.

I detoured through a rose garden where a peacock gracefully strolled. What lovely garden is complete without a peacock or two, nature's greatest extravagance? Not understanding peacock behavior, I raised my camera and approached from the rear, hoping it would turn and spread its shimmering feathers. It took a few steps away from me, still with its back turned, and slowly opened its outrageous fan of feathers—what luck! It rotated its body—the fan making a "whoosh" sound as it met with the air's resistance—lowered its head, and as I snapped a photo, charged. I screamed, stumbled, turned, and ran, embarrassed that I didn't stand my ground, especially since I was being watched by a family with two young children and a granny. STOICs, this kind of behavior can land you in the hospital. I could have fallen backward and hit my head on a rock or impaled myself on a rose bush, and the peacock could have taken advantage of my weakened position and attacked. A Google search told me that peacocks can peck snakes to death, so it could have easily gouged out my eyes and punctured my lungs. A Hindu expression says the peacock has "the feathers of an angel, the walk of a thief, and the voice of a devil." This peacock had the disposition of a black mamba. How ridiculous would it be to arrive at the emergency room following a peacock assault? Did the inspiration for the vicious killer bunny in *Monty Python and the Holy Grail* come from an experience at Kew?

Later in the morning I sat outdoors eating a salad, when pigeons as large as dodos appeared, crash-landing on abandoned tables. If one invades your space while you're trying to eat, slowly push back from the table and run inside. Leave your food behind.

Is the cucumber bitter? set it away. Brambles are in the way? avoid them. Let this suffice. What serve these things for in the world? ...the *nature of the universe hath no such out-place; but herein doth consist the wonder of her art and skill, that she having once circumscribed herself within some certain bounds and limits, whatsoever is within her that seems either corrupted, or old, or unprofitable, she can change it into herself, and of these very things can make new things; so that she needeth not to seek elsewhere out of herself either for a new supply of matter and substance, or for a place where to throw out whatsoever is irrecoverably putrid and corrupt. Thus she, as for place, so for matter and art, is herself sufficient unto herself.*

—*Marcus Aurelius*[98]

CHAPTER X

HAIL MARY

Maybe it's stating the obvious, but STOICs must always budget extra time to leave a place. The flight from London to Lisbon left at two in the afternoon, and I was up and getting ready at five in the morning. I know this sounds irrational, but I want to emphasize that knowing one's routine and the time it takes to accomplish it is critical to successful STOIC travel. Between five and seven in the morning, I washed my hair, repacked everything, and realized before the final zip up I still needed a few things I'd repacked. Removed them. Cleaned the bathroom sink and mirror, swept my hair off the bathroom and bedroom floors, bundled up the trash and left it beside the already full waste bin in the kitchen, wrote my host a thank-you note (I grew up in the genteel U.S. South, where manners and politeness were everything), checked and double-checked the bathroom and room for anything left behind, and got the hell out on the streets.

It was another freezing, dismal, windy May morning in London, and I couldn't wait to arrive in a warmer clime. An uneventful ninety-minute ride on the Tube to

Heathrow seemed auspicious, and a swift and orderly security check-in surely would follow. Heathrow enforces the liquids in a quart ziplock rule, and back in the room I had packed all lotions and sunscreens together for efficiency at the airport. But as I extracted them from the carry-on at the first circle of check-in hell, a panicked thought struck. I flashed back to Mexico and the embarrassment of digging through my bag looking for the immigration form I needed for reentry into the U.S. (more on this later). *Was I given one at entry to Heathrow?* I remembered filling something out that I surrendered to customs, but did he give it back? I had no memory of the hand-off, but I did remember the customs agent. He had a lovely, deep baritone voice that I couldn't help but compliment, so my focus wasn't anywhere near immigration paperwork. There I was back on the well-trodden floor of yet another airport rummaging through the carry-on. No immigration form materialized. Only the usual items were in my bag; no immigration form there, either. No possibility of exit from one country or entry into another pushed me to the edge of panic, but nothing happened on England's end. I had a contingency plan in case it did. I would play the absent-minded-solo-woman-traveler card and maybe conjure some tears. It's worked in the past. I know, not very Stoic.

On the plane to Lisbon, I was seated in the economy section among a huge and excited contingent of Malaysians. They were traveling to Fátima, Portugal, to see Pope Francis, who was visiting to commemorate the hundredth anniversary of the Marian apparitions. In Fátima beginning on May 13, 1917, three shepherd children, Jacinta, Lúcia, and Francisco, reported seeing visions of an angel and then of the Virgin Mary. They described a woman "brighter than the sun, shedding rays of light clearer and stronger than a crystal goblet filled with the most sparkling water and pierced by the burning rays of the sun."[99] The words of shepherd children? I think they may have been media coached by an ambitious poet-uncle. They said the Virgin asked them to pray the Rosary every day to end the Great War (World War I). Jacinta's mother thought it was a joke and told her neighbors, and within a day the entire village knew of the apparitions. Within a few months, thousands of people had flocked to the site, and by August, officials jailed the children to interrogate them. So seeing religious apparitions became an ad hoc criminal offense in 1917 Portugal, and the concept of Miranda rights and child advocacy wouldn't appear for another fifty years. I couldn't help wondering about their interrogation methods. Since they were kids, how did the officials get them to open up and say what happened? If they'd really seen angels and the Virgin Mary, wouldn't they be terrified and just sit in silence when asked about it? Or were the officials versed in child psychology strategies, saying things like, "That must have been scary" or "What was the best part of what you saw?" or "You can go home right away if you tell us what you saw"? Did they shine bright lights in their faces? Did they waterboard them?

Lúcia told her interrogators everything except for certain secrets the VM said to keep under wraps. Her mother hoped that she'd admit it was all a lie. When the children were released from jail, the Virgin appeared to them again and said that two of them would be taken to heaven soon. If I'd received that message as a child, I wouldn't have taken it seriously. I knew from cartoon physics that death was a temporary condition, because when the coyote ran off the cliff and was squashed flat at the bottom of a canyon or crushed by the dehydrated boulder he'd ordered from the Acme Corporation, he'd resurrect and keep trying to capture the Road Runner. Gravity, not death, was the real danger. But in 1918, Jacinta and Francisco died in the flu epidemic.

Lúcia became a nun and died in 2005, in her nineties, but not before revealing the secrets. Here's the gist of secret number one:

> Our Lady showed us a great sea of fire which seemed to be under the earth. Plunged in this fire were demons and souls in human form, like transparent burning embers, all blackened or burnished bronze, floating about in the conflagration…[100]

Well, nothing new there. It's a pretty clear description of hell. Secret number two promises an end to the war, but only if people stop offending God. The VM warns that a worse war will erupt during the Pontificate of Pope Pius XI. Russia's impiety is the culprit.

> To prevent this, I shall come to ask for the Consecration of Russia to my Immaculate Heart, and the Communion of reparation on the First Saturdays. If my requests are heeded, Russia will be converted, and there will be peace; if not, she will spread her errors throughout the world, causing wars and persecutions of the Church…various nations will be annihilated.[101]

Over one hundred years later, the message still hasn't reached Moscow; Catholics comprise a teeny minority in a country of 144 million people. Curious that the VM mentioned Russia instead of the malign influence of the Nazi movement in Germany or another godless superpower-in-the-making. The other piece of the prophesy, as relayed via her underage shepherd mouthpieces, was right on the nose. Pope Pius XI was indeed head of the Catholic Church when World War II was declared in September 1939.

Secret number three is all about Armageddon and annihilation.

We saw an Angel with a flaming sword in his left hand; flashing, it gave out flames that looked as though they would set the world on fire; but they died out in contact with the splendor that Our Lady radiated towards him from her right hand: pointing to the earth with his right hand, the Angel cried out in a loud voice: 'Penance, Penance, Penance!'[102]

Bishops, priests, men and women of the Catholic faith, and the Pope make their way up a steep, corpse-strewn mountain toward a cross hewn from the trunks of a cork tree (Portugal produces nearly half of the world's output in commercial cork, so of course the cross is made of cork). Groups of soldiers fire bullets and arrows into the crowd, killing everyone. Could the children's mothers have accidentally fed them ergot-laced bread for breakfast? Were they reading Dante's *Inferno* to them at bedtime? Could

some poisoned gas have wafted over from the war in
France into Fátima?

> Beneath the two arms of the Cross there were two
> Angels each with a crystal aspersorium [a vessel for
> holy water] in his hand, in which they gathered up the
> blood of the Martyrs and with it sprinkled the souls
> that were making their way to God.[103]

The Vatican had intended for secret number three to be
under seal forever, but in May 1981, a former Trappist
monk, expelled from the order for slugging a superior in
the face, hijacked a plane and demanded that Pope John
Paul II make public the third secret. The monk, *a former
tour guide at the shrine of Fátima*, visited the airplane's loo to
douse himself with gasoline, forced his way into the cock-
pit of the airplane, and ordered the pilot to land in France
to refuel for a flight to Tehran. No wonder everyone in the
Malaysian group was so excited. Fátima promised more
drama and thrills than you'd ever encounter at, say, the
Holy Land Experience in Orlando. The best *they* offer is
Trin-i-Tee mini golf and a gruesome mock crucifixion of
Jesus.

When we reached cruising altitude, the flight attendants served us scraps of bread and a single ounce of mango
juice each, the airline's own version of communion. One of
the patriarchs of the group was positioned directly behind
me, and every few minutes he'd kick my seat, jump up, and
start taking photos of his ancient, sleeping mother directly
across the aisle. The patriarch would present either his ass
or his belly to my face, and like a squirrel haltingly negoti-

ating a street, would scamper backwards and forwards to get exactly the correct angle to photograph his slumbering mother. I wondered, *Am I missing an important opportunity by not going to Fátima? Should I change my plans? Will I see an apparition and become a Catholic? Will Lisbon empty out because everyone's making the pilgrimage, so restaurants, banks, museums, and stores will be closed and transportation will be spotty, in the way São Paulo becomes a ghost town during Carnaval?*

Near the end of our journey, a flight attendant made an important announcement. Since the Pope was visiting Portugal, no entry documents were required up to May 14. It was May 8th, and my plans were to leave on the 11th. Thanks to the Virgin Mary and the three shepherd children, I was legal.

· · · · ·

Like São Paulo's sidewalks (*calçadas*), Lisbon's are made of curvy patterns of black-and-white cobblestones, designed to hypnotize you as you drag your suitcase along, traversing the streets of the neighborhood over and over, looking for the Anos 66 bar at which you're supposed to turn left. Lisbon's hills, its cobblestone streets, and bad directions to the Airbnb threatened the integrity of my wheeled suitcase carry-on like no other place had. The sound of the wheels struggling against these uneven and rough surfaces made me wish I'd packed a backup set and a screw driver. If your carry-on can survive Lisbon, it can survive anywhere.

Lisboans are well aware of the challenges their sidewalks present to suitcases and their owners and have responded with cheap luggage superstores that are numerous and fairly easy to find. So no need to worry about this problem in Lisbon; you're covered. Did you dog-ear page 48? If not, remember: *Wherever I am in the world, I will intersect with a duplicate of the needed object left behind* (or in this case, destroyed). *And if I don't, I have the internal and external resources to get it, or to find a reasonable substitute.*

. . . . .

I learned an important lesson in the Lisbon metro: never be without lots of change and small bills. (Wait. Didn't I learn this lesson in the Mérida bus station?) When the day came to leave, I arrived at the metro station to travel to the airport for the 10 a.m. flight. It was 7 a.m. on a Thursday morning, and the metro was practically empty. A desperate-looking man approached me and asked, in English, for spare change to get something to eat. I fished around in my pockets and gave him what I had, 0.75 euros, then headed for the two side-by-side ticket machines that were a few feet away. The first one rejected my credit card, then its twin rejected the card, too. My change depleted, I had no small bills, and no one staffed the ticket booth at that early hour. In full amygdala hijack, I seriously considered jumping the gated turnstile and pulling my bag underneath its doors. When I was almost convinced that was my only option, other than going above-ground again and paying for an expensive taxi, another passenger appeared and stepped up to one of the machines to buy a ticket. His card didn't work either. When he noticed me, a forlorn woman in distressed circumstances, he so kindly offered to come to the rescue.

A forlorn state is the condition of one who is without help. For a man is not forlorn merely because he is alone, any more than a man in the midst of a crowd is necessarily not forlorn… For according to the nature of the concept the 'forlorn' means the person who is without help, and exposed to those who wish to injure him… it is not the sight of a human being as such which puts an end to our forlorn condition, but the sight of a faithful, and unassuming, and helpful human being.

—*Epictetus*[104]

But when he discovered that he didn't have enough change to buy tickets for the both of us, he bought his and vanished. Just as a metro official materialized and pointed me to a set of two machines down another hallway. The card worked; yet another crisis averted.

The point is to underscore how important it is to have a plan B *always*, especially when you're trying to catch a plane. It's even more important with a free around-the-world ticket, because if you miss one leg of the trip, your entire trip cancels.

The Lisbon airport is one of those designs that works well for long-distance runners or for those who delight in maneuvering around obstacles. Parkour training confers advantage. As you vault, jump, climb, roll, and sometimes get down on all fours, the path to your gate meanders through a labyrinth of shops that, for the most part, are like any other international airport shops. The exception is the high-concept sardine emporium whose design team must have apprenticed on a Ringling Brothers project. This sardine superstore, decorated in the brightest oranges, yellows, and reds imaginable, features walls stacked with sardine cans, a small carousel, and youthful employees wearing dresses that, if the place went under, could be repurposed as rodeo clown costumes. As the employees circulated throughout the store, I expected to hear the loud slapping sounds of oversized, red, rubberized shoes. A can of sardines, retailing for five euros (nearly six dollars USD at this writing, over triple what a can of sardines goes for at Wal-Mart), is the ultimate offbeat vanity purchase. The cans have labels that mark each year from 1916 to the present, arranged by decade. So if the boy- or girlfriend or the newborn baby you left behind on your solo trip needs a can of sardines labeled with his or her birth year, you've come to the right place. Or for the boss who begrudgingly let you have the month off: quick, text her secretary and ask him to sneak a look at her driver's license. A can of sardines would be the ideal gift to take to Fátima for Pope Francis (born in 1936). Sardines, the perfect stocking stuffer!

CHAPTER XI

O-C IN MOROCCO

Spotlessly Clean

Take a piece of paper, fold it accordion-style until you have a dozen or so pleats, cut a diamond shape out of the paper, and open it up to see the chain of linked shapes. The exterior of the stunning and spotless Marrakesh airport looks as if this chain of paper diamonds had inspired the architect's design. The arrival area features a truncated, geodesic glass dome that supports what looks like the world's largest mid-century modern boomerang table with holes to accommodate giant Slurpees. On either side of the dome, like Mexican punched tin, the beautiful Islamic eight-pointed star is used as a motif repeated in huge swaths of undulating bronze-colored metal. Inside, the hot Moroccan sun streams through high ceilings, evocative of Islamic lattice window screens, creating a play of light and shadow on the floors.

Women wearing what look like white nursing uniforms mop the floors back and forth and back and forth, endless-ly. Women posted in the bathrooms supervise handwashing and drying and point you to the sink they want you to use. Their eyes follow you as you walk into the stall, walk to the sink, walk to the air blaster dryer, and walk out of the room. The bathrooms are their domain; the ceaseless battle against dirt and germs their mission.

Since I, too, live in a desert, I know what they're up against. A careless stroll across the wooden floor in my home's living room can leave dusty, gritty, clingy footprints. By the end of a party, half of the front "yard" is in the house, and post-party cleanup becomes a multistep operation that starts with leaf blowing some of the bigger drifts back outside. When it's just me in the house, inside shoes are stationed at each exit so that when I reenter from the outside, I can remove the outside shoes and leave them at their post. That way I'm never scampering around the house looking for a pair of inside shoes and, in the process, widely distributing dirty footprints. Outside shoe removal must be done delicately. You can't just kick off your shoes when you enter a New Mexico house; if you do, the dirt acts like an aerosol and hangs in the air, ultimately descending onto your off-white sofa and your kitchen counters, settling onto the tops of pages of your book collection and clinging to anything with a static charge like CD cases, microfiber pillows, and hair. I also position Mopnado spin mops and floor cleaner in strategic places to keep the dirt under control. O-Cs have to fight the urge to clean constantly, so we develop strategies like these to cope with dirt invasions at their source. I can only imagine what dirt nightmares these diligent white-uniformed women face on a moment-to-moment basis.

My final destination in Morocco was Fez, where Virtù and I planned to rendezvous for the World Festival of Sacred Music. Travel from Marrakesh to Fez was the one aspect of the around-the-world trip planning that was a black box. To book a flight or train online from the U.S. isn't possible unless you're a Moroccan credit card holder, so this part of the journey presented a big question mark. The options were to fly, to take a train, to take a non–air-conditioned bus (worst-case scenario), or to take a taxi (most expensive scenario). At least there were options. This not-knowing, although it sounds very Buddhist and serene and immersed in the present moment, generally does not work well for STOICs. The art of surrender and mindfully letting go are not quite the same concept as Stoic indifference; it's another skill set entirely. We're all about being in command of our destiny and knowing what's around the corner, and if it feels like it's going to be a drop into the abyss, we need to make a controlled descent on a fixed, secure rope.

The domestic flight from Marrakesh to Fez was hugely expensive, and flights were infrequent. Because the airport architecture, efficient customs officials, and industrious cleaning women scattered throughout the airport had made such a positive impression, I was expecting something more Southwest Airlines-ish, like their hourly flights between Houston and Dallas. But I was facing either a seven-hour wait in the airport for the one-hour fight to Fez, or I could take the train and see the countryside. Both options yielded the same arrival time in Fez, so I opted for the train.

The Marrakesh train station was equally beautiful and spotlessly clean and also populated with nurse-women mopping nonstop. By the time I arrived I was desperate for a bathroom but feeling guilty about making more work for the cleaning staff. I looked for the toilets and saw, contradictorily, a sign pointing up to the second floor and on the second floor, a sign pointing down to the first floor. Thinking there may be an in-between floor, I rode the elevator up to floor two. Morocco being a Muslim country, a man was standing by to push the elevator button for me. We ascended and exited the elevator, and I started down the steps, one by one, lugging the carry-on, my cross-body bag, and camera. I quickly discovered there was no in-between floor, or, if there were, it existed in some alternate dimension to which I was refused access. From the McDonald's on the first floor, where I'd passed only moments earlier, I felt pairs of eyes on me, and I felt their ridicule.

Because of our anxiety profiles, STOICs are susceptible to "earworms", songs that stick in our brains and repeat themselves relentlessly. I think you know already which one hijacked my brain when I boarded the train in Marrakesh. In fact, I'll bet the first time you read the M–word in this chapter that it happened to you, too. But the song and the actual train ride had little in common. The train meandered through a landscape that was mostly flat, the tracks lined on either side with wheat fields that in May are a beautiful Naples yellow. Urban areas we passed through consisted of row after row of mid-rise concrete apartment blocks. Somewhere near Casablanca, about three hours into the journey, the train started to parallel the Atlantic

Ocean, the blue in the distance a welcome break from the monotony of the landscape. The song was still tormenting me.

A first-class ticket buys you a place in an air-conditioned compartment seating six, and I was lucky to get a window seat. A middle-aged French couple, a twenty-something modern Arab woman who talked on her cell the entire time she was on the train, and a djellaba-wearing Arab woman about my age shared the compartment with me. My Arab contemporary and I bonded over Portleos, the Moroccan version of Oreos, which I had bought from the porter who walked up and down the aisle selling coffee and snacks. Except for the eight-point Islamic star design stamped into the cookies—appropriately, a symbol of fullness and regeneration—the Portleos were exactly like Oreos. In any culture, food is a great icebreaker, inspiring people to extend their goodwill to each other, so I offered her some of my cookies. She reciprocated in a tender and intimate way that touched me deeply. Whenever I stood to stretch my legs, leaving our compartment to stare out the opposite side of the train for a while, she followed behind. I'd feel a purposeful tug on my shirt and cardigan, reminding me of my mother, who was always rearranging my clothes, even when I was no longer a child. Being mothered was comforting. Whenever a train passed going in the opposite direction, making a thunderclap of sound, we jumped out of our skins and laughed. She made the journey beautiful in these small ways.

Regardless, a STOIC should never expect any return for good deeds; they should be performed for their own sake. But when you're traveling and encountering new situations and strangers all the time, they often come back to you almost as quickly as you dole them out.

A horse at the end of the race...A dog when the hunt is over...A bee with its honey stored...And a human being after helping others. They don't make a fuss about it. They just go on to something else, as the vine looks forward to bearing fruit again in season. We should be like that. Acting almost unconsciously.

—*Marcus Aurelius*[105]

The train ride to Fez lengthened from seven to nine hours, and my Arab friend had long ago reached her destination. When we finally arrived at the station, lit with orange, high-pressure, sodium-vapor lamps and eerily abandoned, I felt a panicky disorientation that I tried to calm by installing an earworm of my own, to the tune of "Follow the Yellow Brick Road". I'd read about Morocco's petit taxis and how they're painted different colors depending on the city. Fez's were red. "Find a red petit taxi" was the phrase I sang to myself as I walked toward the exit.

Even late at night, the streets surrounding the train station were choked with petit taxis, and a driver approached me as if we had arranged ahead of time to meet. He asked the name of my riad (my lodgings), and when I answered, he said he was friends with the owner. In my disoriented state I thought I was being scammed, so I asked him to ring the riad to see if Virtù had arrived safely. When he started to dial the number, the name of the riad popped up on his phone. So it was true. I hopped into his taxi and we took off as if we were driving the Paris-Dakar rally.

Though I can show you that you have resources and endowment for magnanimity and courage, do you, pray, show me what resources you have to justify faultfinding.

—Epictetus[106]

It's true that you have to travel really far from home to see something different, and I'd never seen anything that even remotely resembled the old city of Fez. A ribbon of road followed mile after mile of tall, fastidiously polished sandstone walls—the perimeter of the medina, the old quarter of the city—colored in surreal orange light. I wondered what it must have been like, a few centuries back traveling by camel, to see those ancient walls during a full moon. Like the Marrakesh airport and train station, the roads of Fez were spotlessly clean. The riad I had booked was only one of hundreds within the medina, nestled somewhere in the labyrinth of alleyways and accessible via grand and ornate gateways. I couldn't wait to discover what was behind those walls.

When you arrive at night, laying eyes on the medina for the first time, it looks like one big dark alleyway full of strangers, the kind your parents told you always to avoid. In fact, the medina is composed of nine thousand dark alleyways populated by ninety-two thousand Fessi who, as a culture, must have developed a special type of cooperation among its members to be able to tolerate life in such close quarters. If one of your anxieties is claustrophobia, you may want to choose a different travel destination.

The souks, restaurants, private residences, hotels and riads, and streets full of purveyors of goods comprise this complex maze, and the occasional door or archway interrupts the high-walled continuum. Often, magnificent spaces are hidden behind these walls, ornamented with tile and precious stones and carved wood and all manner of Islamic design, symbolizing the organizing principles that codify our chaotic universe. These spaces simultaneously convey a sense of calm and immensity, of the terrestrial and the heavenly—their open ceilings forming an aperture that frames constellations and planets in the night sky.

A riad is a cube-shaped building with rooms surrounding an inner courtyard. Riads are stunning in the extreme, with colorful, patterned ceramic tiles; luxurious fabrics and handmade carpets; and stained-glass lighting that throws splashes of color on ancient plaster walls. Courtyard gardens full of orange trees, palms, bamboo, roses, and jacaranda trees with their purple blooms rise up to the sky through the open roofs. Bougainvillea entwine columns that frame a central pond or fountain, the visual focus of the space. The kitchen, dining, and lounging areas are situated on the upper level. In addition to being cooler and offering a view of the sky and environs, the upper level is a respite from the claustrophobia of the streets, which frequently are only a few feet wide. It's puzzling how objects like beds, wardrobes, sofas, and kitchen stoves manage to travel these passages. After spending some amount of time in a riad, you understand that these spaces and designs all draw the eye upward to the heavens to the glory of Allah or Jesus or Yahweh or whatever it is that keeps the wheels of this crazy universe turning. You realize that the visual cacophony of the Islamic aesthetic actually serves as an ordering device, suggesting the infinite patterns and symmetries of the universe and how they function in concert with one another: in the grand and the small, in the exterior and the interior, above and below.

Sound is another matter altogether. As an acoustic space, a riad creates frightening, nightmare-inducing sounds in the early mornings that disturb your sleep. The profusion of hard surfaces creates a maddeningly reflective effect, so when the neighbor's rooster starts crowing at 3 a.m., it's as if it's perched on the arm of the sofa next to your bed. When visitors above your room walk around, it sounds like they're hammering nails into the floor. When first experienced, the 5 a.m. call to prayer is absolutely terrifying to the hypnagogic brain and can induce the ghastliest nightmares. Chattering children in the school next door become the menacing flying monkeys from *The Wizard of Oz*. One's brain loses the ability to focus on single sounds, as we do when engaged in a conversation in a room full of dozens of conversations, and this creates little fissures in the psyche that disturb one's functioning. At the first light of day, it's best to get out in the open, take deep breaths, and enjoy the sunshine.

Despite its beauty, Fez is a place of subtle dangers. If you let it, the medina can feel like Morocco's heart of darkness. You can be meandering through the crowds in the medina and suddenly a tiny kitten is underfoot. Or you may be walking a plaza and a hole large enough to place a foot into, or even to swallow you up, appears inexplicably. A wrong turn down an alleyway, some barely an arm's length wide, can lead you into a maze of leather and carpet stalls from which there is no escape. There are also not-so-subtle dangers, like drivers who occupy a different space-time continuum from you. You can anticipate crossing a street and, like a well-habituated STOIC, be obsessively looking in all directions before stepping into the intersection when out of nowhere a petit taxi bears down on you as if you don't exist.

Very old places like Fez (founded in the eighth century) have other dangers common to places of long occupancy, and I'm talking about spirits. Even though I'm not of the woo woo persuasion, this is not tongue-in-cheek advice. Everyone needs to know how to protect themselves from jinn, incubi, druden, specters, airy powers, and furies. These spirits may try to catch a ride in a human, and you don't want to take home that kind of a souvenir of your travels. (Some of the best-known malevolent spirit hot spots that you should consider avoiding include the lower level of the Taj Mahal, where Shah Jahan and Mumtaz Mahal are interred; the Tower of London and its grounds, where one hundred and thirty-three confirmed executions took place and Queen Anne Boleyn walks around carrying her head under her arm; the Paris Catacombs, where the bones of millions of Parisians are used as decorative objects; the RMS *Queen Mary*, docked in Long Beach harbor and haunted by a person murdered on board; and just about any place in Edinburgh.) So if you feel a sense of unease or disharmony or experience a rapid-onset weird physical illness or a shift in your normal, well-functioning state of being, consider nonconventional modes of treatment. In my part of the world, it would be a *curandera*; if you're in Brazil, a *pai-de-santo*; in Ecuador, a shaman. In Morocco, I assumed that role.

Virtù had arrived at the riad three hours before me, and Airbnb had not disclosed that others could be in residence in the room during our stay. Ours was a nightmare-inducing nocturnal spirit, not particularly dangerous, and it seemed like he was just kind of hanging around for lack of something better to do. I got a glimpse of him on my night of arrival. After being dropped off by the Paris-Dakar rally driver at around eleven o'clock, when I entered the dimly lit room, I saw a semitransparent man step into Virtù's leather shoes which were sitting on the floor, toes facing the inner courtyard. The image of this man faded quickly after I saw it. I wondered, *am I still in a state of confusion and exhaustion after the flight from Lisbon to Marrakesh plus the nine-hour train ride from Marrakesh to Fez?*

By the morning of day two, Virtù had experienced two nights of disturbed sleep and reported that there was some kind of man-entity inhabiting the room. Late in the morning of day three, while Virtù was catching up on lost sleep because of yet another restless night, I sat in the courtyard writing when one of the riad staff appeared and placed two sticks of lit incense in an urn close by. I felt compelled to fetch Virtù's leather shoes, smudge them with the incense, and firmly ask the spirit to leave—or at least relocate to the room above us and haunt the people pounding nails. I was eager to see if my actions had any effect.

The previous night I had dreamed of a teenage boy named Kyle who was trying to steal my new bicycle. I looked him right in the eye, challenged him, and he backed down. I decided to call the spirit Kyle and think of him as a prankster teenager.

The third night Virtù slept nightmare-free and the next morning reported that she no longer felt the presence of

Kyle. I shared with her what I'd seen and how I'd gotten rid of him. Maybe a career as an exorcist is in my future?

· · · · ·

The Fez medina is the world's largest continuous city free of auto traffic (it's relegated to the streets outside the medina walls). To my knowledge, no comprehensive, useful tourist map of Fez exists, so for an outsider, navigation is challenging without assistance, either human or electronic. You feel that this lack of a useful map is an old tradition to which the Fessi deliberately cling to maintain control of the secrets of their city. However, young men populate every corner of the medina, eager and willing to assist the hopelessly lost tourist to his or her destination, often without expecting compensation. They are playful and affectionate with each other, sport the same kinds of haircuts seen on young New Mexican men—shaved on the sides and high and bushy on top—and wear T-shirts with logos of their favorite European and American sports teams. At public music concerts they dance with abandon in tight groups and sing loudly, almost shouting, along with their favorite songs. For the STOIC, they're a good influence for how to live as if no one is judging you all the time.

Fez has a large cat population, and I never once saw a rat, a mouse, or a cockroach thanks to them, I imagine. Dogs are not popular pets. With all these people living in close quarters and the other inherent pressures of hive living, you'd think Fez would have a horrific trash problem, but it doesn't. Clearly it ends up at a large dump east of town from where a thick plume of black smoke continually emanates. When you walk the streets late at night, which is safe to do, they are swept clean without exception.

Bait and Switch

Morocco transacts in two currencies, the euro and the dirham, and speaks in three languages, Arabic, Berber, and French. English runs fifth place behind Spanish. The dirham is Morocco's official currency, and prices of goods and services are customarily quoted in dirhams but at payment sometimes switched to euros. Hold that thought. I arrived in Fez with clothes covered in dust, pollution, coffee, and food stains from the ten days I'd spent in London and Lisbon. I scoured the riad, desperate for a plastic bucket in which to wash my clothes, and tried to communicate this need to the cheerful on-site housekeeper. The English-speaking riad manager, an Arab version of James Dean, intervened to tell me that on-site laundry service was available: five dirhams for the clothes I had stuffed in a plastic bag (about fifty cents USD or a little over half a euro). I couldn't believe this incredible bargain and availed myself of the laundry service two more times over nine days. When the bill came due at the end of my stay, I questioned why it was fourteen euros more than I expected. "For laundry," the manager said incredulously.

The next day Virtù and I experienced an even more confounding bait and switch. We hired a driver to take us to a forest in the Middle Atlas, a two-and-a-half-hour drive southeast of Fez, an area populated with giant Moroccan cedars and, we discovered, ravenous Barbary macaques, monkeys roughly the size of a human toddler. The driver deposited us in a gravel parking lot near a grove of 200 foot tall cedars, and the moment the vehicle stopped, a huge male macaque leaped onto the hood of the car and peered at us through the windshield, looking for a handout. Turning on the windshield wipers was enough to scare him back up into the trees, but I was triggered. A few moments later a minivan pulled in next to us and the entire macaque family landed on its hood in a series of thuds, aggressively seeking snacks. The dad emerged from the car with a bag of shelled peanuts and his cell phone, walked to a low stone wall nearby, and sat down. The dad macaque followed. With his left hand, the human dad fed peanuts to the macaque dad while with his right hand, the human dad took selfies. His simian buddy sat next to him as if they were watching a Red Sox game together. This human-macaque camaraderie did not extend to other family members. Both sets of mothers and babies were clinging fearfully to each other, and once the macaque dad was sated, he and his family disappeared into the trees.

Virtù and I set out from the parking lot on a dusty road bordered by fossil and mineral shops, an assortment of Moroccan ceramics, Berber rugs, and hands of Fátima jewelry with a group of five macaques following closely behind. Two men leading handsome Berber horses appeared on either side of us, asking in French if we wanted a ride. To me, it was both a rhetorical question and a way to escape our simian stalkers. Of course I wanted a ride! Slender and spirited, the horses were irresistible with their fancy saddles and bridles covered in rich Berber tapestry, silver, and pompoms. Our driver had cautioned us about these guys and had said not to agree to more than thirty dirhams per person. Now pestered from both sides and from the back, Virtù resisted, but my anxiety rendered me extraordinarily persuasive and she agreed. Still speaking French, they offered a two mile ride to a spectacular vista, via the cedar forest, for whatever we wanted to pay. That offer morphed into one hundred dirhams for the both of us, which Virtù bargained down to eighty. To contextualize this amount of money, various sources we had read said the monthly income of a typical rural Moroccan is 150 dirhams, so eighty dirhams was over half a month's income. They agreed, in French, to our counteroffer; we mounted the horses and were led into the forest.

Without circumspection, you will be running here and there like an ape imitating whatever you see.

—*Epictetus*[107]

The ride was pleasant and our Berber guides jovial and attentive. Ten minutes elapsed, and we arrived at a sprawling meadow, not so much a grand vista as an opening in the forest. The older guide of the two, claiming to be a grandfather to over seventy children, picked a fragrant herb from the meadow floor for us to smell. He took copious photos of both of us from the front and side. We rode back. Twenty minutes, tops.

The guides led us to a picnic table to dismount, where earlier we'd watched an aggressive male macaque steal an entire grocery bag of food from a young woman. That's when our hosts' moods shifted. They both were stricken with intractable amnesia that short-circuited their ability to recall what we'd agreed upon earlier. Dirhams switched to euros, and they wanted twenty euros apiece (ninety dirhams), a long way from "whatever you feel like paying." After lots and lots and lots of haggling, Virtù got them to agree to seventy-five dirhams apiece (150 dirhams total) and gave the younger guide two, one-hundred-dirham notes, expecting change. Suddenly neither of the guides spoke French. The younger guide walked away with the money under the pretense of getting change and never re-appeared. This Middle Atlas tourist destination was a den of thieves, both simian and human. Virtù stormed off to sit under a cedar and calm down. I didn't see her again for two hours.

Fleecing Virtù is never recommended. She abhors deceit, and dishonesty is her pet hate. When I found her in the forest, she was still as angry as ever and wanted to hunt down the guides and demand a full refund. After another half an hour I convinced her that they were the ethical losers in the game and that karma would do its work. I was grateful, but kept it to myself, that they didn't lead us somewhere deep in the forest, à la *The Virgin Spring*, rape us, and leave us for dead (sorry, spoilers).

A very ridiculous thing it is, that any man should dispense with vice and wickedness in himself, which is in his power to restrain; and should go about to suppress it in others, which is altogether impossible.

—*Marcus Aurelius*[108]

The bait and switch (BAS) philosophy of conducting business transactions is, unfortunately, transcultural, and at least as old as recorded history. Its proponents even occupy a special subcircle of the Ninth in Dante's Inferno, those who have committed treachery and are frozen in ice. Epictetus writes about the high price of becoming a thief, the essential nature of bait and switch, and how the thieving lose their virtue and become monsters; a good bargain for the thief, in his view. BAS permeates life, from the car dealership that promises the flat-screen TV in exchange for test driving a car (Virtù fell for that one once), to "while supplies last," to Lucy snatching the football out from under Charlie Brown just as he's about to kick it, to politicians (no explanation needed here), to spiders that can replicate the sex pheromones of female moths to attract and trap male moths. The bait and switch is a literary device used in detective stories. There are hundreds of examples. Even the notebook in which I recorded my around-the-world trip's thoughts shorted me a dozen of its purported one hundred pages.

Fortunately, Virtù and I were left with the feeling that Morocco is full of kind and charitable people. A case in point was Hassan, our driver to the Roman ruins of Volubilis. Virtù's asthma required immediate attention that day, and on our way back to Fez, Hassan took us to a clinic, waited the two hours it took for her breathing treatment and for observation, dropped us as close to the riad as he could, and was genuinely shocked when we tipped him generously.

· · · · ·

Leaving Morocco wasn't a matter of getting on a plane in Fez and flying north to my connection in Vienna. It was either take the nine-hour train back to Marrakesh or fly to Casablanca, lay over for four hours, then fly to Marrakesh. After an overnight in Marrakesh, I would fly to Vienna the next day. I needed to leave the riad at four in the morning to catch the once-a-day Fez-to-Marrakesh plane, not something I was thrilled about because I knew it would cause an anxiety uptick and result in lost sleep. Regardless of who I might meet and how lovely they may be, another nine hours on the train was not an option.

The riad manager—the Arab James Dean—arranged for a petit taxi to take me to the airport. When I emerged from our room at 3:30 a.m., he handed me a bag containing a neatly wrapped and delicious breakfast, something I didn't expect and was happy to have. The driver showed up on time, and after emotional goodbyes between me and Virtù and the riad staff, I was on my way. The driver started off in the direction of the airport, changing course from the main road onto side streets. A shortcut, I thought; or were we making an unscheduled stop at a handicraft emporium? After fifteen minutes we arrived at the train station. Had there been a miscommunication? *"Non, non, l'aéroport!"* I said in a minor panic. The driver explained that we were headed to the airport by way of the train station. A colleague approached the taxi and an exchange of papers occurred. Then, in English, he said, "Did I afraid you?"

We are not to lead events but follow them.
—*Epictetus*[109]

· · · · ·

Marrakesh had a distinctly different vibe from laid-back Fez. Taxi drivers at the airport engaged in life-or-death arguments over who would win my business, and once inside the taxi, we were required to pass a checkpoint manned by a big, fierce-looking dude. He stuck his oversize head, wild-eyed and trembling, into the vehicle and asked what amount of money I'd been quoted to make sure I wasn't being fleeced by the taxi driver. The closer we got to the medina, the more I felt a hot, angry chaos emanating from inside its walls. While I was still sitting in the back seat of the taxi at an entrance to the medina, young guides pushed each other out of the way to get my attention, parting just long enough for me to exit the taxi and get my bag out of the trunk. I chose a quiet boy with a sad face and we took off for the riad. As in Fez, there was no way in hell I could have found the place by myself.

When we arrived at the entrance to the riad, two older and much bigger young men materialized demanding one hundred dirhams, about ten dollars USD. Minimum wage in Marrakesh at the time was $1.50 USD per hour, and I had promised the quiet, sad-faced boy twenty dirhams, or about two dollars USD, not bad for ten minutes of work. The more aggressive of the two add-ons erupted in high-decibel shouting, and I tried to be calm and not let his threats turn into a trigger. The second young man chanted in the background, "Give us money, give us money!" A tiny, middle-aged Arab woman, also with a sad face, opened the door and I stepped in. She remained absolutely silent and passive, with eyes trained on the ground. When I realized I was on my own, throwing my hat into the shouting match seemed like the best, most expeditious solution. STOICs, when you find a door between yourself and a threat, it's okay to empower yourself with aggressive displays and posturing. When breaching a boundary invades territory that is off-limits, and your aggressors know it, you have the upper hand. Without crossing the threshold, my opponent leaned in toward me and snatched the twenty-dirham note from my hand. Not an inch from my face, he roared, "Fuck your mother!" Like Kyle, the nightmare spirit back in Fez, the three of them evaporated as quickly as they had appeared, and I slammed the door. Their extortion scheme failed, but my amygdala had grown from the size of an almond to a watermelon.

Remember that it is not he who gives abuse or blows who insults; but the view we take of these things as insulting. When, therefore, anyone provokes you, be assured that it is your own opinion which provokes you.

—Epictetus[110]

An hour passed before I recovered and wanted to leave the safety of the riad. I changed my shirt, tied back my hair, and wore a big hat and sunglasses so if I ran into them again they wouldn't recognize me. When I stepped into the street, the "Give us money" guy was working another tourist. He glanced in my direction but looked right through me. Another loud shouting match was happening close by, a young man raced around the corner toward which I was walking, and we nearly collided. He wore a heavy, spiked chain wrapped around his hand, and his adversary was in pursuit. The Marrakesh medina was lawless and desperate.

· · · · ·

Any long flight passes quickly when you watch a succession of movies, and after two on the ten-hour flight from Vienna to Bangkok, I realized if I wanted to get any sleep and still be alert when we landed, I'd better take a Valium sooner rather than later. But I'd waited too long. When we hit the tarmac, I was still in a fog and unprepared for the Suvarnabhumi Airport, an anarchist intentional community where etiquette rules for personal space are suspended. Suvarnabhumi processes sixty million passengers per year, and I was one of the herd of ninety-six thousand people who passed through during the seven-hour layover. Back in the States I'd read reviews praising Suvarnabhumi, and I was confident I'd be able to fill the time with interesting activities before my next flight. The airport offered short-term sleep and shower boutiques, beautiful gardens visible from inside the space-age terminal, reclining massage chairs with free Wi-Fi, and great food. However, the terminal I was in offered none of these amenities and was more like a third-world bus station. After a few hours of aimless wandering, I realized I'd again blown any opportunity for sleep. I had a mission, though, more important than sleep: to quest for a store, preferably an Apple store, to buy a charging cable for my iPhone. In Morocco, Virtù's had failed and I'd handed mine over, thinking the Bangkok airport offered better odds of finding a replacement than the tiny Berber village in the High Atlas that was her next destination.

More wandering did not produce results. It wasn't clear how to venture into other terminals, but going into town looked easy, so I took the escalator downstairs where tour operators congregated, thinking they'd know the location of the closest Apple store. Tour operators can be extremely skilled at snagging dazed, disoriented tourists, and offering no resistance, I signed up for a two-hour Thai massage with a stop off at an electronics store. The transaction turned into another bait and switch. The handsome and charming front man spoke perfect English and offered to take me to my destinations personally. After he had my money, he disappeared, and a dour, not-as-skilled linguist materialized to do the actual transport. My advice to the STOIC is to expect these BASs often—then if it works out that you *do* spend time with the handsome, charming, English-speaking front man, well, great.

We drove into town in an immaculate white van with glacial air conditioning, passing row after row of ten-by-ten-foot booths covered in blue plastic tarps, a giant flea market. The driver turned in and parked at the electronics "store." I thought, *Uh-huh, they're going to have this specialty iPhone product.* But they did. I'd been rationing cell phone battery power for the previous thirty-six hours, and this was a relief. First-world problems can knock you off your center when you're so exhausted you've lost your STOIC indifference. The two-hour Thai massage was great and exactly what I needed after the long flight, but I didn't remember requesting a breast fondle add-on.

There is a proper dignity and proportion to be observed in the performance of every act of life.

—*Marcus Aurelius*[111]

CHAPTER XII

COUNTRY OF GHOSTS

Even though late arrival at a destination is not advised, sometimes it's unavoidable. The thought of what could go wrong is enough to keep a STOIC indoors for the rest of his or her life, but try to keep your anxiety at a manageable level. Remind yourself that even though you don't know how to get to a place in a strange new city, it's likely that the people at the airport waiting in the tuk-tuks and taxis to drive you somewhere do. It's part of their job description. Remember this and your anxiety will lift.

Phnom Penh at ten o'clock at night was hot, steamy, and chaotic. I knew Number 264 on Street 288 was my destination, and an earlier-in-the-day (unsuccessful) poring over a city map had spiked my anxiety. But my driver, Mr. Solo, knew exactly where to go, even though the streets rarely had names, which had also been the case in Fez and Marrakesh. We navigated potholed avenues lined with the day's trash and hundreds of impromptu food stands all packed with late-night diners. Speeding motorcyclists passed dangerously close on both sides. A loud and ostentatious funeral procession stalled traffic for thirty minutes.

Something wrong with the tuk-tuk compelled Mr. Solo to turn off the engine at every stoplight. I reminded myself to trust that what was happening was normal. Everything would be okay.

Demand not that events should happen as you wish; but wish them to happen as they do happen, and your life will be serene.
—*Epictetus*[112]

I realized I'd forgotten to exchange money at the airport and had no Cambodian currency to pay Mr. Solo, but ATM kiosks were plentiful. We stopped at one inserted between two automotive parts stores, its glass enclosure sweating with condensation from the air conditioning. Again I was in a situation where I needed to abandon my luggage and place my trust in a complete stranger. Once inside the glass enclosure I couldn't see out, and he could have easily slipped away without my noticing. Because I'd had problems with it during other travels, I wondered if my bank card would even work. Would the ATM screens be readable, or in Khmer only? What was plan B if this effort failed? I entered my PIN, typed in the number five hundred, and the transaction was successful. But instead of Cambodian riels, five crisp new U.S. one-hundred-dollar bills emerged from the cash dispenser. I stuffed them into the pocket of my underwear, collected the receipt, walked out into the hot, steamy, chaotic night, and was relieved to see Mr. Solo standing beside the tuk-tuk, smiling.

Forty-five minutes later we arrived in the sector of the city with numbered streets. A grid of numbered streets, what could be more O-C? Amid the trash and mud and street dogs and dilapidated, multistoried cement and cinder block dwellings, we pulled up to a lush tropical paradise that was my accommodation. I had an entire apartment to myself in this building, with a bathroom much more luxurious than the one back home. How was this possible? And for thirty-two dollars per night? I availed myself of the beer in the fridge, took a long, hot shower, and collapsed onto silk pillows covered in fresh jasmine blossoms.

Mr. Solo had explained that the riel is Cambodia's official currency and the USD the de facto currency, solving the mystery of the hundred dollar bill-dispensing ATM. I still couldn't pay him because I had no small bills, but we had arranged to meet again the next day for a tour of the city. He'd agreed we could settle up then.

In countries with underperforming economies, it's dog-eat-dog competition for the tourist business. Even though you're boosting a country's gross domestic product by visiting, the fact that you have the resources to travel, even if you travel on the cheap, generates a lot of guilt for the STOIC and drives you to question your motivations. O-Cs regularly debate most of our actions anyway, and for me, being in Cambodia triggered this behavior in the extreme. Smiling, handsome young men, many of them orphans and most desperate for your tourist business, were the legacy of Pol Pot's failed agrarian socialist experiment. Their parents suffered complete isolation from the outside world and absolute revoking of all their freedoms. Between 1975 and 1979, the Khmer Rouge expelled all foreigners and closed embassies, the use of foreign languages was forbidden, possession of money was illegal, and any outside economic help was refused. The KR pulled the plug on newspapers, TV and radio stations, and the mail system; religion and education were banned. All health care was eliminated; and no assistance organizations, like the Red Cross, were allowed admittance into Cambodia. People's bicycles were confiscated. Children were separated from their parents, and everyone was forced to inform on each other. A quarter of the population was killed during the time Pol Pot was in power, and people of my generation were conspicuously absent. So why was I visiting Cambodia? It had to do with a decades-long fascination with their art and architecture, and specifically to see Angkor Wat. War tourism hadn't even crossed my mind. I had no idea that the horror of the late '70s would still be so palpable.

The next morning, Mr. Solo arrived before our agreed-upon time and didn't seem to mind waiting the fifteen minutes I needed to finish getting ready. We greeted each other with the Cambodian Sampeah (both palms together in front of the chest), and the first thing he asked was, "You want to see the Killing Fields?" I took a pass. Instead he drove me to the Royal Palace, an immense walled compound enclosing a complex of buildings that serve as the royal residence of the king of Cambodia. Walk to the entrance from either corner of the compound and you run a gauntlet of people who have suffered life's cruelties in the most dramatic ways. Men in wheelchairs with missing legs. A clubfooted man sitting on the sidewalk. A woman with a huge, bulbous tumor dangling from her head like a jackfruit. A young man in a wheelchair, with no hands or forearms and only one leg, who can somehow remove his Mao-era cap and hold it in front of his smiling face while he asks you for money. My pockets were drained in a matter of minutes. I imagined a Cambodian Siddhartha living within the Palace walls with a protective father who forbade him to leave the grounds. Seeing his subjects on the other side of the wall would destroy his innocence and inspire depletion of the royal coffers.

The scene reminded me of my own moment of lost innocence. From age three through age ten I wore corrective shoes, black-and-white saddle Oxfords fortified with arch-supporting inserts. Think pink felt poodle skirts and bobby socks, a look from the American '50s that I was not going for. They were big, clunky shoes with leather so stiff that for the first month of wearing a new pair they rubbed blisters on the delicate, pink skin that transitions from the sole of your foot to the top. A middle panel (the "saddle"), the soles, and the heels were black and the rest of the shoe white. Keeping the white parts looking good for more than a few days at a time was impossible. When you walked, the rubber soles made black scuff marks on the white sides of the opposite shoe, and the rubber tripped you up, scuffing the tips of the shoes. Our household had a well-stocked shoeshine kit, including a bottle of foul-smelling white polish with a round, drippy sponge applicator, the kind nurses used. My father was insistent on maintaining spiffy shoes, so I was expected to polish the saddle Oxfords nightly. Those shoes were a nuisance. Their bold black-and-white pattern created a spotlight effect and drew undesired attention to my feet. I've often wondered if saddle shoes marked the genesis, and reinforcement, of my introversion.

My mother had taken me to the orthopedist where I was diagnosed with incipient flat feet, and the only remedy at the time were saddle Oxfords with their ironclad arch support. I resented having to wear such ugly shoes when all the other girls were wearing patent leather Mary Janes or comfortable strappy sandals. Nobody else at school had to wear saddle shoes, so there was no one with whom to share my feelings about this indignity. At the beginning of each school year, mom dragged me to a local shoe store to re-place the outgrown ones from the year before, and these were not happy occasions.

Entering the first grade was a big deal because it meant you were going to learn to read and write in earnest as a full-time student. I would rather have gone to school bare-foot than wear shoes that signaled I could be developmentally challenged. As we entered the shoe store, the back-to-school displays featured the latest Buster Browns in multiple colors, and my eye landed on a red leather pair with pretty straps and bows. I asked my mother if I could have a pair of shoes like the other girls were wearing. She said "No," and I went ballistic. During my display of non-Stoic loss of cool, another child came up behind me and tugged on my dress. He asked if I would unwrap his chewing gum. Still furious, I whipped around and snapped at him, "Do it yourself!" My mother grabbed my hand and dragged me toward the back of the store, the domain of ugly shoes.

Something told me to turn around and have another look at the boy. When I did, I was mortified. I'd seen the shocked and disappointed look on the boy's face, but I'd missed an important detail. The little boy toddling away from me had only one arm.

When I arrived back at the Palace entrance an hour later, the same group was outside and most of them approached me again, but I needed to keep the money I had left to pay Mr. Solo. The wheelchair-bound young man with no hands and one leg did not like to be refused and pursued me down the sidewalk yelling, "Give me money, give me money!" I'm not sure how he kept up, but I lost him at the corner, feeling bad for the privilege of being able to run on well-arched feet.

Places where Cambodians were tortured and killed were not on my list of tourist must-sees, but Mr. Solo insisted that I visit S-21, the Tuol Sleng ("poisonous hill") Genocide Museum. A large sign at the entrance told visitors that between 1975 and 1979, inside the converted high school, the Khmer Rouge tortured seventeen thousand people and delivered them to the nearby Killing Fields for execution. Imagine all the inhabitants of Pacific Grove, California; St. Augustine, Florida; or Madison, New Jersey, executed over a five-year period. Kang Kek Iew, whose nom de guerre was Comrad Duch, was a mid-level leader of the Khmer Rouge, former teacher, and manager of Tuol Sleng. Perhaps borrowed from General William Westmoreland, the commander of U.S. forces in Vietnam from 1964 to 1968, Duch said of his victims, "To spare you is no profit; to destroy you is no loss."[113] Westmoreland had famously written, "The Oriental doesn't put the same high price on life as does a Westerner. Life is plentiful; life is cheap in the Orient."[114] Somehow seven people survived Tuol Sleng, and one of those survivors was a daily visitor to the Museum, selling his autobiography from a small folding table under an umbrella. He was one of the last living re-minders of the horror.

Sometimes it is an act of bravery even to live.
—*Seneca*[115]

As history recounts ad nauseam, nations with special in-terests champion the actions of despots, even with incontrovertible evidence of their crimes. In the case of Cambodia, Pol Pot's primary supporters included China, the United States, and Communist sympathizers from Sweden. The Khmer Rouge gained recognition for their government from a total of sixty-three countries, and for five long years the world trivialized their atrocities. I'll spare you the grislier details of Tuol Sleng, and it's enough to say that I couldn't handle what I was seeing. As I stopped to read the narrative of a wall text, I realized I would have been shot simply for wearing the reading glass-es I was using to read about being shot for wearing reading glasses. According to another text, the outfit I had chosen to wear that day, an olive-green shirt and black pants, was the preferred dress of the Communists. My embarrassment was as profound as if I'd worn a swastika armband to visit Auschwitz-Birkenau. During Pol Pot's regime, Tuol Sleng's classrooms were converted to cells, and in each cell, regulations had been posted on blackboard fragments:

1. You must answer accordingly to my questions. Don't turn them away.

2. Don't try to hide the facts by making pretexts of this and that. You are strictly prohibited to contest me.

3. Don't be a fool for you are a chap who dare to thwart

the revolution.

4. You must immediately answer my questions without wasting time to reflect.

5. Don't tell me either about your immoralities or the essence of the revolution.

6. While getting lashes or electrification you must not cry at all.

7. Do nothing. Sit still and wait for my orders. If there is no order, keep quiet. When I ask you to do something, you must do it right away without protesting.

8. Don't make pretext about Kampuchea Krom [southern Vietnam] in order to hide your secret or traitor.

9. If you don't follow all the above rules, you shall get many lashes of electric wire.

10. If you disobey any point of my regulations you shall get either ten lashes or five shocks of electric discharge.

Children between the ages of ten and fifteen were trained as guards and enforcers of these rules. Because children are easy to exploit and abuse, they were also conscripted into the Khmer Rouge army, as children have been conscripted into armies for thousands of years. An intimidating adult, a father figure for an orphan, a child with no options, beatings and deprivations—any of these conditions could turn children into soldiers. And pretty self-evident, the prospect of being shot motivates obeisance to authority. Thousands of kids were forced to the front lines to fight the North Vietnamese, armed with a gun called a Carbine, a shortened and much lighter version of a rifle used in close-quarter situations. If a child refused to cooperate, let's just say that dissent wasn't tolerated. *To destroy you is no loss.*

I raced past hundreds of black-and-white photographs of Pol Pot's victims, like pictures from a high school yearbook, some of them wearing smiles in defiance of what lay ahead. The exhibit culminated with dozens of cabinets and vitrines full of skulls of victims, collected and exhibited as if they were seashells. Our brains are not wired to process horror of this magnitude. Well-worn comment books were full of platitudes like "We need to make sure this never happens again" and "Peace to the world." I was without words. Tuol Sleng was difficult to experience but respectful and honest. To the museum's credit, nothing was Disneyfied.

I even rushed past the elderly survivor selling his books. We acknowledged each other with the Sampeah greeting, but I should have stopped, paid respects, bought a copy of his book, and looked deeply into his eyes. But I was ashamed of my country's complicity in Cambodia's misery. And angry. At that moment I could have dispatched Johnson, Nixon, Kissinger, and Westmoreland Jackie Chan–style. But in this Buddhist country where Pol Pot, when captured, was allowed by his compatriots to continue living under house arrest, four more deaths among thousands would be a meaningless gesture, nothing more. The elderly man's survival was an expression of a great mystery, his presence a profound teacher.

"What?" I say to myself; "does death so often test me? Let it do so; I myself have for a long time tested death." "When?" you ask. Before I was born. Death is non-existence, and I know already what that

means. What was before me will happen again after me. If there is any suffering in this state, there must have been such suffering also in the past, before we entered the light of day. As a matter of fact, however, we felt no discomfort then. And I ask you, would you not say that one was the greatest of fools who believed that a lamp was worse off when it was extinguished than before it was lighted? We mortals also are lighted and extinguished; the period of suffering comes in between, but on either side there is a deep peace. For, unless I am very much mistaken... we go astray in thinking that death only follows, when in reality it has both preceded us and will in turn follow us. Whatever condition existed before our birth, is death. For what does it matter whether you do not begin at all, or whether you leave off, inasmuch as the result of both these states is non-existence?

—Seneca[116]

Like all philosophers, the Stoics struggled with the notion of good and evil. It wasn't a good fit with Stoic indifference. Their thinking went something like this. The Stoics wrote that adult human beings are governed by irrational impulses known as *pathē* or "passions" and that *pathē* was not found in inanimate objects, animals, or children. *Pathē* was considered a perturbation, a disturbance of the soul, like the flight of a flock of birds when startled. They also believed that human beings possess a vital tension between the spirit and the body, and when this tension is weak, intense passions and excessive impulses develop and we revert to a childlike state. When the tension has given way, reason is disobeyed. And when adults have lost their reason, evil becomes possible.

The early Stoics believed that

Moral evil arises from an impulse toward what is good which is insufficiently restrained and goes too far. Evil arises from within good.[117]

So while an evil might be great, it is an inescapable consequence of something that is good. The small bones of the head, like those in the jaw and the cheeks, facilitate eating, talking, and facial expressions, but they're also vulnerable to injury. A snake's poison is deadly but may also be used for medical purposes. The presence of mice makes us store our food carefully. But later Stoics, our heroes Epictetus and Seneca in particular, emphasized that virtue is sufficient for happiness and all moral corruptions are equally vicious. Without rationality, authority becomes dangerous and deadly. As much and as hard as I think about it, I can't come up with a single rationale for how genocide, and specifically the killing of children, arises from something good. I think our Stoic triumvirate would have agreed.

Virtue alone affords everlasting and peace-giving joy; even if some obstacle arises, it is but like an intervening cloud, which floats beneath the sun but never prevails against it.

—*Seneca*[118]

Later that day, after showering, I looked into the fogged mirror and watched it clear. It seemed like a good metaphor for something.

The next morning Mr. Solo arrived a half hour earlier than our arranged time to take me to the airport. I'd booked a flight to Siem Reap to visit Cambodia's famous temple complexes. He was his usual cheerful self, but something about him was a little off. He was nervous. It was an election day, and traffic was heavy. Five minutes into the ride an anxious thought arose: *What if we break down?* I could hire another tuk-tuk—dozens pass by every minute—but could I abandon Mr. Solo? I wanted to prove my loyalty.

Ten minutes later, the drive chain was on the ground. Mr. Solo made a phone call, examined the engine, and said, "Five minutes." He struggled to replace the chain but after a few minutes gave up and hailed another tuk-tuk. I handed over the twenty I'd intended to give him for the ride to the airport. He said, "All this for me?" In Phnom Penh, tuk-tuk drivers earn about two hundred dollars per month. This hard-working and Stoic-in-his-own-right man deserved much more in life: the keys to a brand-new tuk-tuk and a gas card paid up for the next ten years came to mind. I hated leaving him crouched and sweating by the side of the road—dangerously close to the rush of Phnom Penh's midmorning traffic—oil, grease, and grit soiling his hands, struggling with his disabled vehicle.

The new driver owned a much nicer tuk-tuk: a Ferrari compared to Mr. Solo's beater. The closer we came to the airport, the more my anxiety lifted, but suddenly he pulled over next to a gas station and stopped. He disconnected a thin hose from a large plastic reservoir and removed it from the engine. Had we run out of gas? Next he ran not to the fuel pumps but to a large, dense cluster of ornamental bushes. He forced the reservoir into the middle of the bushes and turned on an invisible spigot, filled the container with water, ran back to the tuk-tuk, and reconnected it.

He performed these actions with the precision and speed of someone who's done this many times before.

All I had were twenties for a five-dollar ride to the airport. He had only tens in change. So the ride to the airport cost thirty dollars, the cost of the Santa Fe to Albuquerque airport shuttle. Giving away money had become my travel raison d'être, and I was grateful I had the resources to do it.

· · · · ·

For cheap, fast, scenic, and safe transportation in Cambodia, taking a plane is your best option. The flight from Phnom Penh to Siem Reap cost eight dollars one way, plus tax. From the air, flooded rice fields and undulating rivers reflected the sun like burnished mirrors. Dense jungle conceals ancient temple cities—and some six million land mines placed throughout the countryside during three decades of war—both yet to be excavated. We flew directly over Tonlé Sap, the largest freshwater lake in Southeast Asia, populated along its edges with clusters of colorful fishing villages. The temple complexes of Angkor Wat and Angkor Thom could be seen in the distance.

When the prearranged tuk-tuk from the Siem Reap airport to the Airbnb didn't materialize, a driver named Mr. Phalla offered me a ride—at tuk-tuk prices—in his airconditioned Lexus. During the ride into town he ran through his repertoire of silly jokes and wordplay, so off that it was funny. "How do you feel tomorrow?" "I feel fine yesterday." "Are you traveling alone? Well, now you're not because you're with me." "Are you from New

Zealand? Well, I'm from Old Zealand." I liked the way his jokes played with time and with the absurdities of using incorrect tenses, and how the same humor might be found in the joke repository of an eight-year-old. He put a different spin on the "Are you traveling alone?" question, creating something right out of the pages of *Mad* magazine's ("What, Me Worry?") "Snappy Answers to Stupid Questions." The New Zealand/Old Zealand joke showed that he understood the notion of shifting expectations. Telling jokes that actually get laughs, in a language radically different from one's own, is extremely difficult.

Mr. Phalla and I were together for the next two days, and he was an excellent tour guide and a fun companion. We talked about the politics of our respective countries, the costs of living, cars, tourists, and our shared signature quirks: O-C and introverted. On the first day he drove me to Angkor Wat and Angkor Thom, patiently waiting while I obsessively explored both places. On day two we visited several outlying temples, all fascinating for different reasons. Koh Ker, the pyramid temple, suggested El Castillo at Chichén Itzá in Mexico, and both were built in the twelfth century. Beng Mealea, another twelfth-century structure, purportedly served as a movie set for *Raiders of the Lost Ark*, but that wasn't the draw. Beng Mealea is largely untouched by architectural conservators and far from the crowds at Angkor, and I wanted a temple experience less managed and touristy. Often large areas of walls surrounding the temple complex were still in excellent condition, with entire buildings standing except for a collapsed roof. Perfectly preserved interior structures were frequently juxtaposed with a tumble of stones, suggesting the aftermath of a powerful earthquake. The incursion of nature made Beng Mealea even more enigmatic and bizarre. Strangler figs encased structures within their meandering root systems, creating undulating, asymmetrical lines reminiscent of Art Nouveau designs. A patina of deep green mosses and lichens colonized perfectly cut stones, revealing a fragment of a dancing figure or an intricate, carved pattern. Experiencing these great collaborations between man and nature was both humbling and exhilarating. Beng Mealea was mysterious, deep, and powerful. Wandering the grounds, I felt a suspension of time, my anxiety profoundly quieted.

Angkor Wat is the largest religious complex in the world and a work of transcendent perfection. Originally constructed in the first part of the twelfth century as a Hindu temple dedicated to Vishnu, by the end of the century, the Buddhists had taken over. For a group of people known for expounding on the impermanence of the moment and of life as a continuum of these moments, the Buddhists have preserved the original intent of the Angkor complex with the meticulousness of an art conservator attempting to arrest the effects of time. Laid out in a series of square mandalas, one enclosing the other, Angkor is its own universe of narrative carvings and ornamentations fashioned in repetitive patterns. Thousands of sculptures called *apsaras* depict female spirits of the clouds and waters, and over two thousand feet of carvings, representing stories from Hindu mythology, line the outer walls, creating the world's longest bas-relief.

Angkor Wat suggests some kind of outside help from a big-shot architect who was winning the important commissions of the day, a Frank Gehry or a Le Corbusier, an astrophysicist/architect who understood how to align buildings with respect to celestial events, sometimes that cycle over thousands of years. No mistakes in construction could be tolerated and there could be no afterthoughts, like reducing the size of a bathroom to make a bigger closet in the master suite. An estimated three hundred thousand Angkor Wat craftspeople, assisted by six thousand elephants, traveled more than twenty-five miles to the nearest mountain, Mount Kulen, to cut nearly ten million stones and float them down canals to Angkor's site. The project had a tight deadline: thirty years. And it looks like it was made by a single person.

Like structures at Chichén Itzá, Chaco Canyon in New Mexico, Tikal in Guatemala, Stonehenge, and many other sacred sites with astrological significance, Angkor Wat is an incredibly sophisticated expression of cosmic forces and alignments, sacred geometries, and, as Joseph Campbell wrote about sacred sites in general, a tool for psychic transformation. On the vernal equinox at Angkor, the sun rises in alignment with the tallest tower, positioned exactly in the middle. The tower is a symbol of Mount Meru, a mythological peak Hindus believe to be the home of benevolent supernatural beings. Amateur archeologists studying the Angkor complex realized that its various buildings mirror the positions of the main stars in the constellation Draco as it would have appeared in the sky in 10,500 BCE, also at the vernal equinox. Angkor was part of an explosion of Late Middle Ages temple and church building that created a World Wide Web of sacred sites. These structures, sharing mathematical, astrological, and aesthetic similarities, suggest some kind of intercultural communication, and it's fun to contemplate what that delivery system could have been.

After walking across the long stone bridge that spans the Angkor Wat moat, I entered a small temple, kind of an atrium that funnels people into the complex. Immediately I felt a serious assault on my being. As I've written, I don't align myself with the tribe of woo, but it felt like something was trying to knock me off balance. What seemed like mild electric shocks overwhelmed my brain, and the room started to spin. Was I being psychically frisked? Had I brought Kyle the nocturnal spirit with me from Morocco? Something from Tuol Sleng? Or was this a group of not-so-benevolent supernatural beings? Was it merely an unremarkable, momentary drop in blood pressure? When disturbed, O-Cs run the gamut of possibilities, as you've probably realized by now. After a few moments I felt like I'd passed inspection, the dizziness cleared, and I was allowed to proceed.

Not to wander out of the way… and ever to be careful to attain to the true natural apprehension of every fancy that presents itself.
—*Marcus Aurelius*[119]

Once inside the temple complex I encountered a large tour group, its members trying to out-talk each other while standing near a sign requesting guests to respect Angkor as a sacred space by speaking, if at all, in a whisper. STOICs, we've all observed that some extroverts and entire cultures of people are happiest when a loud utterance is issuing from their mouths, and a parking lot full of tour buses may signal the presence of such people. I wondered, *How can a person find meaning in their experience of Angkor if they're talking distractedly about the Trump White House or recounting tales of a cruise down the Danube or discussing the issue of putting clothes on pets? Or fumbling with their selfie sticks while trying to find that perfect background?* Some people just don't do quiet.

This compelling need to vocalize is related to the Buddhist concept of the hungry ghost, a being who is insatiable in some way. Generally, it's contextualized as an individual with such a small mouth that the stomach must be fed continually to feel sated. This is a variant. The mouth is huge and the brain small, and the hungry ghost must talk continually in order to maintain consciousness. Content is nonessential.

Because we are *solo travelers*, STOICs can escape situations offensive to the ear and challenging to our personalities, placing us at a huge advantage over introverts trapped in a tour bus group or held hostage by friends they thought would be great travel companions but have turned into their boss or their parents. At times I had the outlying temple complexes to myself, but at Beng Mealea a fellow tourist subjected her Cambodian guide to nonstop blather about her problems back home in a voice much louder than necessary, the way some people do with speakers of other languages, as if volume increases comprehension. Clearly, even though alone, she was not a STOIC. He smiled politely and led her through the labyrinthine temple grounds while I let my Stoic indifference guard down.

I am always surprised to see some people demanding the time of others and meeting a most obliging response. Both sides have in view the reason for which the time is asked and neither regards the time itself,

as if nothing there is being asked for and nothing given. They are trifling with life's most precious commodity, being deceived because it is an intangible thing, not open to inspection and therefore reckoned very cheap; in fact, almost without any value… It is generally agreed that no activity can be successfully pursued by an individual who is preoccupied… since the mind distracted absorbs nothing deeply.
—*Seneca*[120]

Some naturally occurring sounds, like the insects at Beng Mealea, are inescapable and you have no choice but to tolerate them. When I exited Mr. Phalla's Lexus and heard them, I thought either I was undergoing another spiritual hazing or my chronic tinnitus was acting up. As I strolled the long path to the entrance I realized they were, indeed, rainy season insects that vocalized at exactly the frequency playing in my head. When I turned my head left to right or up and down, a strange and disorienting phase shift occurred between the inside/outside sounds. It was surprisingly intense and painful. As well-prepared as I was for the trip, it never occurred to me that noise-cancelling headphones would be required in the jungle.

These audio assaults got me thinking about temple photographs I'd seen taken from the air. What if the designs for these temples were based on audio data materialized—in stone? Before my trip, I'd been reading about the 21st century version of this very thing, 3D prints of audio waveforms. Seen from above, Angkor Wat and a neighboring temple called Banteay Srei (the Women's Temple), without too much of a stretch of the imagination, suggest these 3-D visualizations of sound waves. If reverse engineered to pure audio forms, could the temples be, literally, visualizations of ancient Hindu chants? Could they hold secret messages for humanity, like who we are and why we're here? Again, fun things to think about.

Similarly, viewed from the ground, Angkor Wat's towers also suggest sound waves frozen in stone. Like colossal church bells, the towers resemble huge resonators struck by an enormous hammer, the sound vibrating up from their bases like ripples in a pond, the waves becoming more concentrated as they travel up the tower, culminating in a single peak before disappearing into the air: a musical moment captured in time and memorialized in architecture. Viewed from directly above, the design of its nested-box walls implies sound propagation in a different dimension, traveling out from the center instead of up from the ground, the waters of the wide moat surrounding the complex functioning as an amplifier of these sounds. Analogously, at an observatory not too far from the Cosmic Campground in New Mexico, an astronomical survey had detected and measured ripples created by sound waves generated after the Big Bang. These ripples grew until the universe cooled enough to fix matter in place, the earliest instance of sound waves materialized. Could its architects have intended Angkor Wat to be a model of the origin of the universe? More fun things to think about.

· · · · ·

If any people match STOICs in obsequiousness and readiness to say "I'm sorry," it's the Cambodians. They will apologize over and over for the tiniest infraction, sometimes days later. "I'm sorry" is almost a greeting there. Throughout my stay in Cambodia, I often wondered what this was about. Was it generalized anxiety disorder? A Buddhist sutra I'm not familiar with? Was it because of what Nixon and Kissinger did to their country (and their parents) back in the '70s, and the kids grew up to be mortally afraid of Americans? It was both endearing and exasperating, because as a chronic apologizer, I know how vulnerable it makes you to exploitation by not-so-nice people. Mr. Phalla was an apologizer, too.

On the second day of our tour, we lunched at a thatch-roofed, open-air jungle restaurant with red plastic chairs and Coca-Cola logo tablecloths, devising strategies for him to attract and retain a more respectable type of clientele. As a tour driver, many, many times Mr. Phalla had been both stood up by tourists and cheated out of money earned. While eating barbecued wild boar, I suggested he learn something about the places most of his customers come from in order to impress them with his worldliness and sophistication, easy knowledge to gain right from a cell phone. Maybe then he wouldn't come across to others as naïve and someone to cheat. I also suggested he follow up relentlessly with people who had scheduled his time, sending reminder texts and emails and requesting replies. In my STOIC experiences, I've noticed that once you schedule travel with a company or individual, and particularly if they have your money, you must beg them to tell you where you're expected to meet and when. Being an overzealous communicator would make him stand out. I promised to post a photo and an enthusiastic review on TripAdvisor when I returned to the States, and I'm happy to report that this strategy caused an uptick in his business.

Backgrounding our conversation was an American tourist haggling with a merchant selling Cambodian drawstring pants in a variety of beautiful fabrics. Cambodia is known for its exquisite silks and cottons woven in small lattice patterns, difficult and time-consuming activities involving many steps, from growing mulberry trees whose leaves feed the silkworms to harvesting cocoons and processing the thread to creating the end product. This American was arguing over two dollars. Cambodia, I'm so, so sorry.

After lunch, Mr. Phalla drove me to a nearby restroom—a clean, modern facility catering to tourists. A young boy followed me in, and when I emerged from the stall, he led me to the sink by my elbow, helped squeeze soap into my hands from the dispenser, turned on the water, and handed me a paper towel to dry my hands. I'd left my money in the car and signaled to him to follow me. When I pulled two dollars out of my wallet, Mr. Phalla encouraged me to give him a five. I handed over the five, embarrassed by my stinginess.

On the two-hour drive back to Siem Reap from Beng Mealea and the other outlying temples, we encountered a long procession of hog farmers traveling to market on their motorcycles, driving in the opposite direction. Up to three huge hogs on each motorcycle were lying feet-up, lashed to bamboo frames attached to the backs of their bikes. The hogs were utterly placid as they zoomed past, as if they rode motorcycles all the time and it was no big deal. We also passed dozens of roadside stands selling what looked like bamboo flutes, but some were charred at one end. Mr. Phalla said the lengths of bamboo were filled with a rice and sugar solution. I wanted to stop and sample one, but he seemed intent on getting home.

That night after dinner at the Airbnb, one of the employees, who called himself Steven, apologized over and over for not having ice cream available for dessert. And he was still obsessing about not connecting with me at the airport for transport to the Airbnb. Three days later Steven was in the obsessive apology-loop again, and nothing I said helped relieve his anxiety. I wondered if most Cambodians live in this state of continual tortured self-flagellation and worry.

There are more things… likely to frighten us than there are to crush us; we suffer more often in imagination than in reality.
—Seneca[121]

Worth mentioning are a few strange place-names, products, and practices I encountered in Cambodia. While touring Siem Reap with Mr. Phalla, we passed a hotel called Angkor Embrace Latex. It's as if the committee that named the place took an English-language porn magazine and an industrial equipment supply catalog, cut out some words, threw them in a hat, and chose them at random. Another place, named New Hammer Massage, had a sign featuring a Neanderthal-looking Khmer guy wielding a huge wooden mallet. As far as I could tell, no customers were sitting in the waiting area.

Siem Reap's city center features a spa where, after a long day of temple-hopping, you can submerge your calloused feet into a tank of fish that nibble off the dead skin from your heels and toes. If you're inclined to try this ichthyic version of a pumice stone, I recommend you ask how often the water is changed. Related is Snail White, an all-in-one face cleanser that could be a flawed translation of "Snow White." Perhaps this cleanser is also a whitening solution. Or an add-on at the dead skin–eating fish place, where snails applied to the skin slowly crawl around, leaving bleaching and moisturizing slime trails.

When the time came, I wasn't ready to leave Siem Reap and its mystical temples. Plus Mr. Phalla and I had become friends and I was sad to part company. We stay in touch via email.

Ponder for a long time whether you shall admit a given person to your friendship; but when you have decided to admit him, welcome him with all your heart and soul.

—*Seneca*[122]

During the short plane ride back to Phnom Penh, I was convinced of the absolute necessity for noise-cancelling headphones while traveling in Cambodia. I'm sure the same group of loud tourists encountered at Angkor Wat were also on board, and two of their biggest bloviators were seated in the row immediately behind me. Even though they sat only inches away from each other, except for a few brief interludes, they shouted for the entire flight. I heard my mother's voice in my head saying, "Give them the benefit of the doubt; maybe they're hard of hearing." The interludes were not moments of silence. The guy directly behind me coughed into the space between my seat and the window, then hacked up unknown substances and deposited them in unknown places. In addition to noise-cancelling headphones, a full complement of personal protective equipment would have been good to have along, too.

What could be more agreeable than the needs of your own nature?

—*Marcus Aurelius*[123]

CHAPTER XIII

DOWN UNDER, UPSIDE DOWN, AND BACKWARDS

An absolute must for the STOIC is to know your travel weaknesses and develop strategies for coping with them. How do you recognize a TW in the first place? This can be extraordinarily difficult because O-Cs are already engaged in critical self-examination nearly constantly. One effective way to recognize TWs is to generate a record of travel situations that trigger an anxiety and/or fear response and maintain an accurate accounting of these triggers. Include the nature of the trigger, the time of day, time of month, how long you spent in the anxiety abyss, if you cursed and was it aloud or to yourself, how you worked the problem, and the outcome. Doing this exercise will reveal your TWs and may diminish the O-C on your next trip.

My primary travel weakness is a big one. I have a difficult time reading maps and most kinds of 3-D orientation of myself on the planet. Hints of this challenge emerged in a Fort Worth, Texas, first grade class. An introduction to maps was coincident with my realization that the world was much larger and contained far more content than our homes and backyards. Ancient Egypt was the first unit we studied, and the teacher gave us a mimeographed map to color. I was familiar with the shape of Texas, and Egypt's borders were not distinctive or memorable. But I was obsessed with the word "Egypt" and its three letters, nestled in between "E" and "T," that reached below the solid blue line on our writing paper. I'd stare at the word "Egypt" and think it was the most perfect word ever conceived. We were told to code Egypt's land masses with colors suggestive of the landscape. Areas bordering oceans or other bodies of water were to be colored a deep blue that faded to light blue. Of course, Egypt is mostly desert with green areas flanking the Nile, and it shares a border with the Mediterranean, so it was an easy assignment. Being a visual learner and already a highly developed obsessive-compulsive, I spent way too much time coloring the map of Egypt to perfection and not understanding it as a place with cities and airports and schools with children and trash collection and TV and moms and dads.

Throughout the year these map-coloring exercises expanded to include the Tigris and Euphrates rivers and surrounds, Italy for its singular shape, the rest of Africa, and the U.S. We weren't even made aware of Australia or Central and South America. Maps became more of an art project than anything else, so learning to read one and understand its contents and symbolic meanings was a big leap I never made successfully.

Fast forward thirty years to Delhi, India, where a friend and I embarked on a ten-day journey through Rajasthan. We decided that she would be the interpreter of maps and

I would be the interpreter of language, thereby combining our respective strengths. Five years later I was in Hong Kong for the Handover. I noticed that whenever I emerged from the subway, often my impulse was to take off in the wrong direction. In parts of Hong Kong, like in New York City or São Paulo, the buildings are so lofty and close together that cues from the natural world are unavailable and your internal navigation system is compromised. Fortunately, I was traveling with a local, so, again, map-reading wasn't an issue. Orientation was deferred to someone else.

Traveling around the world underscored the gravity of my bad navigation skills. Emerging from an underground station onto the street with my bags and purse and camera and laying eyes for the first time on the maze in which I'd booked a room tested my Stoic indifference. In these situations, the STOIC must try to maintain a rational emotional state. We are serene and confident, regardless of appearances and in spite of annoyances.

No matter how great your host thinks he or she has done with directions, they seldom take you to your destination reliably. For the STOIC, these moments of uncertainty between the train/metro and our cozy new digs plunge us into the deepest circle of traveler's hell like nothing else. You might as well be wearing a scrolling LED sign on your back that declares "lost first-world solo traveler, vulnerable, utterly defenseless, carrying hundreds of dollars in secret pocket underwear." You attempt to maintain a confident air and upright posture while your eyes dart back and forth looking for the landmarks your host may have mentioned. In Lisbon my host told me to "turn left at the Anos 66 bar," a place I never did find during my five days there. Another host said to "just walk up the hill after you exit the Metro." But which one of three different exits? All of them pointed you up a hill.

Then there was the tiny sign bearing crucial information partially hidden behind a large, leafy bush in a neighborhood populated with dozens of identical mid-rises with similar-sounding names and confusing addresses. The sign read, "buildings A, C, D, E, and F." No building B, which was the one I was looking for. Some cities have lodgings with similar names, like the Rydges Plaza Cairns and the Rydges Esplanade Cairns and the Rydges Tradewinds Cairns in Australia, and you might not have known this until you're dragging yourself and your luggage around. On your meticulously detailed itinerary you may have abbreviated your destination as "the Rydges," so it's a one-in-three chance you'll land at the correct hotel on the first try. This is far preferable, though, to thinking that you've booked a flight to Memphis, Egypt, and you land in Memphis, Tennessee—or Ithaca, New York, and you end up in the homeland of Odysseus. And yep, there's a Sydney, Canada, in Nova Scotia, also a waterfront city with multiple harbors, but instead of a magnificent opera house, their primary tourist attraction is the World's Largest Ceilidh (pronounced "kā-lē") Fiddle. (A ceilidh is a traditional Scottish or Irish social event with music and dancing.)

You may even find yourself at the mercy of inaccurate maps, which in a totally unfamiliar city can be a terrifying experience for the STOIC if you let it. Having endured an obscenely early flight from Phnom Penh to Bangkok, a seven-hour layover in the Bangkok airport, and an eight-hour flight to Sydney (Australia) that arrived at 6:30 a.m., I had the entire day ahead of me to explore. My Airbnb host kindly provided me with a map of the harbor and surrounds and gave me the lowdown on what was happening in Sydney that day. I noted with excitement that we were located within walking distance of the Royal Botanical Garden and the Opera House, a two-and-a-half-mile walk one way, and I headed off in that direction. What a great introduction to the strange flora and fauna of Australia. I wandered among giant Cook pines that lean toward the equator as they grow and shared the sidewalk with black-faced ibises scavenging for food. Rainbow lorikeets fed on the nectar of huge bottlebrush blooms the size and shape of corn on the cob. Squawking flocks of cockatoos flew overhead. The weather was absolutely perfect.

It does good to take walks out of doors, that our spirits may be raised and refreshed by the open air and fresh breeze.

—Seneca[124]

I made my way to Sydney Harbour to take the ferry to Manly Island, named for the manly indigenous people who once populated the island, but this over-the-top tourist trap was a turnoff. I strolled half a mile down Manly's main street, and that was enough to realize I wanted to catch the next return ferry. My plan was to walk through the Botanical Garden back to my room and crawl into bed to sleep off the long journey.

Around Sydney Harbour the city had installed signs with colorful area maps, no doubt to help confused tourists, and I began relying on these maps rather than the one provided by the Airbnb host. But something odd happened in the Botanical Garden. I'd make my way to one of the exits, then discover I was on the wrong side of the garden. I'd backtrack and still be on the wrong side of the garden. I'd try another route and end up at another wrong exit. At that point I was consulting both the city map and the host's map obsessively. I zigzagged through the park, not finding my way out, and felt like I'd stumbled into some bizarre alternate reality. By then I was beyond deliriously tired and also a little panicky. How could this be happening? I let go of some tears and a few choice expletives, aloud. STOICs, when this filter is gone, you know you're in trouble. Here at the bottom of the world, like everywhere else but in the U.S., my phone worked only in Wi-Fi hot spots. It was getting dark.

Call good sense to your aid against difficulties: it is possible to soften what is harsh, to widen what is too narrow, and to make heavy burdens press less severely upon one who bears them skillfully.
—Seneca[125]

A travel challenge like this shifts the amygdala into full alarm mode and a part of the brain that is largely inactive lights up. The euphonious Alan Rickman voice arises and delivers the solution in a gentle, unassuming kind of way. "Why don't you look at both maps and compare them more closely?" The city map and the map provided by my host were indeed different. The city map showed the harbor bridge and the Sydney Opera House to the south, while the other map showed the bridge and the Opera House to the north. They were 180° off from each other.

When I held the host-provided map so the writing was up-side down, the two maps matched. I found my way out.

We have diviners within us.

—Epictetus[126]

Sydney also taught me how much my public transportation skills were seriously compromised. When you've never been without personal transportation, you don't fully appreciate the extent of the advantages conferred by automobile ownership. Obviously, never having to wait for your ride to materialize is the big one. The privilege of jumping in your car and driving somewhere is huge. Standing in the rain at night and realizing you missed the hourly bus that goes to your destination, while groups of drunk and rowdy young men stagger up and down the sidewalk behind you, leaves you feeling vulnerable. Plus, being ignored by the driver of the hourly bus the next time around is supremely exasperating. When you board the wrong bus and realize you've made a forty-five-minute mistake that will take a big chunk out of your travel day, your gratitude for having a car back home in the garage soars.

All this getting lost taught me an important lesson. I realized that what will deliver a solo traveler from extreme anxiety mixed with full-blown anger (in addition to the wisdom of the Stoics, of course) is to consult Google Earth prior to your trip. Look at street views of all planned destinations—accommodations and places you intend to visit—and get a feel for the neighborhoods, unless you like the challenge of being lost. I never welcome this challenge, and my guess is that my fellow STOICs don't either. Although this strategy will generate more paper to lug around on your trip, create printouts of your destinations' façades and include buildings on both sides to contextualize. Once the paper photos have helped lead you to your target, they can be recycled. Here's another reason to do some pre-trip sleuthing using Google Earth. Usually Airbnb hosts, if they provide exterior shots at all, will photograph their properties in a way that excludes the immediate environs so the muddy, rut-filled, trashed-out street lined with mangy, aggressive dogs (Tulum, Mexico) that you must navigate isn't visible. If you don't scrutinize a neighborhood ahead of time, you run the risk of amygdala hijack.

The following exercise may help you decide which Airbnb to choose if you're conflicted about venue and can't make up your mind. If the Airbnb's cancellation policy is flexible, book it so you can see the address. Type the address into Google Earth, then check to see if there's a grocery store, a metro, and a coffee shop nearby, or rows of projects covered in gang graffiti. If you don't like what you see, cancel the reservation and book another one you were considering. Your money for the original reservation will be refunded. You may not like that neighborhood either, and, if so, keep looking and booking. This process will provide valuable, sometimes unexpected information and will boost your solo travel confidence. You will thank yourself for taking this extra step.

You may be thinking, *Why don't I just do a screenshot of the Google Earth street views instead wasting all that paper and ink?* Here's the reason. When you're not near Wi-Fi and you want to look at photos of documents/screenshots on your phone, only very low-resolution versions of these images are available. Your itinerary and other important documents that you patted yourself on the back for so cleverly photographing in advance of your trip may be totally unreadable.

Another word about maps. STOICs often connect to a type of map anxiety more visceral and understated than a non-STOIC map reader might experience. A map is a direct conduit to our first-grade selves, when maps were aesthetic experiences and countries were populated with people and places fascinating and alluring and hometown-boring. Because pleasurable activities and compulsiveness itself trigger your reward system, coloring those maps probably contributed to your current-day O-C, and, in addition, laid the foundation for wanting to go everywhere and see everything. These feelings become somatic, insinuating themselves into our bodies and surviving into adulthood. So when you look at a map of Australia, for example, and see Sydney on the east coast, Cairns to the north by the Great Barrier Reef, Darwin to the west of that, and Ayers Rock in the middle, remember this continent is 2,485 miles wide from east to west. You'll feel a rush of dopamine that will make you want to conquer the mountains and hike the deserts and snorkel the Reef, but unless you have several months and unlimited funds to spend in Australia, you must prioritize. This lack of focus leads directly to anxiety, so try to reign in the desire to travel everywhere and stick to plans simple and doable. You are the best judge of what "doable" means for you.

There will be no benefit to you in this hurrying to and fro; for you are travelling with your emotions and are followed by your afflictions. Would that they were indeed following you! In that case, they would be farther away; as it is, you are carrying and not leading them.

—*Seneca*[127]

CHAPTER XIV

THE REPUBLIC OF THE EQUATOR

Like many tourist centers, the historic district of Quito, Ecuador, bustles with vendors, tour guides, and people specializing in selling a single product. In Quito, it's cherries, mangoes, and Huggies baby wipes. Curiously, people selling packages of Huggies probably outnumber all other vendors five to one. Were there really that many baby tourists with bottoms that needed cleaning up? And was the Huggies distribution network making a living? I'm still puzzling over that. Young men selling coca leaves to tourists with altitude challenges came in at a close second. El Centro is also populated with tiny *abuelas* wearing typical Ecuadorian dress: a plain, mid-calf skirt; a large alpaca poncho; and a tall, black felt hat that adds six inches to their less-than-five-foot frames. I imagined one of them in the kitchen of my Airbnb washing the dishes. The Ecuadorians have devised an ingenious dish drying rack system that sits above the sink. You wash the dishes, place them in the rack, close the cabinet door, and water drips into the sink. Great for those of us over five feet four inches, but a tiny grandmother averages only four and a half feet tall. Working in a kitchen like this would require either painter's stilts or some kind of grasping and reaching device. A step stool could create a falling hazard.

As often as not, Quito's taxi drivers do not know their city, even if they're locals. They can be as unpredictable as the Quito weather, where it's said you experience all four seasons in one day. Maybe they've never done exploratory driving because they don't want to fight the traffic, which in Quito is considerable, or pay for gas on their own dime. Other drivers can be fantastic. You don't actually know which kind of driver you're with until you've been riding around for ten or fifteen minutes. You then have two choices: commit to the trip, offering whatever help you can, or politely excuse yourself and exit the vehicle. Choice number two does not guarantee that your next driver will be savvier, so it's best to stick it out.

One afternoon, my destination was a small travel agency on the fringe of the historic district, a twenty-five-minute drive in non–rush hour traffic from the Airbnb. At the first stoplight it was clear that I was with an unseasoned driver. He even admitted it, and when he wasn't working the problem, I did what I could with my limited resources, which consisted of the address of the place, their phone number, and vague directions scrawled on a half-sheet of paper. As I've mentioned, away from Wi-Fi my phone is useless, so I suggested he call dispatch for directions, but his phone was out of minutes. We stopped at a tiny convenience store in between two ice cream shops so he could refill the minutes on his phone, and I gave him the number of the travel agency. Ten, fifteen minutes elapsed; he reap-peared, and we were off, randomly crisscrossing the steep hills of Quito. One more stop, to ask directions from a policewoman wearing a black cap bearing the word "SWAT," and we were at the destination within five minutes. By then I'd recognized the neighborhood because I'd walked the area the day before, a five dollar cab ride from the Airbnb. He was demanding ten, and I was paying for the time it took him to reload his phone and for his Quito geography lesson. Ten dollars was half of my food and discretionary budget for the day, and as I fished around in my pocket underwear for an additional five, I was mad at myself for letting this guy exploit me. I'd already lost my patience back at the convenience store.

This also thou must consider, that many things there be, which oftentimes unsensibly trouble and vex thee, as not armed against them with patience, because they go not ordinarily under the name of pains, which in very deed are of the same nature as pain; as to slumber unquietly, to suffer heat, to want appetite: when therefore any of these things make thee discontented, check thyself with these words: Now hath pain given thee the foil; thy courage hath failed thee.
—*Marcus Aurelius*[128]

Like in Cambodia, the official currency of Ecuador is the U.S. dollar. Many transactions cost five dollars and under, and guide books recommend bringing only ones and fives into the country. Since I was there for three weeks, at the beginning of my trip over four hundred bills were stuffed into my underwear, and I felt like a pole dancer after a successful night. Public transportation is ridiculously affordable. Local buses cost a quarter, and long distance travel by bus costs one dollar per hour of travel. So the thirteen hour bus ride from Quito to Cuenca costs thirteen dollars. Most cab rides anywhere in the city cost between three and five dollars. After I calmed down I reminded myself that five extra dollars was not a huge loss for me and was probably meaningful to him.

His taxi didn't have a meter, so the behavior I changed before getting into the next taxi was to do a meter check and see if it was turned on. What I didn't notice was the fresh, thick coat of Armor All that covered the back seat and transferred to my purse, backpack, and the seat of my pants. Normally this would have triggered a cleaning compulsion, stopping all other activity until there was no trace of Armor All on any of these surfaces. But the cab had just merged into traffic when I noticed, and Epictetus reminded me to wish events to happen as they do happen. Travel, informed by Stoicism, had interrupted the compulsion cycle and calmed my obsession.

On my last day in Ecuador, a local told me to never, ever get into a Quito taxi solo. The driver may not know where he or she is going, but worse, robbery or kidnapping are a real possibility. Of course, I'd taken dozens of taxis by then, and I'd been robbed in a benign way by being overcharged. About half of the experiences had been positive and the other half less than satisfactory, and I felt lucky nothing worse had happened.

The best tourist attraction in the Quito area is the Mitad del Mundo, the Middle of the World. At the Mitad, employees are standing by to take your picture while you straddle both the northern and the southern hemispheres simultaneously, planting your feet on either side of a four inch wide red line painted on the concrete and feeling the dizzying effects of being in two electromagnetic worlds at once. (The Mitad experience involves some suspension of disbelief, since latitude 0°0'0" varies according to time of year and the revolution of the Earth.) A tour guide demonstrates the Coriolis effect in a sink of water, settling once and for all the burning question of hemispheric vortex rotation. Strangely, water went down the drain in a clockwise direction in the Northern Hemisphere side of the red equatorial line and in a counterclockwise direction in the Southern Hemisphere side of the line. The tour guide merely moved the portable sink to one side or the other of the line, threw a few small leaves in with the water to help us see the rotational direction, and let the water drain into a bucket. There was no sleight of hand or deception involved; the vortex changed direction, QED. Also at the Mitad, you can try to balance a raw egg on the head of a nail (according to our guide, possible but difficult because of the convergence of opposing electro-magnetic forces), and you can see a real shrunken head. A model of an indigenous tribesman displays how his penis is cinched in an upright position against his lower abdomen for protection. There's something for the entire family at the Mitad.

Cuenca, Ecuador, is a weather obsessive's dream. Instead of Quito's four seasons in one day, Cuenca has two seasons in one year: wet and dry. The wet season is from January through May, the dry season June through December. A wet season Cuenca day begins in mist and fog, with church bells at 5:30 a.m., not exactly pealing but banging out the two-note shark motif from *Jaws* on what sounds like a couple of big aluminum kettles. The church

bell snooze button allows an extra fifteen minutes of re-
pose, then they're at it again. Final alarm sounds at 6:30
a.m., and if you're not up by then, you're officially lazy,
one of the three cardinal sins in Quechua indigenous culture (the other two: lying and theft). Since Cuenca is also
near the equator, one can expect the same sunrise and sunset time every day and basically the same weather. During
the wet season, the morning's fog dissipates by 10 a.m. and
you can look forward to mostly sunny skies until 2:30 or
3:00 p.m. Thunderstorms appear from the east and dump
torrents of rain for two hours, then it's pleasantly cool and
cloudy until the next morning. Every. Day.

Cuenca is the home of the delicious three-dollar prix
fixe lunch. Excellent cuisine, bakeries, and ice cream stores
can be found throughout downtown. Immediately behind
the Catedral de la Inmaculada Concepción, a large, mid-
century–inspired coffee and lunch spot sits at the intersection of Simón Bolívar and General Torres. I'd bought a
ticket for a tour of the cathedral and had an hour to kill,
and cappuccino and chocolate cake sounded like a great
way to spend it. The friendly waitress brought a substantial
piece of cake to the table, and I ate it slowly and deliberately, relishing every bite. Halfway through the cake, a huge
pigeon flew into the restaurant and landed on the table at
which I had originally considered sitting and began desperately flinging its body against the plate glass window,
trying to escape. A few minutes elapsed before the staff
reacted, then a young man working behind the counter
removed his apron and strolled confidently over to the pigeon. He grabbed it with his bare hands, walked to the
open front doors, tossed it into the air, and returned to his

task. I relished a few more bites of cake and went to the counter to ask for a box. Instead of handing me one, he grabbed the plate and slid the cake into the box with hands covered in pigeon. I carried it around the rest of the day in my backpack, but the cake ended up in the trash.

When I walk the streets of any city, I look down as much as I look up. An occasional glance downward helps preclude falling, but the real reason to look down is because the ground can be as interesting as a church ceiling. Anyone who has walked the streets of São Paulo will tell you this. The *paulistanos'* use of tile and ceramic is whimsical and imaginative, as if they were the rebellious offspring of their much more rigid tile traditionalist parents from Lisbon. Cuenca's beautiful cobblestone streets are occasionally inlaid with flower motif tiles, and Quito's historic center features streets that to this day can be trod in the highest of heels, its stones are so perfectly fitted and laid. Very gratifying to those of us who are O-C.

My history of discovering lost or hidden treasures on the ground is long and varied. As a child I was always the one of us three siblings to find the golden egg at family Easter egg hunts, infuriating my older sister. I found a man's ring in the woods behind our house, set with a ruby flanked by two diamonds. I've found arrowheads and fossils and Native American potsherds. A few exposed molars lying in the dirt were attached to an upside-down possum skull, probably buried at the site for years. Single earrings are a regular find. I carry a special marble unearthed from a field in Vilcabamba, a village south of Cuenca. The ground is interesting in the way the verso side of a painting with a varied provenance is interesting. Like the painting, the ground can tell you who's owned it, the kinds of things that've happened to it, and can reveal cryptic messages to those curious to dig a little deeper.

Admiring a Quito historic center street one day, I noticed something small, shiny, and black lying on the ground. It had four distinct, lighter stripes and a shape suggesting a scarab beetle, and I flinched as I watched someone step on it. When it survived, I realized it was a rock. I noticed rocks like this a few more times in Quito and thought they were river stones dislodged from the concrete. But they had a distinctly different character and always the four stripes. Then in Cuenca I came across one near the central plaza. If I'd observed this in the U.S., I would have assumed it was someone's conceptual art work. The black stones with the four lighter stripes were signifiers of something the artist found meaningful: the four seasons, four directions, a square, the four rivers flowing through Cuenca. I decided to do a little research. I Googled "black stones" and was connected to a black version of the Flintstones and a bunch of gemstones and crystals websites explaining their meanings, symbolism, and powers.

> Black gemstones symbolize self-control and resilience. Black stones have protective energies in the sense that black is the absence of light, and therefore, can be used to create invisibility.... [Onyx] can help release negative emotions such as sorrow and grief... and helps in recognizing personal strength.

Indulging in some magical thinking, I liked the idea that these black stones appeared specifically to protect me, but I also began to consider the quantum mechanical take on what was going on. Was this another case of spooky action at a distance, like what I thought I'd experienced at the Cosmic Campground? Was it quantum tunneling, a virtual particle popping in and out of existence? Scientists admit that the boundary separating explainable, physical phenomena and what seems like magic is sometimes blurry. I saw the rock (or its identical twin) a few more times around Cuenca and decided to name it Heisenberg. I was going to pocket it to take back home to New Mexico, but I wanted to see if it would be waiting for me in the driveway when I returned from my trip.

Having spent two weeks in Quito and Cuenca, both large, bustling, noisy cities, I began to wonder where I could find some quiet. From what I'd read about Vilcabamba, it was an earthly paradise not to be missed, still in a state of Edenic purity. A four-and-a-half-hour drive south of Cuenca, at five thousand feet, Vilcabamba's daylight and weather are also consistent year-round. Getting there meant riding in a twelve passenger minivan with fourteen other people and sharing the road with huge trucks and diesel-belching buses. Along the narrow, winding Andean road, every few hundred feet we'd pass a name and phone number, spray painted in bright red on steep cliff faces, advertising tow trucks outfitted with large cranes. Our driver was also a veteran of the Paris-Dakar rally, and at every turn in the road the rosary that dangled from the rear view mirror leaned either to a 45 or a 135° angle.

Vilcabamba is famous worldwide for being one of the few places on Earth that preserves its inhabitants well into old age. The village is nestled in a verdant, bird-filled valley with a deep, clear river that flows through the town, and a tiny tree-lined zocalo and colonial church is its focal point. Its population of barking dogs was noticeably low. As I lay in bed in the morning at the Descanso del Toro ("the bull taking a break"), watching the sun rise and listening to the chorus of birds, I thought, *This place pre roads and internal combustion engines probably was the real Eden, not somewhere in Mesopotamia.* Even though no highways were visible from my second floor balcony, only thick jungle, a steady stream of traffic produced a background rumble that competed with the sounds of birds, rain, and the river. Even in Vilcabamba, escaping the din of civilization was futile. But to its credit, Ecuador was the first county in the world to legislate legally enforceable rights on behalf of Mother Nature, called Pachamama by indigenous Andeans. Former President Rafael Correa conferred the constitutional right to "exist, persist, maintain, and regenerate its vital cycles" [129] on nature, grandiose and arrogant-sounding but necessary for the conservation of Ecuador's many and varied ecosystems. He was also responsible for modernizing Ecuador's highway system, arguably the best in all of South America, creating jobs and reducing travel times dramatically between major cities. Ten years later, Ecuadorians still loved talking about their great roads. Maybe someday forward-thinking Ecuador will examine the problem of sound pollution and devise a solution.

Vilcabamba is a place where a group of hippies emerged from their 1960s Haight-Ashbury wormhole. I kept thinking I'd run into a former college roommate who, back then, never left the house without a garland of flowers in her hair and a lilt in her step. She could pull it off, too. Because it's an American expat retirement haven, one does not have to learn Spanish to thrive in Vilcabamba. More than once I heard sixty-year-old Napoleon Dynamites trying to sprinkle their banalities with Spanish, not even attempting to pronounce the words correctly. Was I jealous because the nouveau Vilcabambans were so chill and I am not? That they were comfortable using nonstandard English, drinking more than a few beers in public, and regaling each other with stories of inconveniences gringos experience in foreign lands? These bloviating expats were befouling Eden with their unfocused leisure.

We should say that these are living, not in leisure, but in busy idleness... Tell me, would you say that those men are at leisure who pass many hours at the barber's while they are being stripped of whatever grew out the night before? While a solemn debate is held over each separate hair? While either disarranged locks are restored to their place or thinning ones drawn from this side and that toward the forehead? How angry they get if the barber has been a bit too careless, just as if he were shearing a real man!... These have not leisure, but idle occupation.

—Seneca[130]

I felt sympathy for the locals for having to tolerate goofball expats and us clueless tourists. Because I live in a tourist city myself, where visitors overrun the place during certain times of year, I could side with the locals and see how dealing with *extranjeros* must be challenging. These expats, who seemed to have no personal boundaries, were the antithesis of a STOIC, because STOICs feel like we're always imposing on others' lives. Even if we declared a no-contact-with-the-outside-world day and stayed home, we could conjure something to put ourselves in that who-am-I-inconveniencing-now anxious place.

Do not you know how very small a part you are of the whole? —that is, as to body; for, as to reason, you are neither worse nor less than divine. For reason is not measured by size or height, but by the decisions of its will. Will you not, therefore, place your good there wherein you are equal with the gods?

—Epictetus[131]

. . . . .

Gated expat communities have sprung up all over the world, populated with retirees living a carefree lifestyle, their reward for decades of toil and strife in First World, capitalist societies. Twenty minutes east of the Quito airport, a retiree escape called Kichana Kuska, Quechua for "secret place," was developed specifically for this demographic. Touted as a tropical utopia, Kichana encompasses over eighty acres of land, and every square inch is manicured, maintained by workers recruited from the local pool of recovering obsessive-compulsives. Picture a famous golf course. Superimpose faux adobe houses with Spanish tile roofs onto the fairways. Entangle the houses in bougainvillea and surround them with palm and mango trees and exotic flowers. Create vague boundaries between homes with plants from all over the world. To denote the perimeter, surround the entire property with eucalyptus trees, a tall natural barrier. Never run into another homeowner. This is Kichana.

Kichana is a fortress. It sits atop a land formation surrounded on three sides by deep gorges blasted out by recent volcanic eruptions, a typical Quito-area landscape. Kichana residents can walk to the edges of limestone cliffs, denuded beyond the eucalyptus trees, and see tiny trickles of water at their bases. These bodies of water are wide and rushing rivers originating in the Andes, miniaturized by the sheer depth and steep gradient of the gorges. The only entrance or egress is through a single, heavily guarded, intimidating wrought iron gate. Kichana is an island in the high-elevation skies of Quito, completely fabricated and contrived.

STOICs, even though we can appreciate the high level of O-C that defines Kichana, a place like this is not for us. It oozes the atmosphere of a white-collar crime minimum security prison—a place where the president of Ecuador might be confined under house arrest, or where Julian Assange, an Ecuadorian citizen currently living in their Embassy in London, might be secretly squirreled away someday. Kichana is a zoo exhibiting species of *Homo retiredii* from around the world. The homes feature huge picture windows, integrating the outside with the inside, and the various workers and groundskeepers who roam the property throughout the day challenge your privacy. The fishbowl effect is further enhanced by a lack of walls, fences, or dense hedges to insulate one property from another. The homes are lavishly and copiously furnished as if a huge party could erupt at any moment, but the place is conspicuously devoid of revelers. On the other hand, Kichana is the perfect place to go underground. It wouldn't be surprising to learn that Vladmir Putin was a homeowner or that Kichana is a weekend getaway for Meghan and Harry.

Everything Kichana is controlled and managed, down to single blades of grass. An O-C paradise, you might think, but to me, achieving this level of perfection when nature is more of a stochastic, chaotic system borders on the creepy. I suspect that if you live in Kichana for some amount of time you develop an inability to contend, in any meaningful way, with the outside world—which is what I imagine prison does to a person. STOICs need a variety of stimulating situations, and the utter isolation of Kichana, though beautiful to look at, takes a special kind of individual to endure. During a two-day incarceration at the end of my stay in Ecuador, I recalled the original meaning of utopia: "no place."

We crush ourselves, close ourselves in.

—*Epictetus*[132]

CHAPTER XV

TRAVELING WITHIN

For the past ten years, a spindly, anemic San Pedro cactus (*Echinopsis pachanoi*) has been clinging to life in my kitchen, reaching for whatever sun it can scrounge through the sliding glass doors that lead to the backyard. I inherited the San Pedro from Virtù before she moved to Brazil and have been determined to keep it alive. However, I don't believe in holding plants hostage in pots or encouraging the displacement of plants from their native environments by buying exotics, and someday I'd like to return it to the Andes of Ecuador or Peru, where San Pedro grows abundantly. But until I can figure out how, it will stay in the kitchen. Because it's a hallucinogen, there may be laws prohibiting the possession and transportation of San Pedro. I'm not sure.

San Pedro contains a number of alkaloids, including mescaline, the same molecule found in peyote buttons (*Lophophora williamsii*). Mescaline is an entheogen, a chemical ingested to produce a non-ordinary state of consciousness, and mescaline is one of those time- and mood-altering drugs that neutralizes anxiety for some us-

ers. U.S. researchers and psychiatrists have shown a re-
newed interest in the therapeutic potential of
hallucinogens for treating conditions like O-C, depression,
and phobias—dusting the cobwebs off some very promising research from the 1950s—but are still experiencing
pushback from the FDA. Indigenous Ecuadorians have
consumed San Pedro ritually for at least three thousand
years, and when the Spanish imposed their Catholic belief
system on the locals in the mid-1500s, they also tried to
suppress its use. But the Spaniards themselves must have
indulged because San Pedro is so appropriately named. It's
called *wachuma* by the indigenous, but the Spanish gave it
the name that stuck. According to the biblical reference,
Jesus gave San Pedro (Saint Peter) the keys to heaven and,
as users of San Pedro have blogged, the distillate of the
cactus delivers an experience echoing the divine. For whatever reason, those in power are invested in pocketing the
keys, depriving the rest of us of paradise.

For years I'd wanted to know if San Pedro could diminish my anxiety or at least reprogram my brain to reject
anxiety as part of everyday functioning. The three-week
trip I'd booked to tour Ecuador was not specifically to experience San Pedro, but I was excited to find, via the
Internet, a place a short bus ride from Cuenca where I
could participate in a ceremony. When I arrived in Cuenca
on a Sunday, the anxiety of anticipating the San Pedro experience, eight days into the future, intensified but created
the effect of slowing down time. The two weeks I'd already
been in Ecuador began to feel like several months. The
San Pedro ceremony was scheduled at the end of my stay
in Cuenca, and I couldn't control the anticipation angst. So

once again, anxiety robbed me of my ability to live in the present.

We suffer more often in imagination than in reality... What I advise you to do is, not to be unhappy before the crisis comes; since it may be that the dangers before which you paled as if they were threatening you, will never come upon you; they certainly have not yet come. Some things torment us more than they ought; some torment us before they ought; and some torment us when they ought not to torment us at all. We are in the habit of exaggerating, or imagining, or anticipating, sorrow... no fear is so ruinous and so uncontrollable as panic fear. For other fears are groundless, but this fear is witless.

—*Seneca*[133]

I was about to take a trip of a different kind, compounding my anxiety with a new and unfamiliar form of disquiet. What if I didn't return from the trip mentally? What if the people running the operation intended to poison and rob me? Three different Ecuadorians had warned me about unscrupulous individuals who extract a powder from angel's trumpets flowers (*Brugmansia*), blow the powder into your face, then steal your money, credit cards, plane tickets, and anything else of value. The powder renders you both utterly cooperative and an amnesiac, and when you revive, all of your material assets may have vanished. Urban myth? I didn't want to find out. These thoughts tormented me, but once I was on the bus to my destination, the anxiety resolved and I felt confident that everything would be fine.

After two hours of traveling a meandering mountain highway, the bus driver dropped me at a rusty chain-link gate with a crudely painted sign that read "*El Lugar*" ("the place"). Two barking dogs met me at the gate, but I ignored them and started the steep climb up crumbling cement steps to the cinderblock house. The front door was open; I called the names of my hosts but received no response. Per the request posted on the door, I removed my shoes and entered, trying to maintain my confidence. The house smelled like wet dog, locker-room socks, and burnt lentil soup. I found the couple sitting on the back porch with a young client recovering from the previous day's experience, huddled in an Ecuadorian poncho, his bare feet crossed on a coffee table. He seemed of sound mind and body, calm and gentle, which was reassuring. The couple, a man and woman in their mid-fifties, were from central Texas and longtime San Pedro users, with over four hundred experiences between them. She was small, wiry, hyperactive, and a spinner of long, banal yarns. The deeper she dove into a story, the wider her eyes became; the more she tilted her head back, the more I could imagine a Big Bang type of vibrational force popping her eyes out of their sockets. Her partner was the antithesis of her, direct, serene, and comforting, with huge powder blue eyes set in a fleshy, tanned face, a good listener; someone with whom you could feel safe.

While ayahuasca, another entheogenic drink, is said to connect you, via the DMT (Dimethyltryptamine) molecule, to various worlds, entities, and experiences that can sometimes be terrifying, I'd read that San Pedro reveals the secrets of light and nature and happiness. Ayahuasca is ingested at night, and a San Pedro ceremony starts at ten in the morning. My hosts and I got acquainted for half an hour, then the man went to the kitchen to fetch the brew. The young client stood and gave hugs all around—again, reassuring—and left to start his day. Ceremoniously, the man emerged from the kitchen carrying a tray holding a few ritual objects and a large clip-top water bottle full of a chartreuse, viscous substance. He set the tray down on the table and recited an invocation to his spirit guides and to mine, inviting them to participate. When he popped the top, a large amount of gas escaped as if it were a carbonated beverage vigorously shaken. He poured eight ounces, and I was expected to drink the entire thing. The San Pedro looked like a wheatgrass smoothie, and everything I'd read about its taste had made me expect the most bitter, foul flavor imaginable, but it slid down my throat in two big gulps, not lingering long enough on my taste buds to affect a reaction. A tiny belch followed, giving me a hint of its flavor. It reminded me of a fruit I'd eaten somewhere in Brazil, but I couldn't put my finger on it. I expected waves of nausea to follow, but I was stable. There was no turning back, and I felt victorious.

I assumed I'd be outdoors for most of the experience, but when I started feeling the effects, I realized I could not be around the woman with the bulging eyes. In the middle of one of her meandering stories, I excused myself, climbed the stairs to my designated bedroom, and shut the door.

For the next four hours I lay on the bed, my body cold as a cadaver, twitching, shuddering, and jerking violently as the San Pedro reprogrammed me. I was vaguely nauseated the entire time but not enough to purge. Eyes closed, I experienced what I interpreted as an energy field, and later when I researched the kinds of imagery people see while "journeying," others reported what I had seen: the Flower of Life.

The Flower of Life is a symbol made of infinitely repeating, intersecting circles, evenly spaced and overlapping so they form a flower-like pattern with hexagonal symmetry. It's used in architecture, jewelry, quilts and other textiles, and much more. It's even on a box of tissues in my bathroom. Many ancient civilizations created this symbol independently of each other, including societies of people living in Ireland, Turkey, Israel, Egypt, Morocco, China, Greece, Germany, India, and elsewhere, and many called the pattern by the same name. San Pedro showed me that everything in the universe derives from this basic geometry, a concept I'd read about and seen manifest in ways like the Fibonacci number series expressed in plants. But I'd never understood it in terms of myself. I was seeing "me" not corporally but as a creation of the Flower of Life in a field of patterns repeated hundreds of thousands of times. Parts of me were fragmented and discontinuous, and San Pedro was making repairs, removing chunks of damage and replacing them with orderly rows and columns of tiny Flowers of Life, putting me back together again like Humpty Dumpty after he'd fallen off the wall. Such a satisfying experience for an O-C person. Colors indentified with the cool region of the visible spectrum—violets, indigo blues, turquoise—were luminous beyond anything occurring in the natural world. San Pedro purged me of what no longer served and inserted what was beneficial.

The whole contains nothing which is not for its advantage; and all natures indeed have this common principle, but the nature of the uni-

verse has this principle besides, that it cannot be compelled even by any external cause to generate anything harmful to itself... By remembering then that I am a part of such a whole, I shall be content with everything that happens... Acquire the contemplative way of seeing how all things change into one another, and constantly attend to it, Look at everything that exists, and observe that it is already in dissolution and change.

—Marcus Aurelius[134]

In mainstream psychology, the bicameralism of the brain is an old paradigm. But I noticed a definite split, right down the middle, that seemed to separate my mind into two halves. When I turned my head to the left, my inner vision was bright yellow, clear, and positive, and when I turned my head to the right, the colors switched to a dark palette with darker thoughts and indistinctness to follow. When I wanted to examine one or the other, I turned my head. I never felt a warm, loving embrace of a grandfather, as so many people have described, but I didn't feel slapped around by an evil stepmother, either. A few deceased loved ones paid me a visit, and insights about friends and relatives with whom I have conflict helped me understand how I could behave with more compassion. A sister was a landlocked crocodile, captive and tethered in a desiccated swamp, thrashing her head and tail. She snapped at luminescent, colorful orbs that floated around her, just out of reach, and San Pedro said if she could just catch one of them, her suffering would transform into happiness. To her frustration, the orbs eluded her but didn't fly away. I thought maybe if she stopped thrashing they would settle on her body and penetrate the tough, armor-like skin. I saw my adoptive father as a boy, sad and lonely, and my heart split open with compassion. I felt past existences as an old Plains Indian woman, a wounded Comanche warrior, and an old woman from the Indian subcontinent. I was told I would live to be a very old woman in this life. I saw images of the Holocaust and was a shriveled and lifeless body among many.

Periodically I'd open my eyes to observe how San Pedro modified the material world. Straight lines were wavy, and any kind of movement became discontinuous and stroboscopic. Waving my hands in front of my face was endlessly entertaining. A few times I stood up and looked out the windows, feeling the essences of the mountains, clouds, and fog, the green of the Ecuadorian landscape, the cacophony of animal and human sounds magnified, all expressing their distinct character. The world felt rich and vibrant, pulsating with the same energy that I felt in myself, bursting at the seams.

I felt a certain mental thrill, and a transformation unaccompanied by fear, due to the novelty and the unpleasantness of an unusual occurrence... For there are certain emotions... which no courage can avoid; nature reminds courage how perishable a thing it is. And so he will contract his brow when the prospect is forbidding, will shudder at sudden apparitions, and will become dizzy when he stands at the edge of a high precipice and looks down. This is not fear; it is a natural feeling which reason cannot rout.

—Seneca[135]

San Pedro reminds you not to lose your sense of humor. When (what seemed like) a profound thought struck, a bird outside in the jungle (*Forlornus trombonus*) responded with a loud, four-note descending call. The San Pedro was laughing at me. (Spoiler alert: several paragraphs to follow that seemed profound on San Pedro, not so much now.)

Being in Ecuador exposes you to lots of Catholic imagery, and their artists excel at creating explicitly gruesome crucifixes. I'm often repulsed by crucifixes and look away, and I think I figured out why (beyond wanting to avoid looking at something so horrible). In Quito and Cuenca I'd visited many magnificent cathedrals and churches and began thinking about how Jesus's crucifixion mirrors our individual struggles. When we feel shame or self-hatred we crucify ourselves, in a metaphoric way, and as with Jesus, the punishment doesn't fit the crime. In fact, there is no crime. We all navigate life with challenges and hurts and unmet needs and, at times, images of ourselves as failures, and we punish ourselves relentlessly for what we see as weaknesses or failings. We give ourselves harmful, negative messages, when we're really an extraordinary expression of this amazing, mysterious universe. The beauty we see in a flower or a bird or hear in a favorite piece of music is a reflection of the beauty that is part of us and is just a different expression of the essential substance we all share. It is in us and we are in it. We are meant to be happy and enjoy life and just be who we are.

Seek thou that which is according to thine own nature, and whether it be for thy credit or no, use all possible speed for the attainment of it: for no man ought to be blamed, for seeking his own good and happiness.

—Marcus Aurelius[136]

San Pedro also said that the metaphor of the bleeding lamb expresses this innocent condition in which we exist. The sacrificial lamb, the surrogate, concentrates humanity's suffering in one place, and bleeding cathartically releases it. Interesting that these messages were couched in a Catholic context and delivered to a person raised as a liberal Protestant; I was expecting and hoping for aliens or Sasquatch or some other interdimensional creatures.

I write about San Pedro as if we were having a conversation, and it *was* a conversation, but not of the conventional kind. San Pedro didn't feel like a person or like Alan Rickman's voice in my head. I didn't ask it questions and receive answers. I was tossed into a mind stream of a different kind, like a parent throwing a toddler into a swimming pool for the first time. But children are not born with an innate ability to swim. An infant girl isn't physically capable of swimming, holding her breath intentionally, or keeping her head above water. She needs a parent to constantly monitor her condition and guide her through the water. I was that infant conveyed down a gentle stream, sometimes floating on my back, sometimes struggling to keep my head above water, sometimes suffering bumps and bruises. The journey was long and unpredictable, with both disturbing twists and turns and stretches of calm and tranquility. San Pedro was the loving parent whose hands cradled my head and back, making sure I was protected and safe.

I'd read that the effects of San Pedro last from eight to fifteen hours, and after six I began to come down. The next twelve hours were extremely uncomfortable. The environment was overstimulating in a negative way: the constant traffic on the highway not more than fifty feet from the house. The couple's bad taste in music. The bad smells. Her fanatical laughter. I couldn't wait to get the hell out of there, but night was falling, and the next bus back to Cuenca was in the morning. I lay in bed and my heart raced. My water supply depleted, I was dehydrated, and I wasn't sure the house water was safe to drink. San Pedro had rendered me unable to eat. I remembered a scene from Houston's Intercontinental Airport, back before I'd boarded the plane to Ecuador. The water fountains were disconnected and shrouded in plastic, and I'd watched a young woman with a four-dollar bottle of Evian toss her head back and take a long drink. The CIBO Express Gourmet Market, also located in the airport terminal, reminded me of its homophone SIBO, which stands for small intestinal bacterial overgrowth, implicated in chronic diarrhea. Not a great name for an airport food emporium. The image of the terminal as a dystopia where water is only for the privileged and the food is a risk factor for intestinal distress tormented me. Sleep wasn't an option.

I tried evoking the Stoics.

Unthinking panic is incapable of its own self-preservation.
—*Seneca*[137]

It helped to imagine Seneca, Marcus Aurelius, and Epictetus as fellow entheogenic travelers and to imagine the observations they would make about the experience. The jokes Seneca would crack. The serious tone of Marc-A. No-nonsense Epictetus. To feel gratitude for the great

Stoic triumvirate was enough to calm me down but not to induce sleep. Again,

Some things torment us more than they ought; some torment us before they ought; and some torment us when they ought not to torment us at all. We are in the habit of exaggerating, or imagining, or anticipating, sorrow.

—Seneca[138]

Shortly after daybreak the next morning, I stood on the opposite side of the highway in a truck yard blanketed in soot, waiting to flag down the bus to Cuenca. My heart had been pounding for the past fifteen hours, and my anxiety skyrocketed when the first bus passed me by. But the next bus stopped, and as soon as I took my seat, I felt that comforting grandfather's arm wrap itself around my shoulders. Back in Cuenca, at hour twenty-four, I was finally back to normal.

I took a beating and I survived. The negative energy removal and repatterning was worth the "trip", and after another twelve hours elapsed, I felt happy and vigorous. Experiencing the exquisite geometries of the Flower of Life (for examples, visit travelforstoics.com) and getting a reboot was something I think I'd like to do again under different, more agreeable circumstances. A weak undercurrent of anxiety is still in the background, but whenever I think about the experience, I feel like I've got the keys to heaven. STOICs, was there anything for you in this narrative?

Avoid a frequent and excessive mention of your own actions and dangers. For however agreeable it may be to yourself to allude to the risks you have run, it is not equally agreeable to others to hear your adventures.

—*Epictetus*[139]

CHAPTER XVI

AIRLINE SLOGANS

Congonhas Airport is one of four facilities that serve the twenty-two million inhabitants of São Paulo, Brazil's metro area. That's right, twenty-two million, two million shy of the entire population of Australia. When it opened in 1936, the airport was a good distance from any urban areas, but today Congonhas is surrounded by miles and miles of neighborhoods, an amalgam of vast numbers of residential high-rises. The short, notoriously slippery runways and all those high-rises that might get their tops clipped during a takeoff or landing means no aviation wiggle room. Add in the amount of chaos in the airport itself, too small to handle the numbers of passengers that pass through every day, and Congonhas may make your list of least favorite flying experiences. When you notice your fellow passengers making the sign of the cross during takeoff and the flight attendant ending her safety demonstration with "in the name of the Father, and of the Son, and of the Holy Spirit, Amen," you may feel that something is off.

Gol Linhas Aéreas is a Brazilian airline that flies domestically from Congonhas Airport. At the time I flew Gol, the airline had a great slogan: *Adds More Life to Your Time.* I pondered this slogan for days, trying to understand its message, and I think this is what it meant. A takeoff and landing from Congonhas is so scary that it triggers the phenomenon that proves how elastic our perception of time can be. When we are in the grip of fear, time slows down, like the slow-motion car crash that many people have described (touched on in Chapter II). Scientists have studied this phenomenon by making people who are scared of spiders stare at them for a prescribed amount of time, and these arachnophobes always overestimate how many seconds have elapsed. Scientists have also observed the same time-expanding response in novice bungee jumpers. The jumpers all thought the duration of their fall was much longer than it actually was. So on a Gol flight, if takeoff is taking waaaay too long and you think you're about to slam into a cluster of high-rises, time will slow down. It will feel like *more life is added to your time.*

Inspired by Gol's great slogan, I decided to interpret the slogans of other airlines. Here's a partial list:

Emirates: *Hello Tomorrow*
Goodbye today.

Lufthansa (Germany): *Nonstop You*
The preferred airline for narcissists.

Hainan Airlines (China): *Cherished Experience*
Special moments, like sitting next to a screaming baby.

Air France: *France Is in the Air*
Quick, turn off the antigravity machine!

Swiss International Air Lines: *Made of Switzerland*
Runs with the precision of a cuckoo clock.

Virgin Australia: *Here's to Looking Up*
Here's to looking up at you, kid.

Virgin America: *A Breath of Fresh Airline*
As long as you avoid the last few rows in coach.

Japan Airlines: *Fly into Tomorrow. Dream Skyward.*
Ignore that recurring airplane crash nightmare.

Aegean Airlines (Greece): *For Everything Distant You Want to Bring Near*
And for every encroaching elbow you want to push away.

Aeroflot (Russia): *Sincerely Yours*
Alternate slogans they considered: Best Wishes, Warm Regards, Take Care, Cheers.

Aer Lingus (Ireland): *Smart Flies*
Our fleet of common houseflies reengineered for intelligent travel.

WestJet (Canada): *Owners Care*
Do you really have to tell us this?

Vueling (Spain): *Love the Way You Fly*
Hate the way you land.

JetBlue Airways (USA): *You Above All*
And every man for himself when the life rafts deploy.

Azul Brazilian Airlines: *You Up There. It's Brazil Up There.*
Then who are we down here?

TAP Air Portugal: *With Arms Wide Open*
I just flew in from Lisbon, and boy are my arms tired.

TUI Airways (UK): *Discover Your Smile*
You've been grimacing the entire flight.

Air China: *Your World, Our Flights*
And never the twain shall meet.

LOT Polish Airlines: *You Choose the Direction*
And hope that we're all on the same page.

Royal Jordanian: *A World of Stories*
About near-misses, bad airplane food, drunken pilots, and bathroom sex.

Bahamasair (Bahamas): *We Don't Just Fly There, We Live There*
You know where we live, so we're really careful not to piss you off.

Iran Air (a former slogan): *We Take You There, We Take You Back*
End of story.

Scandinavian Airlines: *We Are Travelers*
So who are those people in the cabin?

Lion Air (Indonesia): *We Make People Fly*
We push you out the emergency exit and hope your parachute deploys.

Onur Air (Turkey; a former slogan): *Fly, Turkey, Fly!*
Oh, wait, turkeys can't fly.

Pegasus Airlines (Turkey): *We Didn't Start Aviation in Turkey, but We Transformed It*
Into a mythical creature whose passenger slides off its back, falling to Earth.

Sunwing Airlines (Canada): *Fly Better*
Than…?

Syrian Air: *Syrian Air Means Safety*
Because operations are suspended and all planes are grounded.

Kulula (South Africa): *The Most South African Airways*
Their slogan is already a joke, playing off their competitors
in Botswana, Namibia, and Zimbabwe.

WOW Air (Iceland): Doesn't need a slogan.

CHAPTER XVII

THE ANXIETY OF RETURNING HOME

*Those Nightmares Where You're Running in Slow Motion
Are a Lot Like Trying to Get to the Airport on Time*

Early morning flight anxiety is a STOIC's nightmare. The year was 2009; I'd been visiting Virtù in Jaipur, and I needed to catch an obscenely early flight to Delhi to connect with the flight back to the States. The two of us had been staying in a house built on a brand-new street at the outskirts of town. No tuk-tuks or taxis passed through the neighborhood and no bus service had been established. The street didn't even have a name. We walked to the closest commercial district, only ten minutes away, to hire a driver for the next morning. No one we talked to spoke English, so again thanks to Virtù, who had a command of elementary Hindi, we communicated to a willing driver that I needed a ride to the airport at four in the morning. Because there was no plan B, no Uber, our old-technology cell phones had no GPS, and we couldn't call within India without incurring huge roaming charges, neither of us slept well that night.

My first worry was, of course, what if the driver didn't show up? How would I get to the airport? No good solution presented itself. Imposing on Virtù's Indian host family was out of the question, as was hitchhiking. If I missed the flight, I'd have to taxi to the airport early that same evening, hope to get booked on the next morning's flight, and sleep in a nearby hotel with early morning shuttle service—not a bad scenario because I'd gain an extra day with Virtù. I'd been lugging a massive piece of luggage with compromised wheels around India and my new sitar purchased in Varanasi. My second worry was, if the driver showed up, how was I going to fit me, the huge bag, and the sitar into a tiny tuk-tuk? I'd arrived at the house in Jaipur in a taxi with ample trunk space, so that hadn't been an issue. Alan Rickman's coolheaded voice reminded me, "Entire Indian families ride on a single motorcycle and men balance huge bales of whatever on the backs of bicycles, what's the worry?" My third worry was grim. What if the driver, pissed that he was losing precious sleep for a four-in-the-morning airport run, realized my utter vulnerability and stole my luggage and sitar, demanded my purse, and dumped me somewhere on the side of the road? I had to prepare for this unpleasantness and worse. Being a STOIC even back then, preparation for catastrophe was my M.O. On a piece of paper, I wrote my name, Virtù's cell phone number, the name and address of the Jaipur family, the names and numbers of contacts back in the States, and a goodbye note to Virtù. I stuffed the note along with one hundred dollars in twenties into my socks so that whoever found my body might be incentivized to dial one of the numbers provided.

Prepare yourself and be brave—those unprepared panic by insignificant things.

—Seneca[140]

The driver arrived at the predetermined time. Worry number one eliminated. Virtù and I exchanged sleep-deprived, teary goodbyes as he loaded me and my stuff into the tuk-tuk, the long neck of the sitar case projecting out the left side and the *kadu* (the sitar's body, made of a big gourd) sitting in my lap. Worry number two eliminated. We took off for the airport, only twenty minutes away through a mix of commercial development and the remnants of former farming communities. *Kind of a good dumping ground for bodies*, I thought. The road was deserted at four in the morning, so a traffic accident seemed unlikely; plus, as I've mentioned, Indian drivers are the best in the world. As the number of miles between me and Virtù grew, so did a mix of increased sadness and decreased anxiety. Signs for the airport began to appear, my conflicted emotional state lifted, and I knew I was home free. Worry number three eliminated.

Inside the terminal, I checked the humongous bag and held on to the sitar. Helpful and friendly airport staff arranged for an escort to take me to the plane when it was time to board, where I would have the option to carry the sitar up the conveyor belt and into the cargo compartment, stowing it where I saw fit. They knew what it was and held it in the highest regard—such a contrast to where it eventually ended up, smashed on the tarmac in Detroit, carelessly knocked over by a harried baggage handler in the pouring rain.

After checking in, I went searching for a public phone. When I entered the waiting area for my flight, I spotted a red, 1960s-era rotary phone sitting on a table in a corner. I lifted the receiver and heard a dial tone. I called Virtù's cell, and, astonishingly, the call went through and she picked up. We shed tears of relief and felt the pain of separation. When we hung up, I was in a funk. The sitar and I relocated to the main part of the waiting area, and an empathetic fellow passenger sat next to me so I could watch a cell phone video of a thousand-sitar performance in Delhi.

Welcome all that happens to you.
—Marcus Aurelius[141]

. . . . .

The day has arrived for your return home. You enter the airport terminal feeling heaviness in your heart, fighting back tears when you reflect on the great times you've had and the wonderful people you've met on your journey. You're in line to check a bag, being herded like cattle back and forth between crowd control belts and stanchions, congratulating yourself on the new ways in which you've learned to manage your Solo Traveler: Obsessive, Introverted, Compulsive–ness on the trip. Finally, it's your turn to check your bag, and you cheerfully greet the airline employee, the one who will give you your boarding pass and baggage claim ticket, the first gatekeeper in a series of several who may prevent you from exiting their country.

Be good natured to all.
                    —*Seneca*[142]

She asks for your passport and immigration form. Your immigration form? That important piece of paper you put in a safe place there's no way you'd forget? The first go-to is your wallet, and it's not there. Next is the compartment of your cross body travel bag in which you keep your wallet; also not there. Suddenly an image of placing it in the important documents and receipts pouch comes to mind, but where is the pouch? Here's where your cheery mood fizzles and the O-C goes from zero to sixty in two seconds. You're now forced into a situation of having to rummage, and in a ticking bomb kind of way, because the throng of passengers behind you is growing impatient. You remove your backpack and place it on the floor, kneel as if venerating a powerful sovereign, and extract its entire contents, which includes remaining packets of vitamins, various chargers, the "flat" toiletry bag, a Mexican wrestling mask you bought for your son-in-law, the Grayl water filtration bottle, the aluminum water bottle in which you place the filtered water, the waterproof pouch for your cell phone plus two large safety pins attached to its lanyard, your travel AC adapter, a swimsuit, and your Skechers. The receipts pouch is not there. Now, for all the world to see, you have to open the bag you intend to check and rummage again, facing the possibility of having to remove all of its contents.

Do not be distraught about how you appear to others.
—*Epictetus*[143]

I'm reminded of the times I've seen this scenario at check-in and silently scorned the person engaged in this behavior, judging him or her for not being more mindful of the whereabouts of the important stuff. Now I'm the actor in this humiliating role, trying to control the burn rising in my cheeks and promising myself that I will feel only empathy for the next person I see engaged in this activity. My advice? To avoid unnecessary embarrassment, keep that immigration form in a known, accessible place, and check it often. Stapled to my passport is what I'm doing next time.

Gatekeepers Two and Three were the security personnel stationed at the x-ray machine, and my backpack raised a red flag. As it parted the slatted plastic curtain after going through x-ray and landed on the conveyor belt's aluminum rollers, Gatekeeper Two grabbed the pack, removed a few objects and placed them in a bin, and rescanned the bin and backpack. Again a red flag. He removed more objects and sent the whole jumble through again. This time he found something suspect and triumphantly displayed it to Gatekeeper Three: the two large safety pins. Busted! I was planning to gouge out the eyes of a flight attendant with those lethal little daggers. Again the contents of my backpack were scanned. Gatekeeper Two extracted a fingernail file from the toiletry kit, and as I protested, he impersonated an angry sociopath, making violent stabbing motions with the file. The file disappeared into a bucket of confiscated dangerous objects and probably ended up in his girl-friend's mani-pedi place of business.

Here are despoilers and thieves… they think that they have some power over us because of the paltry body and its possessions. Suffer us to show them that they have power over no one.
—*Epictetus*[144]

· · · · ·

After a long and exhausting flight, you're home. When you open the front door, inserting a familiar key into a reliable lock, your first impression of your clean and orderly house triggers a huge release of dopamine. Driving your car again is a privilege you'll never take for granted, ever again. You may notice that the O-C routines in place before your trip have relaxed, and over the following weeks you're able to hold on to that feeling. Congratulate your-self for completing a STOIC journey and returning home an empowered, confident, and calm human being, exuding Stoic virtue. You've met many STOIC challenges and, with the help of Epictetus, Seneca, and Marcus Aurelius, risen to their demands, enabling you to enjoy the travel experiences you left home to have. Have you effected a lasting disruption of the O-C cycle? There're a few more things we need to discuss.

Is Travel Itself a Compulsion?

Let's reexamine the definitions of obsessions and compulsions from the DSM-5.

Obsessions are defined by (1) and (2):
1. Recurrent and persistent thoughts, urges, or impulses that are experienced, at some time during the disturbance, as intrusive and unwanted, and that in most individuals cause marked anxiety or distress.
2. The individual attempts to ignore or suppress such thoughts, urges, or images, or to neutralize them with some other thought or action (i.e., by performing a compulsion).

Compulsions are defined by (1) and (2):
1. Repetitive behaviors (e.g., hand washing, ordering, checking) or mental acts (e.g., praying, counting, repeating words silently) that the individual feels driven to perform in response to an obsession or according to rules that must be applied rigidly.
2. The behaviors or mental acts are aimed at preventing or reducing anxiety or distress, or preventing some dreaded event or situation; however, these behaviors or mental acts are not connected in a realistic way with what they are designed to neutralize or prevent, or are clearly excessive...[145]

I think it's worth asking the obvious: *What actually qualifies as an obsessive disturbance?* Is it like the old SCOTUS (Supreme Court of the United States) definition of pornography, "I know it when I see it?"[146] What are the parameters, what are the boundaries crossed that create an obsessive disturbance? What is its nature?

Since a disturbance is a perturbation or disruption of the norm, for the O-C person, feeling relief from the O-C condition *is* the disturbance. From the moment we wake up in the morning, our norm is O-C, so just about everything triggers anxiety and distress. We sit up, swing our feet around to the side of the bed, look down at the carpet, and obsess about the footprints that have spoiled the freshly vacuumed evenness. We walk to the window to raise the shade, take a few steps back from it, and readjust it until it's exactly parallel with the windowsill. We make our beds with such meticulousness that any army sergeant would be proud. The dishwasher must be emptied bottom rack first. The food in the fridge must be arranged in categories and placed on specific shelves. And on and on and on... Our entire lives are expressions of restraint, prudence, and fastidiousness, and if we don't follow these obsession rules, our anxiety grows every time we encounter violations of the rules. The only way to reduce the anxiety is by physical acts: constantly adjusting (fill in your compulsion here) until it satisfies your sense of perfection, washing your hands until they're raw, checking and rechecking that you've turned off the stove and locked the doors. The point is, you must remove yourself completely from the long-standing, quotidian triggers to create a meaningful disruption of the O-C cycle, and travel is one of the best ways to do it.

One of the concepts this book has set out to illuminate is that a person's equanimity can be restored by a change of scenery and with help from the Stoics. Solo obsessive, introverted, compulsive travel challenges those elements of a person's "issues" that cause us so much grief and unhappiness back home. Because you are disconnected from your familiar environment and daily routines, you gain valuable insights into exactly what the problems are and how you might mitigate or even fix them when you arrive back home, cross the threshold of your domicile, and resume your normal life. But most important, *Travel for STOICs* encourages you to enjoy your own company and your own life, and achieving the ability to do this is big.

One ought none the less to prepare oneself for this... that is, to be able to be self-sufficient, to be able to commune with oneself; even as Zeus communes with himself, and is at peace with himself, and contemplates the character of his governance, and occupies himself with ideas appropriate to himself, so ought we also to be able to converse with ourselves, not to be in need of others, not to be at a loss for some way to spend our time; we ought to devote ourselves to the study of... our own relation to all other things; to consider how we used to act toward the things that happen to us, and how we act now; what the things are that still distress us; how these too can be remedied, or how removed; if any of these matters that I have mentioned need to be brought to perfection, to perfect them in accordance with the principle of reason inherent in them.

—Epictetus[147]

Travel offers protracted disruption of the O-C cycle but as a behavior is *not connected in a realistic way with what it is designed to neutralize or prevent.* When you return from traveling, the old triggers are still in place but attenuated for a while, at least. Hold on to those new insights your experiences have afforded you. Reference the Stoics when you feel yourself slipping back into the old ways. Wear one of those red wrist bands with the initials WWSD (What would the Stoics do?) to remind yourself of their wisdom. Resume taking low-commitment trips to maintain your travel chops, and remember that when challenging situations arise, you know what to do.

Now you have the tools to help evaluate compatibility with a travel objective or activity and knowledge about your own special place on the STOIC spectrum. The more you travel, the more comfortable you will become, the more travel options you will have, and you may even develop more control over your obsessive-compulsive introverted self in a healthier way. Is there a danger of developing a tolerance for travel and needing more and more travel experiences to keep the obsessions at bay? Perhaps. More important, when you're immersed in STOIC travel, a magical thing happens—by being away from home and released from the grip of situations, objects, and people that activate the O-C, your spirit expands in ways that are impossible at home.

I never bring back home the same character that I took abroad with me.

—*Seneca*[148]

Because travel requires constant problem-solving and adapting to new circumstances, when you accomplish travel successfully—whatever that looks like for you—you realize that everywhere feels like that special place in your heart that is easy, friendly, and O-C–free. Or at least mediated. Solo travel regulates the obsessive, introverted, and compulsive like nothing else, strengthening the "ruling power within us,"[149] and makes us masters of our personality challenges.

How can novelty of surroundings abroad and becoming acquainted with foreign scenes or cities be of any help?... the answer is simply this: you have to lay aside the load on your spirit.
  —*Seneca*[150]

Exactly.

GRATITUDE

Travel for STOICs would not be possible without the assistance and generosity of many individuals. Kelsey Mitchener (hello@kelseymitchener.com), editor extraordinaire, helped shape the book to the requirements of readers of standard English, demonstrating infinite patience for my disregard of punctuation.

Jean-Manuel Duvivier (http://www.jmduvivier.com/) designed the clever, whimsical cover, adding the winged boots at my request. Hermes, the Greek god who sports winged footwear, is associated with travel.

John L. Bowman, author of *A Reference Guide to Stoicism: A Compilation of the Principle Stoic Writings on Various Topics* (http://www.johnlbowman.com) generously gave permission to quote from his work on Stoicism.

Various long-time friends helped shape *TFS*, offering their valued opinions on the fifteen or so covers I designed before giving up and handing it over to Jean-Manuel: Alaine Ball, Dale Conner, Raquel Casillas-Hughes, Susan Matthews, Geoffry Oshman, Suzie Russell, Lucien Stavenhagen, Evelyne and Tim Taylor, and Linda Thornton. Susan Matthews also read parts of the book and made invaluable comments and revisions. Toddy Sewell and Len Eggleston saved me from publishing under a pen name already taken by a writer of soft-core porn. Anatha Attar house-sat while I traveled around the world. Pi Luna helped refine the cover's message. A huge thank-you to all.

APPENDIX A

Mexico: List of Necessities (124 items total)
cross body bag, backpack, and luggage contents

bag:

packed?	item #	description
	1	passport
	2	wallet: driver's license, credit card, bank card, Global Entry card, emergency contact info, U.S. money (6 total)
	3	iPhone + charger (2 total)
	4	Kindle + charger (2 total)
	5	paper items: itinerary, Airbnb contacts, map of Airbnb location, insurance policy, addresses for postcards, Celestún trip voucher, business cards (7 total)
	6	*Lonely Planet Yucatán* (only the pages I needed, photocopied from the book)
	7	Road iD for ankle
	8	receipts/documents pouch (with pesos)
	9	2 pairs of reading glasses
	10	sunglasses
	11	lipstick/lip balm
	12	empty lip balm with $20
	13	comb
	14	earplugs
	15	earbuds
	16	sanitizing wipes
	17	tissues
	18	Valium
	19	three pens, small notebook
	20	chewing gum
	21	flashlight
	38	**total items**

backpack:

packed?	item #	description
	1	paper items: copies of passport, Global Entry card, credit cards, insurance policy, map of Airbnb, Celestún trip voucher, itinerary, and emergency numbers (8 total)
	2	Spanish phrase book
	3	Skechers shoes
	4	inflatable neck pillow
	5	binoculars
	6	water purifier bottle
	7	aluminum water bottle
	8	toothpaste, toothbrush, floss (3 total)
	9	foldable cotton hat
	10	swimsuit
	11	hair curler
	12	electricity adapter
	13	4AA batteries
	14	dietary supplements
	15	electrolytes
	16	Advil
	17	antibiotic for traveler's diarrhea
	18	Imodium
	19	Tums
	20	Lactaid
	21	Benadryl
	22	Calcet (for leg cramps)
	23	Charmin to Go
	24	Band-Aids
	33	**total items**

luggage:

packed?	item #	description
	1	various toiletries (in toiletry bag: liquid make-up, blush, concealer, mascara, eyelash crimper, two sunscreens, hand/body lotion, shampoo, It's a 10 conditioner, Cetaphil, 2 hair clips, shower cap, deodorant, razor; 16 total)
	2	seven shirts
	3	seven underwear
	4	seven socks
	5	sleepwear
	6	T-shirt gifts for hosts (2)
	7	shorts
	8	white jeans, blue jeans
	9	flip-flops
	10	small towel
	11	deet sheets
	12	umbrella
	13	small travel bottle of liquid All
	14	hangers
	15	oatmeal
	16	green tea
	17	*Book of the Maya*
	18	waterproof iPhone case
	53	**total items**

APPENDIX B

Around the World: List of Necessities
cross body bag, jacket, camera bag, and carry-on contents
(136 items total)

bag:

packed?	item #	description
	1	passport
	2	wallet: driver's license, credit card, bank card, Global Entry card, emergency contact info, U.S. money (6 total)
	3	iPhone + charger (2 total)
	4	itinerary, Airbnb contacts (on phone)
	5	insurance policy, addresses for postcards (on phone)
	6	Kindle + charger (2 total)
	7	paper items: itinerary, Airbnb contacts, maps of Airbnb locations, insurance policy, addresses for postcards, business cards (6 total)
	8	2 pairs of reading glasses
	9	sunglasses
	10	lipstick/lip balm
	11	3 empty lip balms with $20 each
	12	comb
	13	earplugs
	14	earbuds
	15	sanitizing wipes
	16	tissues
	17	Valium
	18	three pens, small notebook
	19	chewing gum
	20	flashlight
	39	**total items**

jacket:

packed?	item #	description
	1	lip balm
	2	glasses
	3	money (also carried in underwear)
	4	pen
	4	total items

(carried neck pillow and scarf)

camera bag:

packed?	item #	description
	1	camera with 16-50mm lens
	2	55-210mm lens
	3	extra 64 GB SD card
	4	battery charger
	5	lens cleaning tissue
	5	total items

carry-on:

packed?	*item #*	*description*
	1	paper items: copies of passport, Global Entry card, credit card, bank card, insurance policy, itinerary, maps of and directions to Airbnbs, admission tickets, and emergency numbers (9 total)
	2	water purifier
	3	aluminum bottle
	4	electricity adapter
	5	foldable backpack
	6	four shirts: green rayon, white Indian, navy quick-dry, long underwear top
	7	three pairs of pocket underwear
	8	three pairs of regular underwear
	9	socks: three pairs of footies, three pairs of ankle socks
	10	body scarf
	11	leggings
	12	sleepwear
	13	foldable cotton hat
	14	swimsuit
	15	flip-flops
	16	rain shoes
	17	dietary supplements
	18	electrolytes
	19	Imodium
	20	DiaResQ (natural remedy for traveler's diarrhea)
	21	two kinds of antibiotics
	22	Neosporin
	23	nose spray
	24	Advil
	25	Benadryl
	26	Calcet
	27	Tums
	28	Lactaid

	29	baby aspirin
	30	eye drops
	31	Band-Aids
	32	Q-tips
	33	moleskin for blisters
	34	Dr. Scholl's buttress pad for injured second toe
	35	Dove soap
	36	Cetaphil
	37	deodorant
	38	toothbrush
	39	toothpaste
	40	floss
	41	shampoo
	42	It's a 10 conditioner
	43	shower cap
	44	2 hair clips
	45	comb
	46	hair curler
	47	2 hair bands
	48	hand/body lotion
	49	sunscreen for face
	50	sunscreen for body
	51	deet sheets
	52	face powder, brush, and blush
	53	concealer
	54	razor
	55	fingernail file
	56	fingernail clipper
	57	sewing kit
	58	two safety pins
	59	Tide sheets
	60	sink plug
	61	umbrella
	62	camera raincoat
	88	total items

NOTES

1. https://theunboundedspirit.com/3-mind-opening-epictetus-quotes/
2. John L. Bowman, *A Reference Guide to Stoicism: A Compilation of the Principle Stoic Writings on Various Topics* (Bloomington, IN: AuthorHouse™ LLC, 2014), 15.
3. Ibid., 2.
4. Epictetus, *Discourses and Enchiridion*, based on the translation of Thomas Wentwort Higginson (New York: Walter J. Black, 1944), Book 2, Chapter 16, 129.
5. Bowman, 157.
6. Epictetus, *Discourses*, Chapter 24, 61.
7. Diogenes Laërtius, *Lives of Eminent Philosophers*, R.D. Hicks, Ed., (Cambridge: Harvard University Press, 1972; first published 1925), Chapter 1, Zeno, 2.
8. Epictetus, https://books.google.com/books/about/The_Moral_Discourses_of_Epic tetus_Annota.html?id=LfRtBAAAQBAJ
9. Seneca, https://www.goodreads.com/quotes/699205-all-the-greatest-blessings-are-a-source-of-anxiety-and.
10. Marcus Aurelius, https://twitter.com/dailyStoic?lang=en
11. *Diagnostic and Statistical Manual of Mental Disorders (DSM–5)*. American Psychiatric Publishing; 5th edition, 2013, https://dsm.psychiatryonline.org/doi/full/10.1176/appi.books.97808904 25596.dsm06
12. Bowman, 83.
13. Marcus Aurelius, *Meditations*, trans. W.H.D. Rouse (Darlington, England: J.M. Dent and Co., 1900), Book 2, II, https://en.wikisource.org/wiki/Marcus_Aurelius_Antoninus_-_His_Meditations_concerning_himselfe
14. Seneca, *Moral Letters to Lucilius*, Letter 8, 2, https://en.wikisource.org/wiki/Moral_letters_to_Lucilius/Letter_8
15. Seneca, https://www.goodreads.com/quotes/7689848-remember-that-all-we-have-is-on-loan-from-fortune
16. Bowman, 1.

17. Epictetus, *Discourses*, Book 3, Chapter 8, 193.

18. Epictetus, *Discourses*, Book 1, Chapter 1, 4.

19. Seneca, *Moral Letters to Lucilius*, Letter 13, 12-13, https://en.wikisource.org/wiki/Moral_letters_to_Lucilius/Letter_13

20. Marcus Aurelius, *Meditations*, trans. W.H.D. Rouse (Darlington, England: J.M. Dent and Co., 1900) Book 4, XL, https://en.wikisource.org/wiki/Marcus_Aurelius_Antoninus_-_His_Meditations_concerning_himselfe

21. Epictetus, *Discourses*, Book 4, Chapter 7, 302-3.

22. Seneca, https://dailyStoic.com/memento-mori/

23. Marcus Aurelius, https://www.goodreads.com/quotes/293726-think-of-yourself-as-dead-you-have-lived-your-life

24. Epictetus, *Discourses*, Book 2, Chapter 20, 148.

25. Marcus Aurelius, *Meditations*, trans. W.H.D. Rouse (Darlington, England: J.M. Dent and Co., 1900) Book 8, XXXIV, https://en.wikisource.org/wiki/Marcus_Aurelius_Antoninus_-_His_Meditations_concerning_himselfe

26. Bowman, 111.

27. Epictetus, *Discourses*, Book 2, Chapter 16, 128-29.

28. Bowman, 3.

29. Bowman, 175.

30. Marcus Aurelius, *Meditations*, trans. W.H.D. Rouse (Darlington, England: J.M. Dent and Co., 1900), Book 11, XV, https://en.wikisource.org/wiki/Marcus_Aurelius_Antoninus_-_His_Meditations_concerning_himselfe

31. Bowman, 45.

32. Epictetus, *Discourses*, Book 4, Chapter 1, 269-70.

33. Epictetus, *Discourses*, Book 1, Chapter 18, 51.

34. Marcus Aurelius, *Meditations*, trans. W.H.D. Rouse (Darlington, England: J.M. Dent and Co., 1900), Book 4, XXVII, https://en.wikisource.org/wiki/Marcus_Aurelius_Antoninus_-_His_Meditations_concerning_himselfe

35. Bowman, 86.

36. Bowman, 58.

37. Bowman, 103.

38. Bowman, 94.

39. Bowman, 66.

40. Bowman, 47.

41. Roosh Valizadeh, *Return of Kings*, http://www.returnofkings.com/64452/the-principal-tenets-of-Stoicism-by-seneca

42. Seneca, *Moral Letters to Lucilius*, Letter 58, 23, https://en.wikisource.org/wiki/Moral_letters_to_Lucilius/Letter_58

43. Epictetus, *Enchiridion*, 10, 334.

44. Bowman, 55.

45. Bowman, 30.

46. Bowman, 100.

47. Bowman, 146.

48. Epictetus, Book 1, Chapter 1, 5.

49. Epictetus, *Enchiridion*, 4, 333.

50. Bowman, 172.

51. Bowman, 12.

52. Marcus Aurelius, *Meditations*, trans. W.H.D. Rouse (Darlington, England: J.M. Dent and Co., 1900) Book 4, XXIX, https://en.wikisource.org/wiki/Marcus_Aurelius_Antoninus_-_His_Meditations_concerning_himselfe

53. Epictetus, *Enchiridion*, 9, 334.

54. Epictetus, *Discourses,* Book 3, 197-98.

55. Bowman, 89.

56. Bowman, 8.

57. Bowman, 39/35.

58. Bowman, 36.

59. Bowman, 146.

60. Epictetus, *Enchiridion*, 1, 332.

61. Marcus Aurelius, https://en.wikiquote.org/wiki/Marcus_Aurelius, Book V, 16

62. Bowman, 30.

63. Bowman, 3.

64. Epictetus, *Discourses II*, 18, 4-5.

65. Bowman, 31.

66. Marcus Aurelius, *The Modern Library Collection of Greek and Roman Philosophy* (New York: The Random House Publishing Group, 2002), 49a.

67. Epictetus, *Discourses*, Book 3, 93.

68. Marcus Aurelius, *Meditations*, trans. W.H.D. Rouse (Darlington, England: J.M. Dent and Co., 1900) Book 7, XXVI, https://en.wikisource.org/wiki/Marcus_Aurelius_Antoninus_-_His_Meditations_concerning_himselfe

69. Bowman, 180.

70. Bowman, 23.

71. Epictetus, *Discourses*, Book 3, Chapter 15, 208.

72. Bowman, 54.

73. Seneca, *Moral Letters to Lucilius*, Letter 6, 7, https://en.wikisource.org/wiki/Moral_letters_to_Lucilius/Letter_6

74. Bowman, 86.

75. Bowman, 179.

76. Epictetus, *Discourses*, Book 3, Chapter 15, 208.

77. Bowman, 82.

78. Epictetus, *Enchiridion,* 33, 344.

79. Bowman, 178.

80. Epictetus, *Discourses*, Book 3, Chapter 5, 185.

81. Bowman, 130.

82. Marcus Aurelius, *Meditations*, trans. W.H.D. Rouse (Darlington, England: J.M. Dent and Co., 1900) Book 5, XVI, https://en.wikisource.org/wiki/Marcus_Aurelius_Antoninus_-_His_Meditations_concerning_himselfe

83. Marcus Aurelius, *Meditations*, trans. W.H.D. Rouse (Darlington, England: J.M. Dent and Co., 1900) Book 1, XV, https://en.wikisource.org/wiki/Marcus_Aurelius_Antoninus_-_His_Meditations_concerning_himselfe

84. https://www.mars-one.com/faq/selection-and-preparation-of-the-astronauts/how-are-the-astronauts-prepared.

85. Ibid.

86. Marcus Aurelius, *Meditations*, Book IV, 3, https://en.wikiquote.org/wiki/Marcus_Aurelius

87. Bowman, 144.

88. Seneca, *Moral Letters to Lucilius*, Letter 13, 12-13,
https://en.wikisource.org/wiki/Moral_letters_to_Lucilius/Letter_13

89. Epictetus, *Discourses*, Book 1, Chapter 9, 26.

90. Seneca, *Moral Letters to Lucilius*, Letter 58, 32,
https://en.wikisource.org/wiki/Moral_letters_to_Lucilius/Letter_58

91. Bowman, 88.

92. Epictetus, *Discourses*, Book 4, Chapter 3, 285.

93. Epictetus, *Discourses*, Book 1, Chapter 1, 5.

94. Seneca, https://philosiblog.com/2011/06/04/travel-and-change-of-place/

95. Seneca, https://www.goodreads.com/work/quotes/93900-epistulae-morales-ad-lucilium?page=9

96. Epictetus, *Discourses*, Book 1, Chapter 23, 60.

97. Epictetus, *Discourses*, Book 3, Chapter 14, 206.

98. Epictetus, *Discourses*, Book 4, Chapter 3, 285.

99. Marcus Aurelius, *Meditations*, trans. W.H.D. Rouse (Darlington, England: J.M. Dent and Co., 1900) Book 8, XLVIII,
https://en.wikisource.org/wiki/Marcus_Aurelius_Antoninus_-_His_Meditations_concerning_himselfe

100. Our Lady of Fatima, Catholic News Agency (CNA), September 8, 2016.

101. Santos, Lúcia, *Fátima in Lúcia's Own Words: Sister Lúcia's Memoirs*, ed. Fr. Louis Kondor, Svd. (2011), 123-124; 215.

102. Santos, 123-124; 215.

103. Santos, 123-124; 215.

104. Epictetus, *Discourses*, Book 3, Chapter 13, 229.

105. Marcus Aurelius, *Meditations*, Book V, 6,
https://en.wikiquote.org/wiki/Marcus_Aurelius

106. Epictetus, *Discourses*, Chapter 6/49-50,
https://en.wikisource.org/wiki/Epictetus,_the_Discourses_as_reported_by_Arrian,_the_Manual,_and_Fragments/Book_1/Chapter_6

107. Bowman, 22.

108. Marcus Aurelius, *Meditations*, trans. W.H.D. Rouse (Darlington, England: J.M. Dent and Co., 1900) Book 7, XLI,

https://en.wikisource.org/wiki/Marcus_Aurelius_Antoninus_-_His_Meditations_concerning_himselfe

109. Bowman, 157.

110. Epictetus, *Enchiridion*, 20, 338.

111. Marcus Aurelius, *Meditations*, Book IV, 32, https://en.wikiquote.org/wiki/Marcus_Aurelius

112. Epictetus, *Enchiridion*, 8, 334.

113. https://cambodiangenocideproject.weebly.com/dehumanization.html

114. https://www.nytimes.com/2013/10/10/opinion/for-america-life-was-cheap-in-vietnam.html

115. Seneca, *Moral Letters to Lucilius*, Richard M. Grummere, trans. 1920 ed., Letter 78, 1, https://en.wikisource.org/wiki/Moral_letters_to_Lucilius/Letter_78

116. Seneca, https://en.wikisource.org/wiki/Moral_letters_to_Lucilius/Letter_54/4

117. *Stoicorum Veterum Fragmenta* (a collection by Hans von Arnim of fragments of the earlier Stoics; SVF ii 1170, 1181,1163).

118. Seneca, *Moral Letters to Lucilius*, Letter 27,3, https://en.wikisource.org/wiki/Moral_letters_to_Lucilius/Letter_27/3

119. Marcus Aurelius, *Meditations*, trans. W.H.D. Rouse (Darlington, England: J.M. Dent and Co., 1900) Book 4, XVIII, https://en.wikisource.org/wiki/Marcus_Aurelius_Antoninus_-_His_Meditations_concerning_himselfe

120. Seneca, *On the Shortness of Life*, trans. C.D.N. Costa (New York: Penguin Group, 1997), 9, 12.

121. Seneca, *Moral Letters to Lucilius*, Letter 13, 4, https://en.wikisource.org/wiki/Moral_letters_to_Lucilius/Letter_13/4

122. Seneca, *Moral Letters to Lucilius*, Letter 3, 2, https://en.wikisource.org/wiki/Moral_letters_to_Lucilius/Letter_3

123. Bowman, 89.

124. Seneca, *Of Peace of Mind*, trans. Aubrey Stewart (Bohn's Classical Library Edition; London, George Bell and Sons, 1900), https://en.wikisource.org/wiki/Of_Peace_of_Mind#XVII

125. Seneca, *Of Peace of Mind*,

https://en.wikisource.org/wiki/Of_Peace_of_Mind#X

126. Bowman, 51.

127. Seneca, *Moral Letters to Lucilius*, Letter 104, 17-18, https://en.wikisource.org/wiki/Moral_letters_to_Lucilius/Letter_104

128. Marcus Aurelius, *Meditations*, trans. W.H.D. Rouse (Darlington, England: J.M. Dent and Co., 1900) Book 7, XXXV, https://en.wikisource.org/wiki/Marcus_Aurelius_Antoninus_-_His_Meditations_concerning_himselfe

129. https://web.archive.org/web/20081003211008/http://www.celdf.org/Default.aspx?tabid=548

130. Seneca, *On the Shortness of Life*, trans. John W. Basore (Loeb Classical Library London: William Heinemann, 1932), Chapter 12, 12, https://en.wikisource.org/wiki/On_the_shortness_of_life/Chapter_XII

131. Epictetus, *Discourses*, Chapter 12, 38.

132. Bowman, 28.

133. Seneca, *Moral Letters to Lucilius*, Letter 13, 4/9, https://en.wikisource.org/wiki/Moral_letters_to_Lucilius/Letter_13

134. Marcus Aurelius, *Meditations*, Book X, 6,8,18, https://en.wikiquote.org/wiki/Marcus_Aurelius

135. Seneca, *Moral Letters to Lucilius,* Letter 57, 3-4, https://en.wikisource.org/wiki/Moral_letters_to_Lucilius/Letter_57

136. Marcus Aurelius, *Meditations*, trans. W.H.D. Rouse (Darlington, England: J.M. Dent and Co., 1900), Book 11, XV, https://en.wikisource.org/wiki/Marcus_Aurelius_Antoninus_-_His_Meditations_concerning_himselfe

137. Bowman, 128.

138. Seneca, *Moral Letters to Lucilius,* Letter 13, 5, https://en.wikisource.org/wiki/Moral_letters_to_Lucilius/Letter_5

139. Epictetus, *Enchiridion*, 33, 345-46.

140. Bowman, 146.

141. Bowman, 65.

142. Bowman, 50.

143. Bowman, 139.

144. Epictetus, *Discourses*, Book 1, Chapter 9, 69.

145. *Diagnostic and Statistical Manual of Mental Disorders (DSM–5)*.

146. https://en.wikipedia.org/wiki/I_know_it_when_I_see_it#cite_ref-4

147. Epictetus, *Discourses*, Book 3, Chapter 13, 89-91.

148. Seneca, https://www.quora.com/What-is-your-favorite-quote-from-the-Stoic-philosophers-and-why
and: Seneca, *Moral Letters to Lucilius*, Letter 7, 1,
https://en.wikisource.org/wiki/Moral_letters_to_Lucilius/Letter_7

149. Bowman, 157.

150. Seneca, https://www.quora.com/What-is-your-favorite-quote-from-the-Stoic-philosophers-and-why
and: Seneca, *Moral Letters to Lucilius*, Letter 7, 1,
https://en.wikisource.org/wiki/Moral_letters_to_Lucilius/Letter_7

Eva Rome is a writer and a video artist. As a writer, her experience ranges from screenplays, short stories, poetry she doesn't let anyone read, a novel she trashed about a decade ago, to her first self-published novel *Travel for STO-ICs*. Her screenplay *Nota Ogni Cosa: Leonardo the Artist* won a Gold Award in the Houston International Film Festival and placed in the finals of the Academy Awards Foundation's annual screenplay competition. She has served as a screenplay consultant to the National Endowment for the Arts Media Grants Committee and as a contract screenplay and script writer/consultant.

As a video artist, she has received a National Endowment for the Arts Visual Artist Fellowship and four American Film Institute/NEA Fellowships. Her video art has been exhibited internationally at venues including the

Museum of Modern Art, the Metropolitan Museum of Art, the Pierre du Chardin Gallery (Paris), The Gallery of Modern Art (Rome), and at festivals including the American Film Institute's Film/Video Festival, the Tokyo Video Festival, the Festival du Cinema in Montreal, and at Filmfest (Berlin, Budapest, Hong Kong, Melbourne, Moscow). She has taught at Brown University and the Rhode Island School of Design (both in Providence) and at the University of Houston, and has been a visiting lecturer at the School of the Art Institute of Chicago, Webster University in St. Louis, Walnut St. Theater in Philadelphia, Dom Kultury in Warsaw, Poland, and other venues. She lives in Santa Fe, New Mexico. Her chile preference is Christmas.

.

50912615R00194

Made in the USA
Middletown, DE
28 June 2019